Frederick Andrew Inderwick

The King's Peace

A historical sketch of the English law courts

Frederick Andrew Inderwick

The King's Peace
A historical sketch of the English law courts

ISBN/EAN: 9783337097073

Printed in Europe, USA, Canada, Australia, Japan

Cover: Foto ©Suzi / pixelio.de

More available books at **www.hansebooks.com**

Social England Series

EDITED BY KENELM D. COTES, M.A. OXON.

THE KING'S PEACE

A Historical Sketch of the English Law Courts

BY

F. A. INDERWICK, Q.C.

Author of "Side-Lights on the Stuarts," "The Interregnum," etc.

WITH 15 ILLUSTRATIONS AND 1 MAP

London

SWAN SONNENSCHEIN & CO. Lim.

New York: MACMILLAN & CO.

1895

To the Right Hon.

LORD RUSSELL OF KILLOWEN, G.C.M.G.

Lord Chief Justice of England

this Sketch

is Dedicated

INTRODUCTION

A STRANGER who, passing up the Strand, looks at our Royal Courts of Justice, will be struck with the graceful harmony of the pile standing at the gates of the city and supported by the church of Saint Clement Danes. The building has an appearance at once dignified and symmetrical, and seems to embody the idea of a Royal Court of Justice. On further investigation, however, there is found a noble stone-roofed hall of lordly proportions leading apparently to no result, with no outward sign of any facilities for the despatch of business. But wooden signboards are supplied to point the way to the courts, which are reached by narrow and precipitous causeways leading into crowded and inconvenient passages, where numbers painted on the doorposts indicate the various courts. A consideration of the combined effect of the external and internal arrangements of the building suggests the work of a man who, having in his mind a great sense of architectural beauty and recognising that success depends upon convenience and convenience upon accuracy of detail, has been cramped and harried by pressure to produce something practical, though not necessarily graceful, sufficient for the requirements of the moment without regard to the possibility of future expansion. But this combination of external beauty and internal confusion presents, though unintentionally, a great similarity to the system of judicature for which it provides a home.

The leading motives of our law and our procedure have always been constant, founded as they are upon a spirit of equity and of self-government, and even now, with their suggested crudity, are the admiration of foreign jurists. But we have always sacrificed science and symmetry on the altar of utility. Our judges from time immemorial would rather give an ephemeral judgment doing practical justice between a man and his neighbour than deliver one of lasting reputation dealing with great interests and world-wide principles; our courts, in which all classes of our laymen take their places as spectators, litigants, jurymen, or assessors, have been constructed and altered and reconstructed to suit their varying notions of convenience; and our legislators being men not mainly of law, but of business, have made their laws to meet the daily and hourly requirements of the people and to render more easy and more safe the duties of their social life. For the social life of Englishmen, from the time when they shouted under the uplifted spear to the time when, as now, they sit with apparent content in the wooden boxes which the custom of many generations has consecrated to their use, has ever been concerned with the administration of justice to an extent unknown probably in any antient, certainly in any modern state. When, therefore, it was suggested to me to write some account of our Courts of Law, I recognised that such a theme did form part of our social story and might fairly be a chapter in our national life.

The methods and details of our procedure have moved on with the intelligence and education of our people. In the old Anglo-Saxon and Norman days, when the ordeal of God's judgment was invoked to decide questions of law and of fact and to demonstrate the innocence or the guilt of the accused, the administration of the law which was thus vouched by miracle was a sacred function in which it was a privilege, rather than a right, to take part. As superstition died out, and knowledge was spread over the face of England, the fortuitous success of a fiery ordeal or of a hireling champion was no longer regarded as due to a special intervention of Divine Providence. The law itself became the subject of comment and of discussion; our procedure rapidly assumed a practical character, and was regulated by well-recognised and definite rules, excluding as far as possible the old system of chance. Our forefathers worshipped the sun as the god of life, of heat, and of fertility, and our fathers, wiser than they, while rejecting his spiritual godhead, utilized his beams to bleach their linen and to force their fruits. And thus the determination of legal questions ceased to be regarded as the direct judgment of Heaven, and came to be accepted as the adjudication of a business-like community.

Limit of space has necessarily had its effect upon the thoroughness of this book; and accordingly, with a view to presenting a more compact volume than would otherwise have been possible, I have confined my sketch of the King's Peace (for it would be presumptuous to describe these pages as more than a sketch) to the consideration of what are commonly called the Superior Courts. I have purposely avoided touching upon the Ecclesiastical Courts, as that would involve the consideration of an aspect of social life in England interesting, no doubt, but opening up an inquiry extending far beyond our restricted boundary. Similarly I have avoided any reference to the High Court of Parliament as involving the discussion of other phases of social life from another and a different standpoint. And when I have referred to any tribunals outside of our Superior Courts, I have done so but lightly and in few words.

The Courts and the procedure of the Anglo-Saxons were, until very recently, almost a sealed book to any but the most experienced of antiquaries. Coke, Spelman, Prynne, Selden, Dugdale, and other writers of the seventeenth century, without making a special study of that period, but investigating its laws and customs in common with other branches of the law, have given us their views, in which they generally concur, on many matters connected with this subject. The nineteenth century has produced writers and students who have devoted themselves with unwearied assiduity to the special study of the Anglo-Saxon period, with the result that the nineteenth century finds the seventeenth century to have been ignorant and inaccurate. Such men as Dr. Stubbs, the Anglo-Saxon essayists, Professor Freeman, and others, have evolved a scheme of Anglo-Saxon law and procedure which places before us the lives and habits of the people of this period with a completeness of detail never before attempted. Whether the twentieth century will cause us or our children to

modify these views, and will draw for us an altogether
different picture of the daily life of our ancestors, time
alone will show. There are still, however, many matters,
even after this patient investigation of the subject, fairly
open to discussion. The place of the King in the antient
judicature, whether he was, as always contended by the
lawyers, the fountain and the last resort of justice, or,
as now propounded by the philosophers, merely an over-
lord, whose decrees and judgments could be over-ridden
by the freemen of the County Court, is one of those open
questions upon which the authors to whom I refer may
be read with profit. For my own part, I hold to the
view of the lawyers, and I believe that the further the
question is investigated, the more clearly this will appear. A question more difficult of solution is perhaps
to be found in the consideration how far, if at all,
the Roman had any part in the formation of the English
Common Law. That it had such part in determining
civil rights I cannot doubt; though how far its influence
extended in the formulating of the system actually in
vogue at, and before the Conquest, may be somewhat
doubtful, and is, at all events, a topic well worthy of
the discussion it has raised. Descriptions of Anglo-
Saxon procedure are, however, necessarily speculative.
If A owed B fifty pence, a trustworthy account of the
precise course of procedure to be adopted by B to recover
his money cannot be given.

A study of the social life of our citizens as affected by
successive laws and ordinances and by the varying
provisions of our common law would be especially in-

teresting in these days, when public attention has been directed by some of our deepest thinkers and most lucid writers to the social condition of the masses at all periods of our national history. It would include amongst other topics an inquiry into Saxon and Norman customs and rights, feudal tenures, the varying reciprocal rights and duties of men and women, the course of sumptuary laws, and the changing and gradually civilizing views of the community on crimes and punishments. But these, with many similar considerations, are outside the province of this sketch, and must remain for their elucidation by other writers and teachers of these abstruse and recondite subjects.

It is a remarkable incident in this study that as just one thousand years have passed since King Alfred is said to have set his hand to our judicial institutions, so the history of the courts divides itself by natural selection into cycles of two centuries each. From the suggested origin of our jurisprudence under Alfred to the Norman Conquest is just two hundred years. The duration of the Curia Regis as the Supreme Court of England was two hundred years. Another two hundred years passed from the division of the courts to the end of the Wars of the Roses, after which the time came, with the advent of peace under Henry VII., for a further development of the judicature and the confirmation of the reforms of Edward IV. The period from the advent of the Tudors to the end of the Commonwealth saw us through a cycle of arbitrary government, of personal rule, of an interference with the courts rudely resented by the nation, and of republican attempts to amend the process of the courts and the laws which they administered. And this was accomplished within a fraction of another two hundred years. In the course of 1660 the reconstituted Royal Courts resumed their sittings on, what was hoped to be, new lines of liberty and integrity, and in 1867, just two hundred years afterwards, Sir Roundell Palmer, reflecting public opinion, made his .celebrated speech in the House of Commons, successfully calling for a return to the antient procedure and for the erection of one Supreme Court of Justice for the whole of England. We begin, therefore, under the Anglo-Saxons, with all the functions of justice discharged in and by the several counties of England, each doing completely its own work, with appeals discouraged and decentralization supreme. With the Conquest we have the opposite system, the work of the country collected together and disposed of in one central court by one supreme authority; decentralization is in principle condemned, and centralization is supreme. After a trial of two centuries the Supreme Court is found unable to discharge the duties cast upon it, and by a compromise always dear to the English heart a portion of the Supreme Court is decentralized, and by dividing the labour and increasing the labourers, the central tribunal once more comes abreast of the wants of the country.

For six hundred years the compromise between the Anglo-Saxon and the Anglo-Norman system was effectual to transact, with varying success and slight modifications, the business of the country. But the divided court again became unequal to the pressure put upon it, and now another compromise between the two systems finds us rapidly approaching the constitution of the original Curia Regis, discussing the propriety of abolishing the circuits, and on the high-road to a complete system of centralization.

One of the most valuable elements of our judicial procedure is the right of every litigant in our courts to be represented by counsel of his own selection. When and under what circumstances this right arose it is impossible with any accuracy to determine. It grew with the expansion of our legal system, and we can only distinctly affirm that it existed in the time of Edward I. The Serjeants, the fathers of the Bar, whether described in Latin as *narratores*, in French as *conteurs*, or in English as *counters*, began, as will be seen, as nominees of the Crown and officers of the courts. They continued to increase in strength, affluence, and independence, until, in the great pressure of business, they became almost overshadowed by members of the Bar who never received or aspired to that rank and degree. But though Serjeants were recognised by early statute, neither they nor any other class of counsel were constituted by that or by any other statute or edict, for the entire constitution and position of the Bar rests on custom and tradition. Custom puts their services at the call of every member of the community, grants them freedom and immunity of speech and pre-audience in the courts, and tradition declares them to be agents and ministers of justice in the discovery of truth and in the correct ascertainment of the law. In their professional conduct they are by custom responsible only to their colleagues in council assembled, with an appeal from the judgment of their colleagues to the judges of the Royal Courts convened in solemn session. But the Serjeants, though they have disappeared, have not been abolished, and the same public clamour which rendered necessary the restoration of a Supreme Court might at any time revive the degree and dignity of a Serjeant-at-Law.

As we are still strictly conservative in retaining the antient forms of our judicial process and, so far as may be, of our judicial staff, so it will be seen that we are alike conservative in the outward model and habits of the judges. The fashion and colour of their robes differ but slightly to-day from those of the first judges, who in the time of the Plantagenets sat in the newly erected court of King's Bench; and they are identical in colour and texture with those worn by Chief Justice Gascoigne when he committed the Prince of Wales to prison and by Chief Justice Fortescue when, under Henry VI., he declared the law of England from his seat in Westminster Hall.

During the eight hundred years of our modern procedure various courts have disappeared, numerous methods of trial have ceased, and great judicial offices have been discontinued. And yet no statute has ordered their discontinuance, and no day can be ascertained upon which it may be said that their functions ceased or were determined. As they arose by custom and were confirmed by prescription, so they ceased by non-user, and their cesser was made perpetual by prescription. The Witenagemot dissolved into the Curia Regis, but no date can with precision be affixed to the dissolution of the one or the establishment of the other. The Curia Regis died out, having struggled on into the life-time of its suc-

cessor.   The ordeals of fire and water and other of God's
judgments came to an end through the growing intelligence of the people and the teaching of the Church, and
the wager of battle, being challenged in the present
century, was found never to have been legally abolished,
though no duel had been fought for nearly three hundred
years.   The Courts of the Forest ceased to harass and
plunder when the national sentiment would no longer
permit of their continuance, but no Act of Parliament dis-
established the judges of those courts until nearly two
centuries after the last effective assertion of their authority.   The Courts of Markets and of Fairs came to an end
one hardly knows how or when.   And we recognise in
these gradual changes over a long period of years not only
the beneficent operation of our unwritten law and its
remarkable adaptability to the requirements of the day,
but also in a high degree the power of public opinion
to remove abuses without the active interference of any
ordinance or statute.

Doubts have been freely expressed as to the probable
results of the latest amendment of our judicial procedure.
The change is too recent, and legal, like agricultural
experiments, are too slow in development, to justify any
expression of opinion on this topic.   As our methods are
founded on expediency rather than on any other virtue, as
our present procedure is flexible and our complex legal
system is susceptible of receiving rapid adaptation to
whatever may be the requirements of the time, we may
look forward to a considerable, though a gradual, extension
of the scheme propounded, rather than accomplished, by
the Judicature Acts.   Pessimist predictions have no place

in our national horoscope. From the earliest days of our judicature we have slowly but surely moved on in the path of reform. We have had some melancholy incidents and encountered many impediments in our progress, but we have steadily advanced in freedom of judicial thought, as in freedom of political life. Where in some instances we may seem to have failed in the realization of our ideas, such failure has arisen rather from the promulgation of premature and ill-considered schemes than from the reluctance of our judges to join in the movement, or from the opposition of our people to necessary reforms. A too great veneration for an existing system may somewhat impede the action of Parliament in what many would consider the requirements of modern legislation, but a spirit of steadfastness and caution, characteristic of the Anglo-Saxon strain, is one of the surest safeguards for the purity and integrity of our Courts of Justice. And so long as the law is administered by judges of irremovable tenure, of sufficient means, of independent character, and of legal training, it matters but little to the ordinary Englishman what is the precise nature or construction of the channel through which the stream of justice is compelled to flow.

To bring the view of justice to every man's door, to emulate the Cadi under the palm tree, the justice-seat in the king's gate, the shout of the Wapentake, has ever been the ideal of law reformers. Equally necessary is it to bring to the doors of our people some knowledge of the principles on which our laws are modelled and of the system under which they are administered. No better mode of transmitting this knowledge can probably be

found than by a consideration of the story of our Courts
of Law, their origin, their growth, their disuse, their
modification, and the more freely this subject is discussed
the more clearly will it appear that our laws have been
framed and our procedure has been settled in the
interests of the people ; that for their benefit these Courts
exist; that through the medium of the Courts internal
quiet is secured, contracts are enforced, rights are respected, and injuries are redressed ; and that the safety,
the freedom, and the social happiness of our nation are
mainly dependent upon the fearless and impartial administration of the King's Peace.

WINCHELSEA, *July*, 1895.

CONTENTS

CHAPTER I

CHAPTER II

CURIA REGIS

[A.D. 1066-1268]

CHAPTER III

FROM THE ACCESSION OF EDWARD I. TO THE DEATH OF RICHARD III.

[A.D. 1272-1485]

I

CHAPTER V

FROM THE ACCESSION OF HENRY VII. TO THE RESTORATION OF
THE MONARCHY

[A.D. 1485-1660]

I

II

CHAPTER VI

FROM THE RESTORATION TO THE ERECTION OF THE SUPREME COURT
OF JUDICATURE

[A.D. 1660-1873]

ment of Judges, 213.—Removal of Judges, 213.—The Rebuild-
ing of London, 214.—Sir Matthew Hale, 216.—King James
II., 217.—Judges after the Revolution, 218.—Their Tenure
of Office, 218.—Their Integrity, 218.—Complaints of the
Judicial System, 219.—Mercantile Code established by the
Judges, 219.—Partial Abolition of the Ecclesiastical Courts,
220.—The Court of Probate, 219.—The Court of Divorce, 219.
—Proposals for a Supreme Court of Judicature in 1873, 223.
—The High Court of Justice and the Court of Appeal, 224.—
Further Consolidation of the Courts, 225.—Suggested Fusion
of Law and Equity, 226.—Further Division of the High
Court, 228.—The Chancellor and the Lord Chief Justice, 228.
—The Royal Courts of Justice, 230.—Former Alterations in
the Courts, 232.—The Removal from Westminster to the
Strand, 233.

LIST OF ILLUSTRATIONS

THE KING'S PEACE

CHAPTER I.

THE ANGLO-SAXON PERIOD.

(A.D. 871-1066.)

I.

The Common Law of England—Dooms of Alfred—Of Canute—
Laws of the Confessor—Nature of Anglo-Saxon Procedure—
Subjects for Adjudication — The Land — The Rights of the
King in regard to his Forests—The Prevention and Punishment of Crime—Matters and Causes Ecclesiastical—Counties
or Shires—The Court Baron—Hundred Court or Wapentake
—Trithing, Leete and Lathe Courts—County Court—Trial
between Archbishop Lanfranc and Odo of Bayeux—Institution of the Shireeves Turn—Trial of a Will—The Burh-geat-
seti—The Witenagemot—Civil Procedure—Oaths in Civil
Cases—Criminal Procedure—Compurgator's Oath—The Ordeal or *Judicium Dei*—Ordeal of Water—Ordeal of Fire or
Hot Iron—Trial of Witches—Punishments—Wer—Murdrum.

THE position which King Alfred holds in relation to
English Law and Procedure has been so much exalted on
the one hand, and depreciated on the other, that the icono-
clastic spirit of modern writers raises a doubt whether
his existence as a statesman, a law-giver, and a scholar,
is more authentic than that of King Arthur. Whatever
may be the justification for this scepticism, his splendid
reign is, for many reasons, a convenient epoch from which
to start on the consideration of our subject. We are
told that he wrote a book of his laws; and *Alfred's
Dooms* (A.D. 871-901) contained in an Anglo-Saxon MS.

B

in the Library of Corpus Christi College, Cambridge, was
published with a careful translation by the Commissioners of Public Records in 1840.[1] *Alfred's Dooms*
were followed by a compendium of laws by Canute (A.D.
1017–1035)[2] which continued, with slight alteration, to
represent the English Law till the time of Edward the
Confessor, after which the laws and customs of the realm
were again collected and promulgated as a code or record
of customs under the title of *Laws of the Confessor.*[3]
They have thus become the foundation of all English
jurisprudence, being known by the style and title of the
Common Law of England. Whether this body of law
took its origin, as suggested by Cæsar,[4] from the Druids,
who delivered their judgments under the oak or beside
the cromlech, or whether, as Lord Ellesmere supposes, it
dated still further back, and derived its inspiration from
the first instincts of Nature founded on the Law of God,
the Common Law of England, an unwritten but well-
recognised customary code, had undoubtedly received
emendations and accretions from each of the various
dynasties by which the country had been ruled. The
Roman, the Dane, but above all the Teuton, had given
tone and colour to the mass, so that it became from time
to time suited to the somewhat conglomerate people for
whose use it was framed.

It was an unwritten law, in the sense that there existed
for its exposition no code and no statute, although there

---

[1] *Ancient Laws and Institutes of England,* vol. i. p. 44.
[2] *Laws of King Cnut,* ib., 358.   [3] *Ibid.,* p. 412.
[4] *De Bello Gallico,* lib. vi.

were even then in the hands of the clerks, and of the officers of State, some few writings such as those to which I have referred, in which the law was recorded and explained. But it was mainly preserved in the breasts and in the closets of the clergy, who, as a rule, were the only persons educated in the law; in the knowledge and recollection of the Thanes and the landowners whose lands and whose persons were governed by it; and in the traditions handed down from father to son by the freeholders and the husbandmen who felt its pressure and who claimed its protection. In this respect the English system differed from that of most other countries of the time, inasmuch as the latter had their laws in written codes, to which the learned or the interested could from time to time refer— a contrast which, even as late as the reign of Henry III., struck one of our great juris-consults and legal writers, Henry Bracton, who, writing however with some lack of exact information, remarks, "In all other countries they use written laws: in England alone they rely on custom and on unwritten law." This customary or un- written law, therefore, as it existed at the time of the Confessor, was the Common Law of England, *bonæ et approbatæ antiquæ leges Angliæ*, "the good and well approved old laws of England," referred to over and over again in Charters and in Statutes: the law which the Conqueror swore faithfully to observe when he took the coronation oath, and to which the Barons referred when, in answer to the demand that they should alter the law of succession to real estate, in accordance with Norman custom, they returned the haughty answer, "*Nolumus leges Angliæ mutari."* This is the Common Law of England, which wo speak of to-day as distinguished from the statuto or written law contained in a series of Acts of Parliament passed since the conquest ; and it is typical of the sturdiness and tenacity of the Anglo-Saxon strain, that a great part of the customary law under which we are now governed comes in a direct line from our ancestors before the Conquest. It must nevertheless be admitted, upon perusal of the somewhat imperfect records that we possess of what our distant forefathers regarded as law, that it was of a semi-barbarous character, often cruel, often capricious, and depending, especially in criminal matters, very much upon the law of chance, which in their ignorance and superstition they were apt to regard as the direct interposition of Heaven.

Although there was no great alteration in the law from the death of Alfred to the accession of Edward, there was necessarily some extension and modification in the manner of its administration. During the years which covered this period population had increased, new interests had been created, commerce had grown up internally and externally, there was more education among the upper classes, and the frequent communication between England and Normandy had led to some taste for luxury and refinement. But such changes as there were in the administration of the law were to be traced to German rather than to Norman sources, although King Edward, as a result of his Norman education, is believed to have introduced some innovations. These, however, if any, were small, and the law continued to be administered under him in substantial accordance with the procedure which had been observed under his predecessors.

The subjects to be dealt with, out of which questions for adjudication arose, were :—

(1) The Land. This involved the rights of the King as against his subjects clerical and lay. The rights and duties of the Lords and landowners towards the King, towards each other, and towards their tenants or their villeins.

(2) The rights of the King in regard to his forests and all unoccupied spaces, together with forfeitures and fines.

(3) The prevention and punishment of crime.

(4) Matters and causes ecclesiastical, involving many questions of much nicety and at times of danger to the public peace.

Personal property was of comparatively small account and entered little into legal consideration.

Procedure varied but little in the several states. Alfred and his lineal descendants accepted the plan based on the conception of independent communities, which has ever since been recognised as politic and wise, by which the country was divided into sections, each being under a chief officer with various subordinates, and these sections sub-divided again and again, till every man, woman and child was found to be settled in a community where he was known to all the other members of that community, and was easily accessible for purposes of legal process, of military service, or of taxation. A recognised head of each subdivision, responsible to his immediate superior and through him indirectly to the King, was

thus at hand for every member to whom in time of need
he could apply for justice or protection. These sections
were called *counties* or *shires*, and with few exceptions,
they are identical and co-terminous with the counties of
England as they exist to-day. The county was then
divided into hundreds, the terms implying, as is supposed,
either a hundred hides of land, equal in extent to about
ten thousand acres, or a hundred friboroughs or decades.
The hundreds were again sub-divided into tithings or
tenths, and there were other sub-divisions for various
purposes. The chief judicial officer of the county was
called the Shire-reeve, afterwards the Sheriff. Of a
similiar, if not a more exalted position in social rank
and dignity, was the alderman. And the Baron or Lord
of the Manor (a Thane), was the head of the Manor, to
which a manorial Court is always appurtenant. Each of
these persons and some others (as hereinafter mentioned),
held his Court at stipulated seasons. And as these were
the most antient Courts of the country and their names
still subsist, although their jurisdiction has been cur-
tailed, I will deal with them before passing to the consideration of those of more recent institution.

The MANOR COURT was held under the presidency of a
Thane, a Baron or a head borough, as the case might be,
for the trial of causes arising within the manor, or if
both parties were content to accept the jurisdiction, in
reference to persons or things connected with the manor,
but not within it. If, however, the cause of action was
between persons, one of whom was not subject to the
jurisdiction of the Manor Court, the suit, upon objection

taken, could not proceed, but was removed to the Court of the Hundred, or to such other Court as had the requisite authority. A Manor Court being thus primarily attached to every manor of which the Baron or Lord was the head, there would seem necessarily to have been in the kingdom as many Courts as there were Manors. Some of these, however, were so small as not to be capable of providing a sufficient number of freemen to constitute a Court, and under these circumstances their causes, if tried at all, were disposed of at the Court of the Hundred. The Baron proceeded by appointing from the freeholders at least ten judges or triers, who knew personally or by repute the other inhabitants of the manor or village, and who were responsible for their production when their presence was required, or for the fines imposed upon, or compensation demanded of the manor for injuries inflicted by the inhabitants if the malefactors themselves could not be produced. The Court sat by custom once a fortnight, until Henry III. restrained their sittings to once in every three weeks, and it was held in the Manor House, which had then become not only the home of the Lord of the Manor, but also the local Temple of Justice. I am not aware that any Anglo-Saxon Manor House is still in existence, but the Manor itself is still part of our legal and social system, though facilities are now afforded for enfranchising all manors and turning them into freeholds. There are many, however, which are not yet enfranchised, where tenants are still admitted by quaint devices according to immemorial custom, and where heriots are still due upon the demise of every tenant for life. An

antient building, probably of the 16th century, at Water
Eaton, near Oxford, would give a good example of the
development of the old Manor House. A square-built man-
sion with spacious hall forms the top of a square. Rooms
for servants, and stables for horses and cattle, occupy the
two sides; the dovecote which, in the olden days, a Lord
of the Manor or a freeholder was alone entitled to erect,
and a chapel are close to the main structure; and a square
open space is then left in the centre of the buildings,
where tenants, labourers, and litigants might wait their
turn out of doors, while other business was being transacted within. Some such building, if fancy could people
it with Anglo-Saxons, would give a good picture of what
the Baron's Court would have been in the alternate weeks
of its session.

The HUNDRED GEMOTE, otherwise the COURT of the
HUNDRED or WAPENTAKE, was a Court of higher and
more extended jurisdiction than the Court Baron. It was
recognised by an Ordinance of King Edgar (A.D. 954–
975),[1] who declared that it should meet always once within four weeks, and that every man should do justice to
another. It tried causes civil, criminal, and ecclesiastical, sitting once in each month as ordered by Edgar and
his successors, until Henry III., acting as in the case of
the Court Baron, ordained that its sittings should take
place once in every three weeks. It was presided over by
a Sheriff or an Alderman when in the hundred, who sat
with the freeholders acting as judges, and tried the

---

[1] *Ancient Laws and Institutes*, vol. i. p. 269. Stubbs' *Charters*,
p. 69.

causes. The title of Baron did not originally import any rank of nobility, but commonly denoted a freeman and a landowner, who was the only person qualified for certain important positions. The name still exists in the same sense. Thus the expression "baron and feme" to represent man and wife is well known in legal phraseology. The Barons of the Exchequer, as will hereafter appear, were originally none other than good men and afterwards high officials who sat in the Exchequer to discharge their duty to the King in the due assessment and recovery of his revenue. And the Barons of the Cinque Ports, originally the Mayors and Jurats of those towns, are to this day called over from the Roll of Parliament, as representatives of the Cinque Port towns of Hastings, Dover, and Hythe. The title, however, was probably not used in England before the time of the Confessor.

With the Alderman, who was frequently himself an ecclesiastic, a Bishop or Archdeacon was usually associated as assessor when questions were tried *contra pacem ecclesiæ*, "against the peace of the Church," or when otherwise the interests of the Church were directly concerned. And here, again, the court only had jurisdiction over persons or lands within its territorial limits. Cases beyond these limits were disposed of in courts of more extended powers. The judges in these Hundred Courts were freeholders drawn from dwellers in the Hundred who had personal knowledge, as was supposed, of the reputation of their co-dwellers. They were sworn as compurgators, if willing, in criminal cases, and they decided according to their knowledge on all questions of contract, or of right to land or dower. The judgment of these courts was, therefore, that of a man's neighbours, who knew him from his youth, and could say whether he was a person to be believed upon his oath. And as the parties themselves were their own counsel, the procedure in civil cases must have partaken more of the form of an arbitration than of an action at law.[1] An appeal apparently lay from this to the County Court, but not till after the party had applied again and again to the Court of the Hundred, and had been refused redress.[2]

It is not stated where this Court held its sitting, but it probably did so in the open air, or in any Manor Court which might be available for the purpose.

In the laws of Edward the Confessor, Sec. 30,[3] in illustration of the rude procedure of the period, an explanation is given of the term Wapentake as applied to the Hundred Court. It is there said that when the President of the Court arrived at the appointed place, all the suitors and others, gathering to the accustomed spot, dismounted from their horses and received him under their spears. And then he, raising his own spear in the midst, touched theirs, and was thus confirmed in his post. In justification of this theory, it is said that the words composing

---

[1] Athelstane (A.D. 925) ordered search to be made for men who were known not to be liars, so that there might always be a number of truthful jurors forthcoming when their attendance was required to vouch the character of a litigant. *Laws of Æthelstane. Ancient Laws and Institutes*, vol. i. p. 223. Stubbs' *Charters*, p. 65.

[2] *Ancient Laws and Institutes. Laws of Cnut*, vol. i. p. 385. Dugdale's *Origines Juridiciales*, fol. 29.

[3] *Ancient Laws and Institutes*, vol. i. p. 455.

the name Wapentake are *wæpen* (arms) and *taccare* (confirm), and that thus the assembled warriors bound themselves to uphold by their arms the authority of their chief. The tradition is probably accurate, but the combination of Saxon (wæpen) and Latin (taccare) is not satisfactory.

The TRITHING, the LATHE COURT, and the COURT LEETE, were Courts of a similar character to that of the Hundred, but they tried cases over which the latter had no jurisdiction. The Trithing, or modern Riding, as found in the counties of York and of Lincoln, according to the laws of the Confessor, Sec. 31,[1] was composed of three hundreds, and could therefore try cases over three times the area of the Hundred Court. The Lathe Court had probably the same jurisdiction. This latter was peculiar to the county of Kent, where the territorial division of the county into Lathes[2] still exists, and is said to be composed of three hundreds. The Court Leete, however, had no territorial limit. It was chiefly concerned with the affairs of manors, towns, and cities, and exercised mainly a criminal or quasi-criminal jurisdiction. The *Leete Jurisdiction of Norwich*, recently published by the Selden Society, affords information as to the extent and variety of the pleas in this Court. It appears to have had conferred upon it in more recent times some jurisdiction in regard to offences under the Forest Laws. At a later period, probably about Henry VII., the jurisdiction of these Courts in matters of debt and

---

[1] *Ancient Laws and Institutes*, vol. i. p. 455.

[2] The original name is supposed to have been " Lething," a military levy. Lappenberg's *Anglo-Saxons*, vol. ii. p. 330.

damages was limited to forty shillings, a sum, however, which, at that time, would represent about twenty pounds of our present money. Their early course of procedure is subject to much difference of opinion, but I apprehend that the freemen were the judges, as in the Court of the Hundred, and that an appeal lay probably on a denial of justice, to the County Court.

The COUNTY COURT, as it was among the most antient, so also was it among the most active and important in the kingdom. It was held under the Presidency of the Sheriff once in every month, according to the laws of Edward the Elder (A.D. 901–924) and of Canute, at a time and place to be duly appointed.[1] The Sheriff sat in a Court of his own, or in a Manor Court, if there were one convenient. If there were none, then in the open air or a church. Dugdale, who is responsible for this latter statement, refers in support of it to the instance of a proceeding against a certain priest whom the people, suitors and litigants having met together at the church early in the morning to plead, but before the pleading began inquired for the priest to say mass, "found that he had the night before slept with his wife,"[2] which precluded him from singing the early mass, and laid him open to ecclesiastical censure. Further confirmation of

---

[1] *Laws of King Edward*, section 11 : "I will that each Reeve have a gemot always once in four weeks; and so do that every man be worthy of folk-right; and that every suit have an end and a term when it shall be brought forward." *Ancient Laws and Institutes*, vol. i. p. 165. Dugdale's *Origines Juridiciales*, fol. 28: "And so is the County Court holden to this day." Coke, *4th Institute*, p. 259.   [2] *Origines Juridiciales*, fol. 31.

this is also found in the fact that the Bishops resolutely discouraged the practice of holding secular courts in churches and churchyards, and at the Synods of Exeter and Winchester, in 1287, the Bishops formally inhibited the use of churches and churchyards for these secular purposes.

The County Court had jurisdiction in civil, criminal, and ecclesiastical causes, the Sheriff associating to himself a Bishop or an Archdeacon if necessary, together with other ecclesiastical or learned persons, who might aid him in the administration of justice. They tried, as may be seen from the instances recorded by Dugdale,[1] the title to land in the county, the right to tithes, bargains and sales of land, services and customs, and other causes of great moment. They also heard cases in the nature of appeals from the Hundred, Lathe, and Trithing Courts, in regard to any suits where the suitors in the inferior courts complained of the conduct or perversity of the judges or the presidents. The judges of these courts were the freeholders of the county, who were summoned by the Sheriff, and who in this instance were called not the jurors or triers, but *sectatores* or the *suitors* of the court. These decided all questions of law and of fact; the Sheriff or Alderman, as the case might be, who presided, not being for this purpose a judge; and, as far as can be ascertained, their judgment was not required to be unanimous, but in case of difference the opinion of the best men was to prevail.[2]

---

[1] *Origines Juridiciales*, fol. 29.

[2] *Ancient Laws and Institutes*, vol. i. p. 612. The words *et*

Numerous instances are given in the old records of trials of much interest in these County Courts. It will, however, suffice to notice one which took place in the year 1076, the tenth year of King William I., in which Lanfranc, Archbishop of Canterbury, was the plaintiff, and Odo,[1] Bishop of Bayeux and Earl of Kent, half brother to the Conqueror, was defendant. The action was brought to try the title of Odo as Earl of Kent to certain lands in the county which, formerly belonging to the see of Canterbury, had since been seized by Odo under some claim of right. The lands and the parties being in Kent, the case came on to be tried in the court of that county held according to custom on Penenden Heath, a table land overlooking the town of Maidstone. This was formerly a Roman encampment; it is in the immediate neighbourhood of many Druidical remains, and has for hundreds of years been dedicated to the administration of justice, to the execution of malefactors and to public assemblies of freeholders and voters of the county. The court was presided over by Hamo, Sheriff of Kent, with whom were associated Geoffrey de Coutance, a Justiciar of the King, and Egelric, Bishop of Selsey.[2] This ecclesiastic, then

---

cui justicia magis acquieverit are added; but the practice indicated is inexplicable, unless it means that in an equal division of opinion the Sheriff is to have a casting vote.

[1] Odo the Bishop is a prominent figure in the Bayeux tapestry, where he appears in a coat of mail leading the Norman cavalry into action. But carrying out the principle that an ecclesiastic must not be a shedder of blood, he is armed with a huge baston or club instead of the customary sword or lance.

[2] He is usually described as the Venerable Bishop of Chichester: this is hardly accurate. The see of Chichester was not created

of very advanced age, was brought to Penenden Heath from beyond Chichester through the forest in a wagon to instruct the judges in the antient laws and customs of the Realm as "the most skilful person in the knowledge of them."[1] The court, composed of divers barons as suitors, sat for three days, at the end of which period they gave a verdict for the Archbishop, and twenty-five manors in Kent formerly seized by Odo were adjudged to belong to the see of Canterbury.

The SHIREEVE'S TURN was a session of the County Court held twice in the year, in each hundred, by the Sheriff and Bishop, if the Sheriff were forthcoming, or by the Alderman and Bishop if there were no Sheriff. It was called once after Easter and once after Michaelmas, with a Bishop to direct in Divine and a Sheriff or Alderman to direct in secular matters.[2] It enquired into frankpledge and had power to proceed alike against those who broke the peace of the Church, and those who broke the peace of their Lord the King.

Business was taken in the following order :[3]—(1) Eccle-

till after the death of Egelric (or Elfric) when Stigand (not the celebrated Archbishop) was appointed. He died in 1067. Elfric was appointed Bishop of Selsey by the Confessor in 1057, and was continued in that see by William, who consulted him on all questions relating to the national jurisprudence of the kingdom. Lower's *Worthies of Sussex*, p. 101. See also Lappenberg's *Anglo-Norman Kings*, pp. 145–171.

[1] Foss' *Judges*, vol. i. pp. 26, 39. Dugdale's *Origines Juridiciales*, fol. 30. Reeve's *History of English Law*, vol. i.

[2] *Laws of Edgar*, sec. 5. *Ancient Laws and Institutes*, vol. i. p. 269. *Laws of Cnut*, ib., p. 387.

[3] Coke's *Institutes*, vol. iv. p. 260.

siastical. (2) Pleas of the Crown or Criminal Cases. (3)
Causes between party and party. The practice of a
Bishop or other ecclesiastic sitting along with a Sheriff
or Alderman was strongly objected to by the clergy after
the Conquest, who wished to try ecclesiastical matters in
their own courts, and both William the Conqueror and
Henry I. inhibited Bishops and Archdeacons[1] from sitting
in Civil Courts to try ecclesiastical matters, a decree
which did not, however, prevent the clergy sitting as
judges in other cases. And as they were the only
persons really conversant with Roman Law and instructed in the Laws and Customs of England, they were
for many generations necessarily selected as justices
in the King's Courts. It seems, moreover, notwithstanding such inhibition, that the secular courts continued
to try clerics and their causes till the law relieved ecclesiastical suits altogether from liability to be instituted
and tried by the process of Civil Courts. Hallam[2]
gives an account of a so-called trial in the Shire-gemote
in the reign of Canute. But according to the report, the
business partook less of the nature of a trial at law than
of the settlement of a family dispute between a mother
and her son, in the course of which the former declared her
will to be in favour of her daughter and not of her son—
a declaration which appears by leave of the court to have
been recorded in the parish church.[3] The matter does

---

[1] *Ancient Laws and Institutes*, vol. i. p. 213.

[2] *Middle Ages*, vol. ii. p. 280. *Essays in Anglo-Saxon Law.*

[3] It was, however, a common practice of the Anglo-Saxons to
deposit treasure and valuable documents of all kinds in the

not seem to have been tried as a cause, and the court under those circumstances more nearly resembled a BURH-GEAT-SETL, or seat at the town gate, a court which, according to Selden, was convened for the purpose of trying family quarrels and disputes between tenants.[1] The case is interesting, however, as being an early instance of a *nuncupative testament* or verbal will of lands and goods having been given effect to by the court and finding its record on an ecclesiastical and not a secular roll.

These courts were still exercising their functions under the same presidents, and with the suitors as judges, when the Great Abridgement of the Law was published in the 33rd year of King Henry VIII. According to the table contained in that book, the courts of the hundred and of the county tried at that time, among various other plaints, actions on the case, actions for the admeasurement of dower and of pasture, customs, services, debt, detinue, dower, wardship, trespass and nuisance. Their jurisdiction in matters of debt and account was then, however, limited to forty shillings. If they exceeded that amount a prohibition would issue, and further proceedings in the suit would be stayed.

The times of the sittings remained as previously fixed, viz., the Hundred Court once in three weeks, the County Court once in the month, and the Shireeves Turn or

---

parish church for safe custody, and not necessarily for enrolment. —Lappenberg's *Anglo-Norman Kings*, p. 141.

[1] Selden: *Ancient Laws and Institutes*, vol. ii., glossary.

C

Tourne de Vicomte, as it was then called, twice in the year.[1]

The WITENAGEMOT, or meeting of wise men is usually referred to as the court of highest consideration under the Anglo-Saxon system. It sat at the king's palace, was attended by him and by the great officers of State, and did on occasions try cases of great importance, either from the subject-matter of the dispute, or by reason of the eminence of the parties concerned.[2] It resembled, however, a great Council rather than a Court of Justice. Its sittings were spasmodic, and it can hardly be reckoned among the judicial tribunals of the country.

The mode of trial used by the Anglo-Saxons for the determination of civil suits has never been definitely ascertained. The better opinion seems, however, to be that the parties were put to their oaths, and were supported by witnesses on each side who swore, if necessary, that they believed the plaintiff's or the defendant's contention to be true. If this were not sufficient, the witnesses were questioned by the court; and if that failed to secure a determination, they went to the proof by one or other form of ordeal.

The following Anglo-Saxon oaths in civil cases give good examples of the procedure. In the case of a plaintiff

---

[1] *The Greate Abbrigement,* etc., London, 1542, fol. 64, 137. *L'authorité et jurisdiction des Courts de la majestie de la Roygne,* by R. Crompton. London, 1594, fol. 231. "And so is the *Turn* holden *to this day.*" Coke, *4th Inst.,* p. 259.

[2] Reeve's *History,* vol. i. p. 17.

finding the cow or horse which he had purchased to be unsound, he swears as follows:—

"In the name of Almighty God, thou didst engage to me sound and clean that which thou soldest to me, and full security against after-claims on the witness of N——, who was then with us two."

N——, the witness, then swears:—

"In the name of Almighty God, as I here for in true witness stand, unbidden and unbought, so I with my eyes oversaw, and with my ears overheard that which I with him say."

The defendant swears:—

"In the name of Almighty God, I knew not in the thing about which thou suest foulness, or fraud, or infirmity, or blemish, up to that day's tide that I sold it to thee; but it was both sound and clean, without any kind of fraud.

"In the name of the living God, as I money demand, so have I lack of that which —— promised me when I mine to him sold."[1]

In the CRIMINAL PROCEDURE of the period, as in civil process, the party was put to his oath, and was tried by the sheriff or alderman, with triers or judges selected as for civil causes. Once before the court, however, the procedure against the defendant was barbarous, superstitious and illogical. There were two modes of trial for the defendant who denied the charges against him.[2]

---

[1] *Ancient Laws and Institutes*, vol. i. p. 181.

[2] Reeve's *History of English Law*, vol. i. p. 27. Lappenberg's *Anglo-Saxons*, vol. ii. p. 345.

First, if it was not a matter of such notoriety as to admit of no defence, the party could purge himself on a first offence by his oath and the oaths of certain of his neighbours called *compurgators*, who swore that they knew him, and that they believed he spoke the truth in denying the offence. The oaths were as follows. The accused swore in Saxon : [1]—

" By the Lord I am guiltless, both in deed and counsel, of the charge of which N—— accuses me."

The compurgators each swore :—

" By the Lord, the oath is clean and unperjured which he hath sworn."

This amounted to an acquittal. But if it were not his first offence, or if his compurgators did not agree to make the necessary oath, he was put to the ORDEAL, or God's judgment of fire or water. Of these judgments the ordeal of fire or hot iron was applied to noblemen and freemen as being the more honourable and more easy ; the ordeal of water being reserved for husbandmen or persons under the rank of a freeman.

The ordeal was regarded as a religious rite. It was conducted by the priests in the parish church, and the intervention of Providence was thus assumed to be secured on behalf of the innocent. To accomplish this result, the party charged was handed over to the Church to be prepared by prayer and fasting for the trial he had to undergo. After three days' preparation, he was brought into the church by the priests, and stood in the presence

---

[1] *Ancient Laws and Institutes,* vol. i. p. 181.

of his accuser, each party being accompanied by friends not exceeding twelve in number. Certain collects were then read, and prayer was offered up that heaven would interpose on behalf of the innocent. The accused, if the ordeal were by hot water, then plunged his naked hand or arm, according to the gravity of his alleged offence, into a bowl of boiling water, and picked out a stone which was suspended therein; in the former case to the depth of a man's hand, and in the latter to the depth of a cubit. If his hand or arm came out uninjured, it was assumed that heaven had worked a miracle to declare his innocence. If, on the contrary, his hand or arm was injured by the water, he was held to be guilty. In the ordeal by cold water he was, after three days' fasting and preparation, tied with his thumbs to his toes, and in this condition was thrown into a stream. If he sank he was innocent; if he floated he was guilty. Before, however, this was done, the accused was given holy water to drink, and the priest addressed the stream, adjuring it in the name of the Almighty who first created the water; by the baptism of Christ in the waters of Jordan; by His walking on the water; by the Holy Trinity, by whose will the Israelites passed dry-footed over the Red Sea, and at whose invocation Elisha caused the axe to swim, not to receive the accused if he were guilty, but to make him swim upon it.[1]

In the ordeal of hot iron, after the accused had been similarly prepared, the fire was brought into the church,

---

[1] Dugdale's *Origines Juridiciales*, fol. 87.

after which no one was allowed to enter but the priest
and the accused. Nine feet were then measured from the
fire to a mark, being nine times the length of the man's
foot. The iron, weighing from one to three pounds, according to whether it was the single or the threefold
ordeal,[1] was then laid upon the embers, where it remained
while the mass of judgment was performed, until the
last collect was read. It was then placed upon the
stapela (a pile of wood). The hand of the accused was
then sprinkled with holy water and he took the hot iron.
With this he walked the prescribed nine feet, when he
threw down the iron and went direct to the altar where
his hand was bound up by the priest.

After three days the bandage was removed in the
presence of all parties,[2] and his guilt or innocence depended upon the appearance of his hand.[3] If the wound
was clean, he was innocent; if impure, he was guilty.

By another method the supposed culprit walked between red-hot ploughshares a foot apart,[4] and by another,

---

[1] *Ordinances of Edgar* (A.D. 959–975). *Ancient Laws and Institutes*, vol. i. p. 261. Stubbs' *Charters*, p. 70.

[2] *Laws of Athelstane*, sec. 7. *Ancient Laws and Institutes*, vol.
i. p. 227. Dugdale's *Origines Juridiciales*, fol. 86.

[3] " Ce qui doit, je crois, faire entendre que l'on n'était pas
coupable quand la main conservait des marques de brûlure,
mais seulement lorsque la brûlure tombait en suppuration."—
Glanvil, p. 352. Houard, *Traité sur les Coutumes Anglo-
Normandes*, tom. i. p. 577.

[4] The legend that Emma or Ælfgifu, mother of the Confessor,
being charged with unchastity, purged herself by walking bare-
footed over nine red-hot ploughshares in Winchester Cathedral
is now suggested to be without foundation. See Freeman's *Nor-

called *offa cæcerata*, the accused was given a piece of bread from the altar. If he swallowed it, well : but if, like Macbeth's Amen, it stuck in his throat, he was guilty.[1] Another mode was to blindfold the accused and make him select from two pieces of wood, one being plain and one marked with a cross. If he chose that which bore the cross, he was free; but if he chanced on the other, he was guilty.

Sir Matthew Hale is of opinion that this form of trial by ordeal hardly survived the Conquest, having been condemned by the clergy as cruel and inconclusive, and that it was obsolete by the time of King John; trial by battle, an equally illogical plan, being the Norman substitute. Dugdale, however, who was contemporaneous with Sir Matthew Hale, is of opinion [2] that the Ordeal continued till the reign of Henry III., when it was abolished by an ordinance of that monarch, a copy of which he sets out in his book, reciting that the Ordeal was condemned by the Roman Church, and leaving it to the discretion of the justices not to enforce it. This opinion of Dugdale is supported by a perusal of the list of fines paid into the exchequer during the reigns of Henry II., Richard, John, and Henry III.[3] From this it would appear that in the

---

man Conquest, vol. ii. p. 368. Lee's *Wager of Battle*, etc., p. 258. The earliest authority for the story is Richard of Devizes, and it certainly has no inherent improbability.

[1] Godwin is said to have been choked by a piece of bread blessed by the Confessor.— Lappenberg's *Anglo-Saxons*, vol. ii. p. 258. [2] *Origines Juridiciales*, fol. 87.

[3] Madox's *History of the Exchequer*, vol. i. p. 557. *Ibid.*, pp. 544–47. Lyttleton's *History of Henry II.*, vol. iii. p. 214.

12 Henry II. the Soke of Averton was fined ten marks for putting one to the judgment of water without the presence of the king's officer (*serviens regis*); that in the 21 Henry II., Philip, the son of Wiard, and five others, were fined three and a half marks for letting one in a trial by ordeal of fire bear the iron twice with only one heating; that in the 31 Henry II. the town of Preston was fined five marks for putting a man to the water without warrant; and that in the 3 Henry III. the court of the Abbot of Waltham was fined thirty marks for a trespass in putting certain men to judgment by the water.   There were, in addition, several instances of fines for unjust judgments by water, and many others for proceeding in the absence of the king's servants, or serjeants (*servientes regis*).   It is probable, therefore, that the ordeal as practised by the Anglo-Saxons and continued by the Normans did in fact cease about the time of King Henry III.   The efficacy of the ordeal by cold water seems, however, to have become established in the English mind, and to have continued long after the abolition of the other forms of ordeal.   For people of all parts of England still continued to believe in the Divine interposition in these matters, and the ordeal of water was the common and ordinary mode of trying a witch long after the time of Sir Matthew Hale.   This particular mode of investigation was in fact explained and recommended by King James I. in his celebrated treatise on witches.[1]   It was actually practised in England down to

---

[1] *Dæmonologia*, London, 1603, fol. 79. The passage is extracted in *Sidelights on the Stuarts*, p. 142.

the year 1712, when Chief Justice Parker declared that if the trial by water caused the death of a suspected witch, he would hold every person engaged in it to be guilty of wilful murder. And in 1751 a man named Colley, who, notwithstanding this warning, had been one of a party to try a witch by the water ordeal, in the course of which she sank and died, was convicted of murder and executed.

The origin of the system of compurgators lies far back in the history of the Teuton race. But, like many other customs which reach beyond the memory of man, the principle of it still survives in the practice of our criminal courts, where a man is allowed as part of his defence to call witnesses to character. These are sworn, and, speaking from knowledge, declare their belief in his integrity. Their evidence is left to the jury as a part of the defendant's case, and the prosecution is not permitted to traverse their statements by giving general evidence of bad character.

The defendant, however, when convicted, was not, under the Confessor and his Anglo-Saxon predecessors, punished with that severity which might have been anticipated from the mode of trial adopted. For among these people every man had his *wer*, otherwise his money value, and accordingly nearly every offence could be expiated by a money payment either to the Crown or to the person injured, or, in the event of death, to the relatives of the party killed. Whether this system arose from clemency or cupidity it is impossible to determine. Probably both sentiments shared in its inception, and

while the clergy, who then and for many centuries were
the poor man's friends, saw their way to an alleviation of
the miseries of malefactors real or supposed, the monarchs
saw an easy mode, and one generally acceptable to the
people, of replenishing the coffers of the State from the
goods and lands of culprits.   These payments were regulated from time to time by royal ordinance, the most
complete of which was published by King Edward the
Elder (A.D. 901–924).[1]   The payment for a man's life
called the *wer-geld* was thus ascertained according to a
scale of which the King of England came at the head
with 30,000 thrimsas, or £500 of the money of the period,
half of which went to the king's kindred and half to the
State; an archbishop or earl 15,000, or £250; a bishop
or alderman 8,000, or £133 6s. 8d.; a priest or a thane
2,000, or £33 6s. 8d.; a ceorl, or common person, 267, or
£4 9s.   In a similar way a pecuniary fine of smaller
amount would relieve a man from corporal punishment
for various minor offences.

One penalty, however, known as *murdrum*, deserves a
passing remark.   If an unknown man was found dead, it
was enacted by Canute that he should be assumed to be
a Dane, and the fine called *murdrum* should accrue to the
king, unless it were conclusively shown that the dead
body was that of an Englishman.   A similar law was
promulgated by the Conqueror substituting a Norman for
a Dane, the object in each case being to prevent the
killing of Danes or Normans by the hostile English while

---

[1] *Ancient Laws and Institutes*, vol. i. p. 187.   Wer-gilds
Reeve's *History of English Law*, vol. i. p. 28.

their king and protector was away from the country. This gave rise to the custom of *proving the Englishery*, to which constant reference is made in old books and charters ; in other words, proving that the deceased was English by birth or parentage, in which event murdrum did not become payable to the Crown, and the malefactor or the hundred to which he belonged, and which was answerable for him, would only be liable to account to the family (if any) of the deceased.

II.

The Anglo-Saxon Chancellor—History of the Office—Origin of the Name—Charters of Westminster Abbey ; A.D. 1065—The Great Seal—Introduced by the Confessor—Its Custody— Lords Lyndhurst and Brougham—Never leaves the King- dom—Origin of the Custom—Wolsey—Swithin—Chaplain and Tutor to King Alfred—The Anglo-Saxon System —Long- continued Affection for the Laws of the Confessor.

THE position of a King as *fons et origo justitiæ*, the fountain-head and source of justice, as of honours and dignities, seems to be co-existent with the establishment of monarchy itself. The theory of all monarchical constitutions has originally been that the sovereign, as God's vicegerent here on earth, is himself present in his court, personally administering justice to all comers. And as in the oldest times of our national history the King, whether of a province such as Wessex or North- umbria or of the whole of England, as in the case of the Confessor, issued his writs from his Chancery and sum- moned his subjects, or those within the territorial limits of his power, to attend his presence and submit to the

justice there meted out ; so now, in the year of our Lord
1895, Victoria, by the grace of God, Queen, etc., still
summons her subjects and any others to be found within
her dominion to attend in her court at a specified time
and place, to submit their differences to her determination
and to abide by the judgment to be there given. And to
complete the identity of procedure, all such writs now, as
then, are tested or witnessed by the Chancellor.

How far the office or the occupation of a Chancellor as
keeper of the King's conscience and his assistant in the
administration of justice can be traced back in our history, is a subject of antiquarian research about which
there is much difference of opinion. The *Mirror of
Justices* suggests, and Lord Campbell [1] seems to adopt
the suggestion, that there was such an office even in
the remote and fabulous time of King Arthur, and Lord
Coke [2] puts the existence of a Chancellor in the time of
King Alfred as a matter hardly admitting of dispute.
Other writers disagree with this, and from their collected
views I think it safe to draw the following conclusions.
So long as population was sparse and the area of the
King's jurisdiction was small, he might well on occasions sit in person on the seat of judgment and deal
with the varied complaints of his subjects. But, as he
gradually enlarged his borders, and as his subjects increased in number and in wealth, it would become necessary for him to depute to others the duties of judication,

---

[1] *Lives of the Chancellors*, vol. i. p. 3.
[2] *Institutes*, vol. iv. p. 78.

reserving only to himself the hearing of appeals from his
deputies, or the trial of causes of such magnitude as to
be beyond the scope of any but the Royal authority. To
assist him in dealing with these cases he would require
a scribe or secretary, not only to record the proceedings,
but to make out the writs which would be issued in the
King's name to the various defendants. This involved
the regular employment of an ecclesiastic, for the clergy
were the only persons instructed in reading and writing who could be relied upon for knowledge of the
Roman or the Canon Law, and from that class alone
would a suitable scribe or secretary be available. Here,
therefore, the actual necessities of the Sovereign caused
the institution, under whatever name it might have been,
of an officer (not necessarily in the first instance a judge)
charged with the primary duties of a Chancellor, viz. the
preparing and issuing of original writs calling defendants
into court, and stating the reasons for their being summoned. Writs having been issued and local courts of the
nature already described having a recognised jurisdiction in the various counties, petitions to the King
either to hear appeals from the courts, or to sit himself as
a judge of first instance, would again increase, and it
would become the duty of the King's scribe or secretary
to make himself acquainted with the laws and customs of
the realm, to consider these various applications, and to
advise with the King which, if any, were fit and proper
to be granted. The person who occupied this position
and discharged these duties under the Anglo-Saxon kings
was known as the Referendarius or Referee and, accord-

ing to Selden,[1] one of our greatest legal antiquaries, who
took pains to investigate this subject, Referees discharging the primary duties of Chancellors are to be met with
in the reigns of Ethelbert, Edward the Elder, Athelstan,
Edmund and Edred.

The title Cancellarius, or Chancellor, according to the
opinion of some of our older writers, arose in the following manner. The Referendarius and his clerks being
besieged by people wishing on divers grounds for the
King's interference either in civil or criminal matters, for
the re-hearing of causes in the one case, and for the obtaining of pardons or the releasing of penalties in the other,
were separated from the suitors, like the officials in a
Basilica or Roman Law Court, by an open grille or lattice.
This lattice-work was formed by laths called *cancelli*, or
little bars, and the clerks and others who sat behind the
lattice and took in the plaints were thus called the clerks
of the cancelli or chancery.[2] When the name of Chancellor was actually given to this officer seems also to be
subject to some doubt. Writers of the twelfth and
thirteenth centuries refer to all these officers of the
Anglo-Saxons as Chancellors; but the first occasion upon
which the name is definitely ear-marked as attached to
the office is during the period of the Confessor. Towards
the end of his reign this king granted a charter to St.

---

[1] *A brief Discourse touching the Office of Lord Chancellor, dedicated to Sir Francis Bacon*, by John Selden. London, 1677.
[2] Dugdale's *Origines Juridiciales*, fol. 32. Lord Campbell's
Lives of the Chancellors, vol. i. p. 1.

Peter's, at Westminster [1] (Westminster Abbey), which bears the following among other signatures: " *Ego Rembald regis Cancellarius relegi et sigillavi.*" I, Rembald, the King's Chancellor, have perused and sealed. Here then we find in the reign of the Confessor absolute and indisputable evidence of the existence of an officer called the Chancellor, whose duty it was to peruse public documents on behalf of the King, and to put the seal to them when approved by him. It by no means follows, however, that he was at that time the judge of a court, or that there was in fact any Court of Chancery ; and I am disposed to believe that although the office of a Chancery out of which writs were issued, and a Chancellor who ordered their issue and advised the Sovereign on various matters, existed during the Anglo-Saxon period, yet that the judicial functions of the Chancellor and the court of Chancery did not commence till after the Norman Conquest. Nor did the Anglo-Saxon Chancellor, though a person of distinction, occupy a very high position ; for he was, in most instances, one of the King's chaplains, and on his retirement was usually promoted to some dignity in the Church. The Charter of Westminster Abbey, to which I have referred, gives his exact precedence. It is dated 28th December, 1065,[2] and is the earliest existing public document in which the King's Chancellor is so described, and also the earliest existing document which

---

[1] Dugdale's *Origines Juridiciales*, fol. 34. Coke, *4th Institute*, p. 78. Selden's *Discourse.*

[2] " *V. Kalen., Jan., die Sanct. Innocentium*, A.D. 1066." This would be 28th Dec., 1065.

bears the Great Seal. The signatures are as follows:
First the King signs EADPARD in a schoolboy's hand,
and makes his cross; next the Queen Eadgytha; then the
Archbishops of Canterbury and of York; then the Bishop
of London and eight other Bishops; then seven Abbots;
then Rembald the King's Chancellor, who *seals*; then
three of the King's chaplains (capellanus), who sign; then
Duke Harold, and Earls Edwin, Garth and Leoffwine; then
seven deacons (minister); then five knights; and lastly
the notary, who says he drew the charter under the
authority of Rembald the Chancellor.[1] In a second
charter of the same date, the notary, Smithgarus, who
says he drew it, also signs it on behalf of Rembald the
Chancellor. The first of these bears the Great Seal of
the Confessor, in addition to the signatures; the second
bears the signatures only.

It will be remarked that Rembald, the Chancellor of
the Confessor, executed the Charter of Westminster
Abbey by sealing, as well as by affixing his signature.
From this it is assumed that the Chancellor was at that
time the Keeper of the Great Seal which was set to the
Charter of the Abbey. And this gives rise to the
question, When did the *Great Seal* first exist? The
answer to this question can be given with exactness.
Seals were not common, if in fact they were used at all by
any Anglo-Saxon king before the Confessor. It is said [2]

---

[1] An exemplification of this Charter in photo-zincography has
been published by the Record Office, among their facsimiles of
Anglo-Saxon MSS., edited by W. Basevi Sanders.

[2] Dugdale's *Origines Juridiciales*, fol. 33. Selden's *Discourse
of the Office of Lord Chancellor.*

GREAT SEAL OF THE CONFESSOR.

Face page 32.

The obverse shows the king with flowing beard and moustache; a loose robe fastened by a brooch on the right shoulder; an open crown of four points; in the right hand, a sceptre topped with fleur de lys; in the left hand, an orb.

The reverse shows the king with pointed beard and moustache trimmed in the French fashion, enthroned and robed; a helmet with bars; in the right hand, a sceptre with a dove on the top; in the left, a sword resting on the left shoulder.

The legend on each side is " SIGILLUM EADWARDI ANGLORUM BASILEI."

This impression is taken from a leaden cast in the British Museum. The original seal is in the National Archives in Paris, and is the finest known to exist. A full description of the Seals of the Confessor may be found in the Catalogue of Seals in the MS. Department of the British Museum, *by W. de Gray Birch; London, 1887, vol. i. p. 2.*

in regard to certain charters of the Anglo-Saxon period that there were labels attached to them, suggesting the existence of seals which have since disappeared, and that the word *sigillum* (seal) appears in some even earlier charters. In the possession of the Dean and Chapter of Chichester is an original grant, bearing date A.D. 780, of certain lands in Sussex to the Cathedral of Selsey, by Oslac, Duke of the South Saxons. This grant is confirmed by Offa, King of the Mercians, and concludes as follows: "✠ Ego Offa Deo donante rex Merciorum hanc supradictam terram . . . conroborans subscribo ac dominicæ crucis inpræssione confirmabo." *I Offa, by gift of God King of the Mercians, corroborating the above mentioned grant . . . subscribe, and will confirm with the impression of the Lord's Cross.* This points to the practice of attaching gold crosses to important documents, but does not involve the use of any seal.[1] Crompton refers to certain Forest Charters of the Confessor signed with crosses of gold, and sets out a grant by him in that form.[2] Nor am I aware of any duly authenticated seal to any public document before that date. However this may be, seals were undoubtedly in use on the Continent many years before their adoption in this country. The Great Seal

---

[1] A somewhat imperfect copy of this very antient document may be found in *Monasticon Anglicanum*, vol. vi. p. 1163. It is written on vellum and is in good preservation. It was reproduced in autotype *fascimile* under :he supervision of Mr. Walter de Gray Birch, F.S.A., of the British Museum, and a few copies with annotations by him were printed for private circulation.

[2] *Crompton*, fol. 147, and see post cap. IV.

D

of England was therefore introduced by the Confessor,
whose long pupilage in Normandy had imbued him with
Norman customs and ideas. Examples of the Confessor's
seal, whence we may confidently derive the Great Seal
of England, are still to be seen. One in very perfect
condition is at the British Museum. It represents the
king in his royal robes, seated on his throne, holding a
sceptre in his right hand and a sword in his left, and
bears the legend, " *Sigillum Edwardi Anglorum Basilei.*"
This was the first of the Great Seals of England, for whose
custody a high official is appointed and to counterfeit
which is an act of high treason.[1] It was in old days
kept in the treasury of the Exchequer at Westminster,
in an oaken, iron-bound chest, which also contained the
original Domesday Book. This was fastened by three
several locks, of which the keys were kept respectively
by the Justiciar, the Chancellor, and the Treasurer.
Some other great seals of later date, as they came into
use, were deposited in this chest, such as the seals of the
King's Bench and of the Common Pleas, of the Principal-
ity of Wales, of Calais and the English possessions in
France, and of certain Bishoprics when the sees were
vacant.[2] In each succeeding reign a new seal was made,
and the old seal became the property of the Chancellor
who was in office at the late King's death. Lord Lynd-

---

[1] 1 Edward III., c. 6.

[2] Hall's *Antiquities of the Exchequer*, p. 46. A drawing of this
oaken chest, which still exists, is given as a frontispiece to Mr.
Hall's book.

hurst and Lord Brougham discussed with some energy
which of them was to have the reversion of the Great
Seal of George IV., Lord Lyndhurst having been in office
when the King died, and Lord Brougham being in office
when, the new seal being completed, the old seal was
rendered useless.[1] The dispute was settled by William
IV., who after the approved precedent of King Solomon,
ordered the Great Seal to be divided into two parts,
and half to be given to each claimant. Unlike the rival
mothers in Israel, the legal litigants accepted the royal
judgment, and decided by lot the destination of the respective parts.

One other matter should be mentioned in reference to
the Great Seal. By the customary law of England as
at present established the Great Seal never leaves the
kingdom. When the Plantagenets left home for their
foreign ventures the Great Seal was usually deposited in
the care of the Chancellor or of some other great official.
The monarch, however, on one or two occasions had a
duplicate seal in silver, made for his own use, though it
was never recognised as having the same authority as
the Great Seal. King Richard being in Sicily on his way
to the Crusades, Master Roger Malus Catullus, who is
described as Vice-Chancellor, was sent over sea to obtain
the King's signature to certain charters, the Chancellor
himself (William de Longchamp) being not only keeper
of the Great Seal, but acting Viceroy of England in
his master's absence, and accordingly unable to leave

---

[1] Campbell's *Lives*, vol. i. p. 27.

the realm. On his way home the Vice-Chancellor was drowned off Cyprus and the King's Seal was lost, being, as is said, hung round his neck, and the charters had to be re-executed.[1] Whether, however, this was the Great Seal of England which had been sent out by the hands of the Chancellor's deputy, or, which is much more probable, it was the King's Privy Seal, authorizing the Chancellor to sign and seal in the King's name, does not very clearly appear. In June, 1253, when Henry III. was going to Gascony, and William de Kilkenny, the Chancellor, was sick, the Great Seal was committed to the custody of Queen Eleanor under the King's Privy Seal until the Chancellor's recovery in the following year.[2] These, however, seem to be the only authenticated cases of an early date when the Great Seal was committed to the care of a person who was not himself to execute in effect, or in name, the office of Chancellor; and they tend to corroborate the view that the Great Seal never properly leaves the country. Great pomp and ceremony also accompanied the deposit of the Great Seal in the chest of the Exchequer when the King departed from his kingdom, and its resumption by the monarch on his return. The details of this function are given by Madox, who also informs us that when so deposited it was kept in a bag or purse of white leather, sealed with the Chancellor's Seal. In the reign of Edward I., however,

---

[1] Madox's *History of the Exchequer*, vol. i. p. 77. Campbell's *Lives, etc.*, vol. i. p. 117.

[2] Selden's *Discourse, etc.*; Madox, vol. i. p. 68, where the writ is set out in a note.

there is some evidence that the Great Seal did leave the kingdom, for it is stated that the King, when leaving England for Flanders in 1297, in one of the Winchelsea ships, called the *Cog Edward*, took the Great Seal on board with him and delivered to his son, as regent during his absence, another seal, which was accordingly used by the Chancellor during this period. The King on his return in 1298 took back the regent's seal in exchange for the Great Seal then restored to the Chancellor.[1] It also appears that Henry V. had the Great Seal of England with him during his French campaign, and that he actually lost it with his baggage at the battle of Agincourt.[2] Whether, therefore, the theory, which has now obtained the dignity of a customary law, that the Great Seal never leaves the kingdom, was founded on convenience or superstition it is impossible at this time to say. There is no written law, edict, or ordinance to that effect, nor does the Chancellor in his oath of office swear not to convey the Seal out of England ; and I am disposed to believe that it originated merely in a matter of convenience. It certainly was not safe for the King or his Chancellor to travel with the Royal Seal in foreign parts, when the King and the Seal might both be taken prisoner and held to ransom. And thus the act of precaution which led to the Great Seal being duly and safely deposited in the Exchequer might well have given rise, as many such customs do, to a belief among the people that there was something sacred attached to the Great Seal, and that,

---

[1] Foss' *Judges*, vol. iii. p. 8.   [2] *Ibid.*, vol. iv. p. 186.

like the bones of a saint, some national calamity might
be expected to follow its removal from England. Lord
Campbell says [1] that one of the articles of impeachment
against Cardinal Wolsey was that he took the Great Seal
out of England and sealed writs with it at Calais. His
Lordship, however, gives no authority for this statement,
and I am unable to find any except the exceedingly
doubtful authority of Shakespeare,[2] who puts this charge
into the mouth of one of the lords when reviling Wolsey
after his fall. The only articles given by Coke, among
the forty-four which he copied from the original [3] impeachment, which bear upon the point are the second and
third. By the former Wolsey is charged that being an
ambassador in France he made a treaty with the Pope
and the French King without the knowledge or assent of
the King; and by the latter that being the King's ambassador in France he sent a commission to Sir Gregory
de Cassalis under the Great Seal to conclude a treaty
with the Duke of Ferrara without the knowledge or
assent of the King. The gist of these offences seems,
therefore, to have been, not that he took the Great Seal
to France, but that he made treaties on his own account without previously ascertaining the wishes of the
monarch.

Of the officials holding the post of referee, secretary,
or chaplain to the Anglo-Saxon kings, one at least deserves mention, Swithin, Bishop of Winchester, who,
while discharging the duties of Referee or Chancellor,

---

[1] *Lives of Chancellors*, vol. i. p. 27.
[2] *Henry the Eighth*, Act 3, Sc. 2.   [3] *Institutes*, vol. iv. p. 88.

was Chaplain to King Ethelwulf, and at the same time tutor to Alfred, the future king. Swithin, afterwards canonized and known as Saint Swithin, was a man of great parts, of singular and unaffected piety, and his name lived long in the memory of the people. He taught his young pupil all the learning that was to be had in those days, and accompanying him to Rome, instructed him in the history and showed him the remains of art and of literature in that country. Before the death of Ethelwulf he retired to his cathedral at Winchester, withdrew himself from the world, and died in peace. He did not live to see his former pupil on the throne, but to a careful and judicious training, and to the good principles imbibed during his youthful days, the success of King Alfred's reign may possibly be ascribed.

Thus, far back in the history of our country, long before the institution of Justiciars, Chief Justices, or Chief Barons, do we trace the origin of the Chancellor and of his jurisdiction. Gradually, as will be seen, he rose from the position of a subordinate clerk or secretary of the monarch to be the monarch's rival, if not his controller. Skilled in the common law, but not bound by its rigours, representing the conscience and mercy of the king, as distinguished from the justices of the various courts, who by their impartial administration enforced the strict letter of the law, he entertained the appeals of the people and moderated their burthens by giving effect to those equitable considerations which reason or clemency might suggest, but which other judges of the country were without authority to apply.

These, then, were the Courts in which justice was administered under the Confessor. They proceeded upon the principle that the application of the law should not be left in the hands of one adjudicator; that a man's judges should be his neighbours and his fellows; that the best evidence in a case was the evidence of the litigant's character and reputation, and that the Manor, the Hundred, or the County in which the parties resided should alone provide freemen for the trial of all complaints arising within its limits. Though such trials could not accurately be described as trials by jury, as we now understand the term, yet they involved the principle of such trial, and demanded a certain power of organization to arrange the details. They also had this advantage, that they brought justice down to every man's door, and they probably enjoyed, what are now regarded as essential requirements, cheapness and dispatch. Advocates were not required and probably not permitted, as a man's judges were his neighbours, many of whom had probably been called in from time to time according to the practice of the age to be witnesses to his contracts, and could say from their own knowledge of his life whether he were a person of integrity whose word was to be believed. The Sheriff, and the Earl or the Alderman who presided, were persons of station in the county, usually of good education and well skilled in knowledge of the law; and the courts were held frequently, so that there would probably be no considerable delay in bringing causes to a hearing.

But speed in judicial affairs is not the great boon that

an unreflecting public is apt to regard it. *Præcipitatio est noverca justitiæ.* Haste is the step-mother of justice, says Lord Coke, and he instances the Courts of TRAIL-BASTON (quick as your stick), instituted by Edward I. in order that justice might follow complaint as swiftly as you could trail a club, but which, owing to numerous errors and repeated appeals, came to an end by general consent in the reign of Richard II.[1] And these Anglo-Saxon tribunals must also have had the disadvantages common to courts where justice is administered in local centres, under local presidents, with local judges. Much injustice, as Sir Matthew Hale[2] points out, may have been done through the ignorance of the freeholders who were judges, notwithstanding the advice of the Sheriff and the Bishop, if indeed in all cases these persons were competent to advise. The diversity of rulings in the different courts must also have led to great uncertainty in the law, each county establishing for itself certain precedents conflicting with, or contradicting those of another and, it may be, a neighbouring shire. We know even now the inconvenience which arises from the custom of the country as to the outgoing tenant, differing in agricultural matters widely between county and county. And we have also the conflicting customs of the country as to the devolution of land, where in most counties the eldest son born in wedlock is the heir-at-

---

[1] *Institutes*, vol. iv. p. 186. Reeve's *History of English Law*, vol. ii. p. 169.

[2] *History of the Common Law*, p. 169. Littleton's *History of Henry II.*, vol. iii. pp. 207–209.

law, but in Kent and some parts of Sussex the custom of
gavelkind prevails, by which the land is divided equally
between the sons; and in parts of Surrey, Middlesex,
and some other counties, where the custom of borough-
english governs the succession, and there the youngest
son takes the land over the heads of his older brothers.
But, above all, in such local courts the presidents and
the judges being well known beforehand, solicitation and
bribery were encouraged and parties took sides, so that
he best succeeded who could make for himself most
friends and supporters among the thanes and the freeholders. Men of great influence in the county could
thus easily overbear others of less importance and more
moderate fortune, and the only chance for a small man
lay in the possibility of an appeal: for an appeal lay
from the County Court direct to the King in every case
in which it could be shown that the appellant, after
repeated applications, had failed to get justice in the
courts below.[1]

Such, however, as they were, with all their imperfec-
tions, these Anglo-Saxon courts commended themselves
to the good-will and the intelligence of the people. They
were homely, and their procedure, if crude, was simple
and intelligible. That a man should be tried upon his
general reputation was the accepted mode of trial for

---

[1] *Ordinances of Edgar*, A.D. 959–975. *Laws of Cnut*, A.D. 1016–
1035. *Ancient Laws and Institutes*, vol. i. p. 385. Stubbs' *Charters*
pp. 70–72. An instance of an appeal from the County Court in
the reign of Ethelred is given in Pulling's *Order of the Coif*,
p. 53.

many generations of Englishmen, and that his triers should be his neighbours, with whom it was his business to live on good terms, followed reasonably enough. Equally reasonable and intelligible was it to them that the kindred, or in their default the gild, should be answerable for the misdeeds of any of their number; for no man lived among them of whom they could not give account, and strangers were warned from their limits unless they could warrant their life and occupation. If the trial by ordeal is objected to as cruel and superstitious, it must be borne in mind that the word cruelty represented different ideas in the Middle Ages and in the Nineteenth Century: that no one on the continent of Europe was then shocked by the infliction of torture in pursuit of truth, and that superstition, the foster-brother of ignorance, pervaded all classes and all nations. The general effect of their criminal procedure was also to this extent similar to our own, that although it may in some cases have borne heavily on the innocent, yet it gave to the guilty more chances of escape than the procedure of any other country in the civilized world. Whether for these or other reasons, certain it is that for many a year after the Conquest, so long as a community of fair-haired Anglo-Saxons existed in England, so long did they cry aloud for a return to the antient and beneficent laws of the Confessor. For more than a century after these laws had ceased to have any possibility of operation, when the local courts, no longer trusted to do justice as between the weak and the strong, had been forsaken for the greater security of the Court Hall of the. King; when

Justiciar, Justiciaries and Barons had taken the place of the Alderman and his fellow hundredors; when the ordeal had ceased to be practised and the Church was no longer amenable to the Law people, who could only have known this procedure by tradition, swore their monarchs to observe the laws of the Confessor, and still professed to regard them as the perfection of justice and the embodiment of mercy. And even down to the period of Edward IV. the arms of the Confessor, side by side with the Lions of England, were emblazoned on all the courts of Westminster Hall.

CHAPTER II.

CURIA REGIS.

(A.D. 1066–1268.)

Anglo-Saxon and Norman Systems of Jurisprudence—Curia Regis —The Chief Justiciar—Law Terms—Westminster Hall—The King's Exchequer—The Exchequer Chamber—Process of the Exchequer—Burning of the Tallies in 1834—The title of the Exchequer—Hearing of Causes — Troubles of Richard de Anesti—Institution of Judges' Circuits—Trial by Jury— The Great Assize — Wager of Battle — The Court Rolls— Royal Progresses—Chief Justice of the Common Bench— Decline of the Chief Justiciar—Position of the smaller Courts —The County Court—The Rise of the Chancellor—Thomas à Becket—His connection with Westminster Hall.

WHEN the Conqueror had by force of arms compelled England to accept him as her monarch, and had, as the result of his vigour, effected a momentary tranquillity, it became necessary to formulate a scheme for administration of the law, so as to satisfy his new subjects that justice would be duly meted out to them, and at the same time to assure to his companions in arms and to the crowds of Normans who flocked to England for gain or advancement, a safe and secure abiding place for themselves and their possessions.

The divergence between the Norman and the Anglo-Saxon systems of jurisprudence was vast and manifest. The former was founded on a system of centralization, while the latter was based on a system of self-government. In the former the Grand Justiciar, or Chief of the Law, had in his hands all the power of the judicature; in the latter each community judged its own offences and tried its own cases, with no right of appeal except to the clemency of the Crown. It was impossible, therefore, to expect the Normans to submit to the primitive and Teutonic system approved by the English; and at the same time it would have been impossible to induce the English to accept in a moment a procedure which was contrary to all their pre-conceived notions of justice and law. And surmounting all these considerations was the almost inevitable hope of William, that in due time England and Normandy should be but one kingdom, with one race of subjects, of whom the Norman, having gained the supremacy, would retain the guidance. With this object doubtless at heart, and pressed by his difficult situation, he adopted the Norman model, and superseding the Witenagemot of the Saxon kings, instituted one Supreme Court and one supreme officer of justice. He refrained, however, from interfering with the action of the existing Anglo-Saxon tribunals, except in so far as he withdrew from their cognizance any criminal jurisdiction over the offences of the clergy. The court thus constituted was called indifferently *Curia Regis*, or *Aula Regia*, the King's Court, or the King's Court Hall. It was attached to the king's person, was held in the hall of his palace, followed him wherever he went, and was the embodiment of justice administered by the king himself. It was the only Royal Court as distinguished from the English Courts, which were under the Sheriffs of the counties, and it was furnished with all the pomp and splendour which attached to the service of

the Norman dukes. It was a court of unlimited jurisdiction, although its primary object was the determination
of questions relating to the king and his affairs. It entertained appeals from inferior courts, and questions of
importance between private individuals, having exclusive
jurisdiction in those cases where the king had granted to
certain of his subjects the privilege of suing and being
sued only in the Royal Court. It was presided over by
the *Chief Justiciar*, a great officer of the State, who was
not only the chief magistrate, but the King's lieutenant
throughout his kingdom, and his Viceroy whenever he
departed the realm. The Justiciar's companions on the
Justice Seat were the Chancellor, who now began to
assume a definite position, and such of the barons,
ecclesiastics, and other learned persons as were from
time to time summoned to his assistance. The difference
between the Witenagemot and the Aula Regia thus
became clear and pronounced. While Anglo-Saxon England, represented by the thanes and prelates assembled
in the Witenagemot, with the actual presence of the
King in their midst, bound the Crown by its judgments,
and reversed his decrees [1] if not made in accordance with
their view of the law; the Norman Aula Regia, on the
other hand, being the representative of the King, presided
over by the King's nominee, in the actual or constructive
presence of the King, bound the people by its judgments,
and took its inspiration directly or vicariously from the

---

[1] As in the case of the monks of Worcester, when the Witenagemot over-ruled the king. Stubbs' *Constitutional History*, vol. i.
p. 147.

Crown, which was thus only bound by decrees of its own initiation.

William was a monarch of great splendour and display. Three times in every year he "wore his crown," or, in other words, he held a Court, when lavish hospitality was dispensed, when all the great men of England were summoned to meet him, when matters of state were discussed, and when justice was administered by the king himself. These special occasions were at Christmas, at Easter, and at Whitsuntide, and as there were sittings of the Curia Regis after each of these festivals, they are supposed to have been the origin of the law terms, the fourth term being co-incident with the meeting of the Sheriffs and others to render their accounts in the Exchequer after Michaelmas Day.

In the appointment of his Viceroy, William sought for a man of learning, of courage, and of devotion to himself. In Odo, Bishop of Bayeux, his half-brother, he found all those qualities, and made him his first Justiciar without regarding certain other qualities of his, which would in after years have suggested a disqualification for the post. He was, however, of a respectable learning, having been trained for the Church, and holding the position of a Norman bishop. He was of undoubted courage, as his conduct at the battle of Hastings, when he led the Norman cavalry, and in his previous campaigns against the King of France, undoubtedly testified; and his devotion to William was unquestionable, as in addition to family ties, his own personal interests were bound up with those of the Conqueror. By Odo, therefore, and by his assis-

tants, Geoffry of Coutance and William Fitz Osborne,
justice was administered during the reign of the Conqueror in the Curia Regis which followed the king, at
Westminster, at Winchester, at Gloucester, at Windsor,
and at Salisbury. In what particular part of London
the Court sat at its first inception is not very certain, as
there was no building suitable for such purpose then in
existence, either in or near the capital. The old building, known as Edward the Confessor's Hall, which formerly stood in Old Palace Yard, even if it existed in the
time of the Conqueror, was too small for the grand hospitality and display affected by the Norman kings. The
King's Palace was, however, at Westminster. The rebuilding of the Abbey had been nearly if not quite completed by the Confessor, who had endowed it with special
privileges, had declared it the perpetual depository of
the crown and the regalia, the place for the coronation
of the sovereigns of England [1] and a perpetual sanctuary;
and it is probable, therefore, that the Court during the
reign of the Conqueror, was actually held in the neighbourhood of Westminster Hall.

On the accession of William Rufus steps were at once
taken to provide the King with a hall suitable for regal
hospitality and ceremonies, and for the more frequent sittings of the Curia Regis. For this purpose the Red King
caused a building to be erected in immediate contiguity
to his own palace and the Abbey. At Whitsuntide, A.D.
1099, he wore his crown, and sat for the first time in the

---

[1] Crulls' *Antiquities of St. Peter's*, p. 5. London, 1711.

royal justice seat in Westminster Hall.[1] And in this
venerable building, which, though it has undergone
many changes, and has passed through the ordeals of fire,
of flood, and of renovation, is still the old hall of the
Norman Conquest, justice was administered with unde-
viating regularity, not only in times of peace and of
prosperity, but in years of pestilence, of anarchy, and of
civil war.[2]

The building of this hall and of certain adjoining
houses, long since destroyed, had also become necessary,
not only for the requirements of civil and criminal
justice, but for the courts and offices suitable for the
due entertainment of the judges, the clerks and others
employed in the all-important duty of collecting
and auditing the royal revenue. This was effected
through the machinery of the *King's Exchequer*, itself
a component part of the Curia Regis. That there was,
long before the Conquest, an office answering to the description of an Exchequer, and a more or less efficient
audit of the royal accounts, may fairly be assumed.
Though of what nature it was, where it was located, or
by whom superintended, it is difficult to say, there being
no definite information on the subject. It is believed
that there was a system of audit as early as the reign of

---

[1] Madox, *History of the Exchequer*, vol. i. p. 9. Campbell's *Lives
of the Chief Justices*, vol. i. p. 15.

[2] An interesting and learned architectural history of Westminster Hall will be found in the report of Mr. Pearson, R.A.,
to the Committee of the House of Commons which sat in 1885–
86.

Alfred, and that it was carried out through the officers of the treasury, but here again we are involved in speculation. It must also be borne in mind that owing to the deficiency, or rather the non-circulation, of coin, payments were made in kind, a practice which continued many years after the Conquest, various articles such as bacon, and even hawks, being taken at an estimated value. That there was a Treasurer under the Conqueror is hardly open to question, nor can we doubt that he did his best to get in the King's revenue, but information is wanting as to how or where he exercised his functions. The Exchequer, therefore, as an institution of the country cannot be taken as precisely ascertained before the time of William Rufus and the opening of Westminster Hall. From this date, however, its practice and duties appear to have been settled. The Court and offices of the Exchequer were a part of the King's Court. The name was *Curia Regis de Scaccario*, the King's Court of the Exchequer, and its duties were to receive the accounts of the Sheriffs and of all other accountants and collectors for the Crown, to give acquittances to those who paid, and to issue writs and orders to enforce payment by those in default. The subjects and the varieties of the claims were innumerable, and to assess these and decide between the demands of the king and the excuses of the subject were among the duties cast upon the supreme court of the realm. The staff, which was necessarily administrative as well as judicial, accordingly consisted in the first instance of the Justiciar as President, the Chancellor as Moderator,

the Treasurer as Chief of the office and claimant for the
Crown, the Chamberlains and various other barons, lay
and clerical, summoned by the king. Added to these
were the tellers, the assayers, the ushers, and many
others, who, with the judicial officers, sat at the usual
half-yearly terms and heard the cases brought before
them. Their house was situate on the northern side of
the Palace, and was two stories high, with cellars and
residences for the permanent clerks, together with some
description of lock-up for the temporary accommodation
of the prisoners of the Marshal. The official staff, who,
between one half-year and the next, made the necessary
computations, kept the tallies and other records, and were
responsible for the bullion, the gold and silver plate, the
jewels and other valuables of the Crown, sat in an apart-
ment on the ground floor, while the President, the Chancellor, and the judicial barons occupied a court on the
floor above. This was a large room with a gallery
supported by pillars of chestnut wood, and was in
existence until 1821,[1] when it was pulled down. The
fittings of this court, which was known as the Exchequer
Chamber, and was used in after times for private
conferences of the justices, were somewhat primitive,
but well adapted for the rude process of accounting.
This process was rendered more laborious by the fact
that the only silver money in circulation was the penny,
or somewhat later the silver groat: the noble not having

---

[1] See *Mr. Pearson's Report.*

Sketch of the room adjoining Westminster Hall in which the Barons of the Exchequer sat to transact the revenue business; afterwards the Exchequer Chamber.

See page 52.

The Great Exchequer Court (looking North)

From a drawing by W. Capon. 1822.

been introduced into England till the initiation of a gold coinage by Edward III.

In this room, therefore, sat the treasurer representing the king, and here one after another the accountants came before him, bringing their payments or offering their excuses. The centre of the room was occupied by a table with a cloth or carpet, scored across with lines in chalk or paint like a chess- or draught-board. The table was surrounded by a ledge sufficiently high to prevent the coins or counters falling to the ground. Each space had a numerical value counting from right to left, beginning at the right with pence and ending at the left with thousands of pounds. Around this board sat the barons of the Exchequer.[1] At the head was the Justiciar, as president of the court. To his left sat the Chancellor and the Chamberlains. To his right were the Treasurer with his clerk, and the Chancellor's clerk, afterwards called the Chancellor of the Exchequer, with one or two scribes to write up the rolls. At the side sat the Chamberlain's clerks with their counter-tallies, and the tellers who added up the money and arranged the counters on the board. At the bottom of the table opposite the Justiciar or other presiding officer sat the Sheriffs or other accountants with their clerks, who brought their tallies, bullion, and other materials for making out their account. There were also present other barons of the Exchequer who had been summoned by the King, the Marshal, the Ushers,

---

[1] *Dialogus de Scaccario*, Madox, vol. ii. p. 264. Hall's *Antiquities of the Exchequer*, p. 115. See article in the *Gentleman's Magazine*, January, 1855.

and other necessary officers of the court. As the accountant came to the table the amount of his indebtedness to the Crown was indicated by counters in the several spaces. As he produced his bullion, his wooden tallies, or his indentures of acquittance, the corresponding counters were swept away, till the checking ended either by his last payment balancing the last counter, by a remnant of counters shewing him to be in so much a debtor to the king, or by a surplus of money shewing the Crown to be in so much a debtor to him. Thus, if a sheriff came forward to account for a year's revenue of say £1,000, counters were laid on the table representing on various squares the sum to be paid. As he produced his bags of silver pennies for say £500 they were counted by the tellers, then weighed, and if any doubt suggested itself as to their purity they were tested by the master of assayes. On passing these tests they were swept into the treasury, and counters corresponding to £500 were removed from the table. He then produced his tallies shewing the sum he had already paid on account, say £300, and on these being compared with the foils or counter-tallies held by the exchequer clerks and found correct, his tallies were allowed, and more counters representing £300 were removed from the table. He then produced his indentures shewing how much he was allowed for disbursements for provision for the King and his servants and for other purposes. If these corresponded with the entries on the rolls, they also were allowed, and he was quit of his account, receiving a tally with a notch cut clean across the face of the width of a man's palm, representing the payment of £1,000. Present at the counting was also the Marshal of the Exchequer with his varlets, ready to arrest forthwith and to commit to his prison any defaulter or misdemeanant. The business of the court being concluded on the account, the Chancellor in the early days, and the Chancellor of the Exchequer at a later period, framed, with the assistance of his clerks, the necessary writs and notices to enable the barons in their respective districts to enforce the claims of the Crown against defaulting debtors.

This rude and simple process, very much resembling the disused procedure of the gaming tables at Homburg or Baden-Baden, was the mode of calculation at the Exchequer for many centuries. It lasted, with some modifications, until the year 1834, when the accumulation of tallies was so great that it was determined to get rid of them and thus end the system and its evidences. They were accordingly burnt in the old Exchequer House by the side of Westminster Hall. But the tallies made for themselves a funeral pyre of magnificent proportions, for the flues, being overheated by the unusual firing, set alight to the old combustible Houses of Parliament which then occupied the palace of the Norman kings, and burnt them to the ground.

The title "Exchequer" has given rise to much learned argument, the common acceptation being that the name is derived from the fact that the court was held in a room with a chequered cloth and hence was called the Court of Exchequer. And it does appear from a drawing of the Court of Exchequer in the year 1808, that the centre of the court was occupied by a large square table with a cloth of black and white squares resembling those of a huge chess-board, although in a drawing hereafter mentioned of the fifteenth century no such cloth is depicted. I do not, however, consider it by any means probable that a court originally constituted of the highest authority in the kingdom, should take its name from the pattern of a cloth which was probably not used for many generations after the institution of the tribunal. The word used is *Scaccarium*, for which there seem to be two derivations : one, the game of chess *ludus scaccarii*, to which the moving of the counters on the one side as the bullion and tallies are produced on the other, may have some resemblance ; and the other, which appears to me the more reasonable, from the German word *schach*, a dummy or counter, signifying the mode of computation by counters adopted in the treasury.

Matters thus proceeded for several generations, the Curia Regis dispensing justice by the Justiciars, the Chancellors and their assistants in the one department, and dealing with questions of the revenue with the barons in the other, until the great increase of business in the time of Henry II. rendered other arrangements necessary. It is stated by Madox in his history of the Exchequer,[1] that causes were heard not only by the Justiciars and other justices in the Curia Regis, but also by the barons in the Court of Exchequer ; a course which seems not improbable, inasmuch as many of the justices

---

[1] Vol. i⁰. p. 73.

of the Curia were also barons of the Exchequer, and the overflow of business in the one department may well have been disposed of by the judges sitting in the other. In the meantime, however, the complexion of the country had undergone great and important changes. The Saxon thane had throughout England been gradually supplanted by the Norman baron. The mutuality and simplicity of the old style had given way to the violence and rapacity of the new comers, and the local courts, the courts of the Wapentake, the County, and the Sheriff, had been overborne by the power and wealth of the Normans, so that the English had but a scant measure of justice in their own courts. And as they had a greater confidence in the integrity and independence of the trained lawyers and prelates of the Curia Regis than in the honesty and steadfastness of their neighbours in the county, they deserted the antient tribunals and flocked to the King's Courts in all cases where life or property was in danger. The King's Court accordingly became blocked with causes, and was impotent to deal with the demands of the country. A remarkably interesting and contemporaneous picture of the delays and difficulties of the law in the reign of Henry II. is to be found in a well-authenticated MS. memorandum made by one Richard de Anesti, setting out, in simple language, his struggles to obtain a judgment as to his right to certain lands in the county of Hertford. His uncle, William de Sackville, being pre-contracted to one Albreda de Tregoz, afterwards married Adeliza de Vere. The latter contract being declared invalid on appeal by the Bishop of Winchester, he returned to Albreda and lived with her till his death. Leaving no issue by Albreda and dying intestate, Richard, as heir at law of his uncle, claimed the land, which was also claimed by Adeliza on behalf of a child, of whom, she alleged, that William de Sackville was the father. Richard relied for his case on the divorce granted nearly thirty years before and acted on by all parties, the validity of which, however, was disputed by Adeliza. He began by sending to the king in Normandy for a writ, which being obtained, he took to the Queen Elinor at Salisbury to be sealed by her, as she held the Great Seal during the king's absence. He then had a day appointed for his cause to be heard before Richard de Luci, the Chief Justiciar at Northampton, and he duly cited Adeliza de Vere and her brother Geoffry. Arrived at Northampton with his friends and witnesses, his cause was postponed by de Luci to Southampton. The matter was then moved into the Court of Archbishop Theobald, who ordered it to be heard at Lambeth on the feast of St. Vincent, from which date it was postponed to the feast of St. Perpetua, and thence to the feast of St. Valentine at Maidstone. After other adjournments he appeared with his friends, his advocates, and his witnesses before the archbishop at Lambeth, when he was again referred to Canterbury, and thence to the King who was in Gascony, where he went with his friends and helpers and found the King at Auvilar. He then returned to Canterbury and followed his suit in journeys between London, Canterbury, Winchester, Chichester, Salisbury, and Normandy. His case then got before the Bishop of Chichester and the Abbot of Westminster, who gave him days in London and at Oxford, but his case was not heard. Delays and post-ponements followed each other, and then his adversaries appealed to Rome, where his claim to succeed his uncle was confirmed. At length his influence at Court induced the king to accept a fine of 100 marks of silver to hear the case before himself and his Chief Justiciar, de Luci. After protracted delays, during which he followed the king's Court for weeks at Romsey, at Reading, at Wallingford, and elsewhere, being unable to get a hearing through the multiplicity and importance of the business to be transacted, the king in person tried the case at Woodstock, and confirmed de Anesti in his title to the land. In this suit, which he tells us lasted *six years*, he spent all his substance in journeys, in payments to his friends, to his advocates, and to his witnesses, and in gifts and fees to the queen, to the king's physician, and to others, detailed particulars of which he gives in his story. And he adds, that having been three years in possession of his uncle's land, he still owes fifteen marks to the King, and most of the money which he had bor-rowed from Hakelot the Jew during the progress of his case.[1] To meet this difficulty of procedure King Henry II., who had formerly sat in the Curia Regis and thus became personally acquainted with its requirements,

---

[1] *Miscellanies of the Treasury*, No. $\frac{2}{4}\frac{8}{3}$. The MS. is believed by Palgrave to be the writing of de Anesti himself, and to be of the date A.D. 1177. See also *Court Life under the Plantagenets*, by Hubert Hall, London, 1890, pp. 98, 204, 250. A portion of the original MS. is reproduced at p. 101.

in the sixteenth year of his reign (A.D. 1170) appointed
justices to perambulate the kingdom with regularity, and
not casually as theretofore, and to hear on the spot the
complaints of his subjects. The first of these, of whom we
have any record, are twelve justices whose names, beginning
with the Abbots of Canterbury and Chertsey,[1] are given
by Dugdale, who were sent to try causes in the counties
of Kent, Middlesex, Berks, Oxon, Bucks, and Bedford.
And here we have the first institution of circuits, which
from that time forward have been part and parcel of
our judicial procedure. In 1176, the number of Itinerant
Justices was increased to eighteen, and they were sent
into all the counties of England from Northumberland
to Cornwall. In 1179, at a Grand Council at Windsor,
England was divided into four parts, and to each part five
justices were allotted. They included in their number
six justices of the Curia Regis, and among these was
Ranulph de Glanvil, one of the fathers of our law. In
1181 Ranulph de Glanvil was appointed Chief Justiciar,
and five other justices were appointed "*ad audiendum
clamores populi*," to hear the suits of the people in the
Curia Regis. Certain justices of the Curia were also
appointed to act as barons in the King's Exchequer, and
they appear to have tried causes indifferently as justices
or barons.

There is also every reason to believe that, at whatever
time the practice may have orginated, trial by jury for
both civil and criminal causes was recognised and adopted

---

[1] *Chronica Series*, fol. 2.

in the Curia Regis by the time of Henry II. Glanvil, in his *Treatise on the Laws and Customs of England*,[1] describing the practice in the Curia Regis, clearly recognizes this mode of trial. The jury was not however at that time limited to twelve, although that was even then the usual number. Nor was unanimity required; but if the jurors disagreed, more jurors were added, until twelve were found who agreed upon a verdict one way or the other.[2] This mode of procedure is not altogether unknown even in our days, where on grand juries, on inquisitions before Coroners, and trials *de lunatico inquirendo* before Masters in Lunacy, jurors are sworn to the number of twenty or more, but a verdict by twelve is accepted. Juries were in the early times selected from the county or the hundred by four knights summoned for the purpose from each district. They were liable to be tried for perverse verdicts by twenty-four jurymen[3] selected in the same manner, and a single juryman who disagreed with the eleven was fined. There was also a distinction in the province of the jury in civil and in criminal trials. In the former the jurors appear to have answered questions put to them by the judges, and thus to have decided issues as to the right to land; but in criminal cases they acted as grand jurors, and declared whether or not they suspected the accused to be

---

[1] Written about A.D. 1181.

[2] Hale's *History of Common Law*, p. 348.

[3] This practice, according to Bacon, seems to have been in existence as late as 1492. See *Life of Henry VII.*; Spedding, vol. vi. p. 160.

guilty of the crime imputed to him. If they did not suspect him, he was acquitted; but if they did, he was put to clear himself. This he did by compurgation if charged with a trivial offence; or if the offence were serious, then by the ordeal of water, if a rustic, or by the ordeal of iron, if a freeholder or a person of higher rank. In either case he might claim his right to be tried by the duel, which was carried out, after what would appear to be much delay, in the presence of a judge or some other officer of the King.[1]

About this time also, at the instigation of Ranulph de Glanvil, the GREAT ASSIZE was instituted by Henry II. The main object of this reform was to give each litigant the option of referring himself and his case to the judgment of the King's Justices, instead of appealing to the ordeal of battle. The delays of the duel were thus avoided, and the truth was ascertained by the oaths of twelve lawful men, rather than by the doubtful evidence to be obtained from the chance victory of a champion. Various regulations were made to encourage this reference, and it was amongst others expressly declared that any tenant who insisting on a trial by duel had thus obtained a judgment for his land, should always be bound to defend it by battle, and never afterwards be permitted to try by the Great Assize against any claimant who appealed to the trial by battle.

This mode of trial seems to have originated in Scandi-

---

[1] See Glanvil, *Tractatus de Legibus*, etc., by Beames, London, 1812. Selden Society's Works, vols. i. and ii. *Pleas of the Crown and Civil Actions, temp. John and Henry III.*

navia, and to have continued, according to Selden, in his *History of the Duello*,[1] until the Christian kings set aside the wager of battle as cruel and unchristianlike, and replaced it by the ordeal of fire or water, called God's judgment, which accordingly continued to be used among the Danes and also among the English. The ordeal of battle was thus discontinued down to the period of the Norman invasion, when the Conqueror reinstated it as a mode of trial to which the Normans were accustomed, and which was well suited to their military and violent habits. This process of arriving at the truth was admitted in civil as well as in criminal suits, and those interested in the subject will find in Dugdale's *Origines Juridiciales*,[2] a minute and interesting account of the exact procedure in real actions or claims to land, and of the arms and defence of each of the combatants, whether the parties fought by their champions or in their own proper persons. He also gives[3] a similarly detailed account of the mode of fighting in criminal cases, the subject being apparently of great interest to this antiquary, who was not only a distinguished scholar of the seventeenth century, but held the post of Norroy King of Arms.[4] A short account of a trial by battle is also given in Madox' *History of the Exchequer*,[5] accompanied by a rough drawing of the

---

[1] London, 1610, p. 38.

[2] Fols. 65–74.   [3] Fols. 75–85.

[4] See also the *Ordenaunce and Fourme of Fighting within the Listes*, by Thomas Duke of Gloster, Constable of England: dedicated to Richard II. *The Blacke Booke of the Admiralty* by Sir Travers Twiss, vol. i. p. 301.

[5] Vol. ii. p. 551. *Selden Society*, vol. i. preface.

period of Henry III., showing sufficiently clearly the kind
of battle that was waged between persons of the lower
rank of life, in the thirteenth century.   The actual entry
on the assize roll is in Latin, of which the following
translation is given by the Selden Society.[1]

" Walter Bloweberme comes and appeals Hamo le Stare of
Winchester, by the same words (viz. of robbery) to wit that they
were   .   .   .   the Cross at Winchester, and there stole certain
clothes and other goods, whereof Hamo had as his share two coats
to wit, one of Irish cloth and another coat half of Abingdon
cloth and half of London burrell : and that he (Hamo) was along
with him (Walter) in committing the said larceny, he Walter
offers to deraign against him (Hamo) as the Court shall consider.
And Hamo comes and defends all of it, (and says) that he will
defend of his body, etc.   Therefore it is considered that there be
battle between them.   And the battle between them is struck.
And the said Hamo has been defeated.   Therefore to judgment
against him, etc.   He had no chattels."

Many a suit and many a crime were tried by the ordeal
of battle under this antient judicial system.   Until a comparatively recent date, the law books contained decisions
of points arising on these contests, and a report is given
by Dyer [2] of the manner of and preparation for one of
these combats, in the time of Queen Elizabeth, in such
quaint detail, that I venture to reproduce it here :—

" Paramour chose the trial by battle, and his champion was
one George Thorne; and the demandant's champion was one
Henry Nailer, a master of defence.   And the Court awarded the
battle, and the champions were by mainprise and sworn to perform the battle at Tothill in Westminster, on the Monday next

---

[1] Vol. i. p. xxix.

[2] Lowe and another *v.* Paramour; Dyer, vol. iii. fol. 301, 13
Eliz. (A.D. 1571).

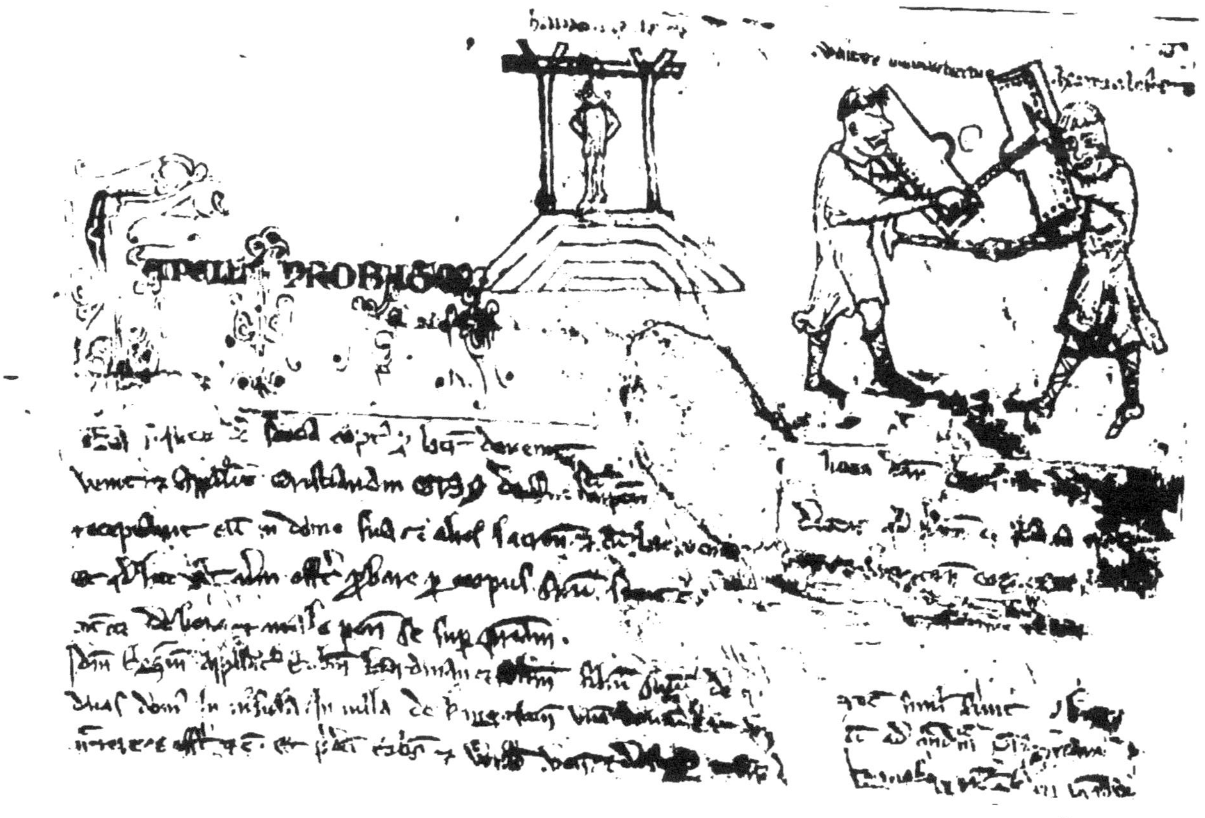

Face page 61.

Reproduction of the Wager of Battle described in page 64. It forms the heading of a roll, of which the record of the battle between Bloweberme and Hamo le Stare is the first entry.

The original roll is at the Record Office. It bears no date, but is of the period of Henry III.

after the Utas of the term, and the same day given to the parties,
at which day and place a list was made in an even and level
piece of ground, set out square sixty feet on each side due east
west, north, and south, and a place or seat for the judges of the
Bench was made without and above the lists, and covered with
the furniture of the same Bench in Westminster Hall, and a bar
made there for the serjeants-at-law. And about the tenth hour
of the same day three Justices of the Bench, Dyer, Weston, and
Harper, Welshe being absent on account of sickness, repaired to
the place in their robes of scarlet, with the appurtenances and
coifs also. And there, public proclamation being three times
made with an Oyes, the demandants first were solemnly called,
and did not come. After which the mainpernors of the champion were called to produce the champion of the demandants first,
who came into the place apparelled in red sandals, over armour
of leather, bare-legged from the knee downward, and bare-headed,
and bare arms to the elbow, being brought in by the hand of a
knight, namely Sir Jerome Bowes, who carried a red baston of an
ell long tipped with horn, and a yeoman carrying a target made
of double leather ; and they brought in at the north side of the
lists, and went about the side of the lists until the middest of the
lists, and then came before the Justices with three solemn congies,
and there was he made to stand on the south side of the place,
being the right side of the Court ; and after that the other champion was brought in like manner at the south side of the lists,
with like congies, etc., by the hands of Sir Henry Cheney, knight,
etc., and was set on the north side of the bar ; and two Serjeants [1]
being of counsel of each party in the midst between them. This
done the defendant was solemnly called again, and appeared not,
but made default, upon which default Barham, Serjeant for the
tenant, prayed the Court to record the nonsuit, which was done.
And then Dyer, Chief Justice, reciting the writ, count and issue,
joined upon battle and the oath of the champions to perform it,
and the fixing of the day and place, gave final judgment against
the demandants, and that the tenant should hold the land to him
and his heirs for ever, quit of the said demandants and their
heirs for ever ; and the demandants and their pledges to prosecute in the Queen's mercy, etc. And then solemn proclamation

---

[1] " In scarlet."

F

was made that the champions and all others there present (who were by estimation about four thousand persons) should depart, every man in the peace of God and the Queen. And they did so *cum magno clamore vivat Regina.*"

In a book containing reports of celebrated trials,[1] it is stated that the Queen ordered that this wager of battle should not take place, and compelled the parties to come to terms, by which Paramour retained his land and Lowe received a sum of money. But in order that Paramour's title should be made secure, it was arranged that the performance of a battle should be prepared, and that default should be duly made. After which Naylor offered to the Chief Justice to play Thorne half a dozen rounds for the diversion of the judges and the spectators. Thorne, however who had much power but little skill, declined, saying he came to fight and not to play. The Chief Justice then commended Naylor for his courage and broke up the court.

This ordeal or appeal of battle, though denounced by the Church, discouraged by the Great Assize, and gradually repudiated by the English people, never ceased to be the law of the land until the reign of King George III. It occurred in the year 1818 that one Richard Thornton was tried at Warwick for the murder of Mary Ashford, and was there acquitted by the jury. The girl's brother, William Ashford, stimulated by a local solicitor who was convinced of Thornton's guilt, brought an appeal of murder in the King's Bench to which the defendant Thornton appeared, and throwing down his glove on the floor of the

---

[1] *London*, 1715, p. 899.

court, declared he was not guilty of the murder, and would defend the same by his body. After much learned argument Lord Ellenborough, with the concurrence of his brother justices, declared that trial by battle was in such cases still the law of England and ordered a battle to be fought, according to the antient rules, in the presence of the judges of the King's Bench. Before, however, the time for fighting arrived, Ashford, the appellant, cried *craven*, and judgment was a second time given in favour of Thornton.[1] An act[2] was then passed to abolish such mode of trial for the future.

To Ranulph de Glanvil may also be attributed the enrolment of judicial proceedings in the Curia Regis, of which the records come down to us from the reign of Henry II. This work was continued and completed by Hubert Walter when Chancellor to King John, who also set on foot the Chancery rolls which commence in the reign of that monarch,[3] and are since that period found to be continuous. The early records of the Exchequer were kept in the *Red Book of the Exchequer*, and the later records in the *Black Book of the Exchequer*. Both these volumes are still existent. The caligraphy of the former, minute and exact in the commencement, becomes larger and less exact in succeeding generations. The binding and bosses are of great antiquity.

---

[1] Ashford *v.* Thornton, 1 Barn. & Ald., 405 ; Campbell's *Lives of the Chief Justices*, vol. iii. p. 171.

[2] 59 Geo. III., c. 46.

[3] *Selden Society*, vol. i. p. 8. The Curia Regis Rolls in the Record Office appear to be undated before the reign of Richard I.

In 1196, under Richard I., there were numerous appointments of judges to the Curia Regis, including those of Hubert Walter, Archbishop of Canterbury, the Bishops of London and Rochester, and several laymen; and similar appointments continued to be made, both to the Curia Regis and to the Justices Itinerant, until the 52nd Henry III. (A.D. 1268), when the system was again altered.

In the meantime, however, dissatisfaction had arisen with the proceedings of the Curia Regis itself. This Court followed the King not only theoretically but actually. Where the King went to hold a Court there also went the Curia in both departments; the Curia Regis with the Justiciar, the Chancellor and the Justices, and the Exchequer with the Treasurer, the Chamberlain, the officers and the treasure. And thus the King in his progresses was accompanied not only by his great and smaller officers of State, but by carts and wagons loaded with bullion,[1] with gold and silver plate, with jewels, and all the personal treasures of the King not deposited in the Abbey or in the treasury at Winchester. Numerous *hanapers*, or hampers of plaited rushes or straw, formed part of the baggage, and held the writs, the records, and the tallies necessary for carrying on the business of the courts. And thither in the wake of the King followed the suitors whose plaints waited determination in the King's Court. These perambulations of the monarch reached their culminating point in the reign

---

[1] Hall's *Antiquities of the Exchequer.*

Hanaper with Tallies & Parchment
(about ⅕ actual size)

Wooden Tally (actual size)

Sketch of a Hanaper in actual use in the XIV. century, with tallies and parchment rolls found within it. The original hanaper and tallies are in the Record Office. This was the kind of hanaper carried about with the royal luggage on the king's journeys through the country.

See page 68.

of King John. When he was out of the kingdom, Archbishop Hubert Walter acted as Chancellor and sat in the King's place at Westminster. When he was at home, he was in constant progress through the country, and in the year 1211 it is said that he sat at no less than twenty-four separate towns.[1] To all these resting-places the unhappy suitors followed, or lost the chance of their causes being tried. And accordingly it was provided, by the 17th clause of Magna Carta, that for the future, common pleas, or causes between party and party, as distinguished from Crown and Revenue cases, should not follow the King in his wanderings, but should be heard and determined in some ascertained and well-known place. "*Communia placita non sequantur curiam nostram, sed teneantur in aliquo loco certo.*" This ascertained place was Westminster Hall, and the Court of Common Pleas retained the name, down to its abolition as a separate jurisdiction in 1875, of *The Court of Common Pleas at Westminster*.

Here then we have the origin of the COURT OF COMMON PLEAS, for although that Court was not actually constituted at the time of King John, nor was there any prohibition against common pleas being heard by the Curia and by the Exchequer, as had hitherto been the practice, yet the provision of the Charter involved the ·continued retention in London, or in the ascertained place to be afterwards fixed, of a sufficient number of justices and barons to compose a court for the hearing of the subjects' causes. And thus it frequently happened that

---

[1] Foss' *Judges*, vol. ii. p. 4.

one division of the Curia was sitting at Westminster
while another division was travelling about the country,
either with or without the King, as the case might be;
the Justiciar being sometimes with the judges in the
country and sometimes with the judges in London.[1]
Numerous instances also occurred where, the Justiciar
being absent, questions of law were left for him to decide
on his arrival, or were sent to be discussed before him at
Westminster. One of the questions so reserved was
whether on proof of his ancestor's absence for twenty
years, an heir at law could enter upon the land of the
missing owner, and take possession of the freehold, on
the presumption that his ancestor was dead.[2]

Henry III. confirmed the Charter of his father in this
as in other respects, and instituted a Court of Common
Bench with duly qualified justices to sit perpetually at
Westminster to hear causes between parties and to have
exclusive jurisdiction in regard to certain claims. It had
no criminal jurisdiction, did not follow the Sovereign in
his peregrinations, and gradually absorbed all the private
business of the country. In 1235, Thomas de Muleton[3]
was appointed Chief Justice of the Common Bench, being
the first Chief Justice of either of the Courts of Common
Law, and from this period personal actions gradually
ceased to be heard either in the Curia Regis or in the Exchequer. To enforce this procedure Edward I.,[4] after the

---

[1] *Selden Society*, vol. 3 p. xviii.　Foss' *Judges*, vol. ii. p. 160.
[2] *Selden Society*, vol. 3, p. 79.
[3] Dugdale's *Chronica Series*, fol. 11.　[4] 28 Edward I., A.D. 1300.

abolition of the Curia, expressly declared that the hearing of common pleas in the Exchequer or elsewhere out of the Common Bench, was contrary to the provisions of the Great Charter.

The natural dissatisfaction which was felt with the Curia Regis rapidly extended to the appointment of Chief Justiciar. The position of this great officer of State was that of a politician and a soldier as well as, or perhaps more than, that of a creator and administrator of the law. Many statesmen of great eminence had held the post. Odo of Bayeux was the first, Hubert de Burgh was among the last. Henry, Duke of Normandy, afterwards Henry the Second, during the later years of King Stephen, was Chief Justiciar and sat regularly in the court. Henry III. also sat in person and delivered a judgment, which is reported.[1] Ranulph de Glanvil, and possibly Henry de Bracton, also occupied the post of Chief Justiciar. Latterly, however, the office had fallen into less competent hands, and when the latter years of King Henry III. showed the scandal of two Chief Justiciars, one appointed by the king and one appointed by the barons, professing to exercise judicial functions at one and the same time as they were leading armies against each other in the field, it was felt that the moment had arrived when the office, with its inconsistent combination of statesman, soldier, lawgiver, and judge, should be brought to an end. Philip Bassett and Hugh le

---

[1] 47 Henry III. *Coram Rege Rolls de tempore Ph. Bassett Justiciarii Angliæ*; Madox, vol. i. p. 100,

Despencer were the two so contending, and after the
death of le Despencer on the field of Evesham, in 1265,
and the subsequent resignation of Bassett, the King's
nominee, the Curia Regis and the Chief Justiciar ceased
to exist.

The Curia Regis had thus been the Royal Court of
England for a period of about 200 years. It sprang into
being when the object of the Conqueror was to establish
an autocratic power and to stifle the existing system of
self-government, and it came to an end when the combination of the Barons had curbed the power of the Crown,
and the growth of a National Parliament had re-asserted
in a modified form the antient rights of self-government.
From that time to the present the judicial has been
definitely severed from the military and executive power,
and succeeding Chief Justices have been lawyers and
lawyers alone.

At the same time that the Curia Regis was drawing to
an end as a judicial institution, the smaller courts of the
country had been insensibly changing. These Courts,
with their suitors, their voting and their popular judgments, had gradually fallen under the control of the
Sheriff, the direct representative of the Crown, who not
only arranged the causes and put his own nominees on
the juries, but being the collector of revenue for the
Crown, conducted business with a primary regard to the
perception of fees so as to show a good balance in his
yearly account with the Exchequer. The vigour and
rapacity of the Norman Barons made them difficult
subjects either for law or for taxation, and the Anglo-

Saxon strain that now permeated the Norman body gave an element of sturdy resolution to their character, so that they, alike with the freeholders and the rest, kept away from the local courts so long as it was possible to do so. But though the smaller courts were gradually losing their importance, the County Court still held on [1] and flourished, and when the itinerant justices came their rounds, directed specially to try causes in each county, they sat in the County Courts. The freemen, the suitors, and the parties, were summoned by the Sheriff to attend the sittings of the King's Justice; but the Anglo-Saxon mode of trial still obtained, judgment was given as of old by the voices of the suitors, and in cases of doubt and difficulty the triple ordeal was still put in force.

The establishment, however, of the Curia Regis, the gradual extension of its functions, the increase of business, and the legal difficulties inseparable from the system of tenure introduced by the Normans gave, year by year, an enlarged importance and responsibility to the office of the Chancellor. From a period very shortly after the Conquest, the Chancellor was the King's principal Chaplain and Confessor. He had the care of the Royal Chapel and of the Chancery,[2] and thus became, in a sense, the keeper of the King's conscience. He sat with the Chief Justiciar in the Curia Regis, and occasionally, as it appears with certain other judges, hearing pleas of the Crown at Westminster and elsewhere.[3] Whether

---

[1] Stephen's *History of the Criminal Law*, vol. i. p. 77. Stubbs' *Const. Hist.*, vol. ii.

[2] Madox, vol. i. p. 60. [3] *Ibid.*, p. 61. Foss' *Judges*, vol. i. p. 198.

the Chancellor at this time heard criminal cases I know
not. He probably, being an ecclesiastic, retired when
any question of blood arose, and was thus never reckoned
among those judges who went on circuit to try the
criminals of the various counties. He also sat, as we
have seen, with the Justiciar and other barons as one of
the chief officers in the King's Exchequer, to assist in the
audit of the accounts of sheriffs and others, and to give
receipts or acquittances to the collectors of the revenue.
In this office he had as his staff a clerk and a scribe, the
former to assist him when he sat as the King's Chancellor
in the Exchequer, and the latter to transcribe the records
for preservation with other memoranda of the Great Seal.
In course of time, however, as the Chancellor's duties
increased, from the charters becoming more numerous and
from the extension of. litigation necessitating a considerable addition to the forms and numbers of writs, and
greater care in their preparation, he gradually,[1] from
about the time of Richard I., gave up sitting as a baron
in the Exchequer, and ceased to take a direct interest in
revenue cases. About the reign of Henry III., his place
was permanently taken by his Chancery clerk, who then
became and was ever afterwards known as the Chancellor of the Exchequer.[2] This official was not intrusted
with the discharge of judicial duties. His place was
simply in the Exchequer, and he moderated while he
supervised the due collection and the auditing of the

---

[1] Madox, vol. i. p. 195.
[2] Hall's *Antiquities of the Exchequer*, p. 83, *Crompton*, fol. 55,

revenue of the Crown. This function he still continues to exercise, and we recognise in the Chancellor of the Exchequer of to-day, not only the holder of one of the most antient offices under the Crown, but the member of the Cabinet specially charged with the care of the royal and the national revenue, and the general auditor and chief accountant of the United Kingdom.

Before the extinction of the Curia Regis, the King's Chancellor appears as *Cancellarius Angliæ*, and afterwards as an independent judge. In addition to sitting with the Chief Justiciar in the Curia Regis, he sat alone to try such matters as came specially under his cognizance, and gave up travelling about the country on judicial business, except on those somewhat rare occasions when his Sovereign required his personal attendance.

Of the early Chancellors after the Conquest the most interesting, from the prominence and importance which he gave to his office, was Thomas à Becket, who administered the affairs of England as Chancellor for a period of eight years, during which time he sat regularly and heard causes in Westminster, in Kent, in Essex, in Lincolnshire, in Shropshire,[1] and probably in many other counties of England, of which, however, there are no definite records. He describes his position at that time as being that of the King's Chancellor, the second man in England, without whose consent and advice no great thing was set on foot or accomplished.[2] According to the account of his secretary and chaplain, he was con-

---

[1] Foss' *Judges*, vol. i. pp. 168, 198. [2] Selden's *Discourse*, etc.

stantly engaged in hearing causes, sometimes alone, but
usually in company with the Earl of Leicester and
Richard de Luci, whom tradition places among the most
eminent of the Chief Justiciars. And I entertain little
doubt that the general love and reverence in which he
appears to have been held by all classes of Englishmen
for many generations were due as much to his merciful
administration and his many reforms of the law, as to
the circumstances under which he met his death. He is
also closely associated with our judicial procedure by
means of his efforts in repairing and maintaining the
fabric of Westminster Hall, which, during the period
between the death of William Rufus and the accession of
Henry II., had fallen somewhat into decay. Mr. Pearson
in his report considers this matter, and is of opinion that
some traces of à Becket's work still remain on the walls
of the antient Hall.

CHAPTER III.

FROM THE ACCESSION OF EDWARD I. TO THE DEATH OF RICHARD III.

(A.D. 1272-1485.)

I.

The Courts of Common Law—The Chief Justice of the King's Bench—The Chief Baron of the Exchequer—Division of business among the Courts—The Common Bench—Judges of the Common Bench—Appointment of Justices of the Peace—Quarter Sessions of the Peace—Permanence of the Judges—Torture—Opinions of successive Judges—The Bar of England—The Order of the Coif—Inns of Court—Writers and Commentators on the Common Law—The Serjeants-at-Law—Their Privileges—Their Duties to the Crown and the People—Counsellors-at-Law—Classification under Richard II.—Courts re-organized by Edward I.—The High Court of Admiralty—The Peace of the Seas—The Black Book of the Admiralty—The Courts of the Cinque Ports—Court of Shepway—Courts of Trailbaston—Court of the Clerk of the Market—An article of Wolsey's Impeachment—The Court of Pypowders.

THE accession of Edward I. found the Courts of King's Bench, Common Bench and Exchequer sitting in Westminster Hall. No Act of Parliament or royal edict had abolished the Curia Regis, but it had come to an end, like many another English institution, because it had done its work and was no longer suitable to the times. The Constitutions of Clarendon (A.D. 1165) had recog-

77

nised the Curia Regis as a tribunal of common resort,[1] where the Bishops sat with the Justiciars and the Barons until cases of blood required them to depart. But since then its jurisdiction as a Supreme Court had been much impaired. The distribution of its business over the country, through the appointment of itinerant justices, who sat in their several counties as justices of the Curia Regis,[2] had tended to this result, and at the same time the prerogative of the Chief Justiciar had been gradually encroached upon by the growing power of the Chancellor as a lawyer and a statesman. Its end was gradual, and the exact moment of its termination cannot be ascertained, for it actually overlapped the new system. The Justiciar and his colleagues held office for some years after the description of the King's justices had been changed from the general appellation of justiciars to the limited title they still hold of justices assigned to hold pleas, *coram rege*, before the King.

The courts thus established, which from that time forward for six hundred years, under the familiar title of the Courts of Common Law, transacted the business of the country, reflected the condition of the English people at the period of their institution. The Normans, who had invaded but not overrun the country, impressed upon its surface their thoughts and traditions; but the Norman Inquisition had only emphasized the Anglo-Saxon practice of open trial by freemen and neighbours. Inter·marriages

---

[1] Stubbs' *Constitutional History*, vol. i. p. 503.
[2] Stephen's *History of the Criminal Law*, vol. i. p. 99.

and territorial settlements had, also, by this time amalgamated the two races into one, so that there was no longer any recognised distinction between Norman and Anglo-Saxon, but all were equally English. And though the Norman blood was thought the more noble, and those families whose ancestors came over with the Conqueror regarded themselves as of a more patrician class, yet the great mass of the people were still of the Anglo-Saxon strain, whose manners and customs still survived. The language of the country was also in a state of transition—Latin was specially that of the learned, English was that of the common people, while French was gradually coming into use by all classes. The polyglot jargon of the courts and the law books belongs to a later date. Thus though the Norman system of Chief Justices and trained lawyers as Presidents of courts was accepted as safe and satisfactory in principle, yet the Anglo-Saxon method of local trials and the judgment of neighbours remained undisturbed, and was recognised as an essential feature of the new procedure. As the county in the Anglo-Saxon times was the unit for judicial administration, so also it remained under the Normans. And as the shire-gemote, formerly presided over by the Sheriff, who convened the suitors and arranged the details of business, was held twice in the year as the Supreme Court of the district for the trial of causes and of criminals, so also under the new system the county remained the unit, the Sheriff summoned the jurors and witnesses and arranged the business, and twice in the year the King's justices, superseding the Sheriff in his office of President, visited each county and tried all causes and offences arising within its limits. Hither also came the witnesses and the suitors, collected from the county, who judged the law and the facts, and found their verdicts from their knowledge of the party's reputation, and of the circumstances into which they had to inquire.

In the 52nd Henry III. (A.D. 1268), Robert de Brus (grandfather of Robert the Bruce, King of Scotland) was appointed the first Chief Justice of the King's Bench. He was a man of noble lineage and of good fortune, who was a lawyer by education and by profession. He had acted for some years as a Justiciar, and had gone several circuits. His position, however, as Chief Justice was limited to the administration of justice: he was no longer a statesman or a viceroy, and the salary, which was 1,000 marks when the Chief of the Court was also Chief Justiciar, was reduced to 100 marks when the office was solely that of Chief Justice of the King's Bench.[1] In other words, £15,000 a year to the Chief Justiciar was reduced to £1,500 a year to the Chief Justice.

The Courts accordingly sat as the King's Bench, the King's Exchequer, and the Common Bench, otherwise the Common Pleas. The King's Bench was presided over by the Lord Chief Justice with certain *puisne* or assistant judges, the Exchequer by the Lord Treasurer with the Chancellor of the Exchequer and other barons, and the Common Bench by the Chief Justice and other

---

[1] Foss' *Judges*, vol. ii. p. 155.

Court of King's Bench.

Face page 80.

THE COURT OF KING'S BENCH, TEMP. HENRY VI.

The Chief Justice and four Puisne Justices on the Bench, a jury in the box, six prisoners at the bar, and one prisoner being tried in chains.

From an illuminated MS. in the Inner Temple.

See page 123.

justices from time to time appointed by the King. It appears that for some time after the division of the Curia into these three separate courts, the Exchequer continued to try pleas between party and party, but in A.D. 1300 that court was ordered by Statute [1] to refrain from hearing such causes as contrary to the Great Charter, and to confine itself to matters touching the King's revenue. Shortly afterwards, in 1303, William de Carleton, a justice of the Common Pleas, was appointed Chief Baron of the Exchequer.[2] This office he held concurrently with that of a *puisne* judge of the Common Bench, and was the first person so appointed. From this date, as vacancies in the office of Chief Baron from time to time occurred, they were usually but not invariably filled from the justices of the Common Bench. The justices so appointed continued to hold the two offices of Justice and Chief Baron, their duties at that period being in no way inconsistent, as the barons could not try causes or hear appeals, and the Common Bench had no jurisdiction over affairs of the revenue.

The business was divided in the following manner. The King's Bench had exclusive jurisdiction in all pleas of the Crown, and in all appeals from inferior courts. The Common Bench had exclusive jurisdiction in all real actions or suits relating to land and in actions between private persons to try private rights, while the jurisdiction of the Exchequer was limited to causes touching the King's revenue with which it had exclusive power

---

[1] 28 Edward I.   [2] Dugdale, *Chronica Series*, fol. 32.

G

to deal. All these judges went Circuit twice a year, the barons of the Exchequer only trying cases on the revenue side, and no baron being permitted to try a prisoner or a civil cause unless he happened also to be a justice of the Common Bench, when he tried prisoners and causes in the latter capacity. The Assizes were held in the County Courts, and those tribunals were for many years after the end of the Curia Regis constituted as before with bishops, abbots, earls, barons, knights and freeholders of the county, the reeve and the burgesses of each township in the county and all those who of old were accustomed to be summoned to attend the business of the court. Itinerant Justices were appointed from time to time for some generations after the accession of King Edward I., and they went circuits equally with the justices of the Courts of Common Law. But the practice was found to be inconvenient. All courts, including those of the Itinerant Justices, were closed so long as the King's Judges of either Bench held their Justice Seat within the County. The Justices in Eyre had accordingly an inferior position and less authority, in public estimation, than the justices in the King's Courts ; there were great complaints of the expense and burthen cast upon the counties for the escort and entertainment of these numerous justices, and in 1335 they ceased to be appointed.

This division of the business of the courts, which was however much interfered with by various devices of the lawyers at a later period, had the inevitable result of throwing the greater portion of the work upon the

COURT OF COMMON BENCH, TEMP. HENRY VI.

The Chief Justice and six Puisne Justices on the Bench; five Serjeants pleading.

From an illuminated MS. in the Inner Temple.

See page 123.

COURT of COMMON PLEAS

Common Bench, which became, as it was called by Sir Edward Coke,[1] "the lock and key of the Common Law," or, more familiarly by Sir Orlando Bridgman, "the Common Shop for Justice."[2] Crown cases were limited in number, and the justices of the King's Bench, after a time, were not only put into an easy position as regarded the work they were called upon to perform, but as in those days their principal source of income was from the suitors' fees, they correspondingly suffered in pocket. The Common Bench, on the other hand, was always full of work, which rapidly increased, with the result that whereas the justices of the King's Bench seldom numbered more than three or four, those of the Common Bench were frequently seven or eight and sometimes amounted to as many as nine. Thus under Edward I. there were at times four, five and six justices of the Common Bench in addition to the Chief.[3] Under Edward II. the Court was ordered to sit in two divisions by reason of the multitude of pleas.[4] Under Richard II. and under Henry IV. there were three justices of the King's Bench and five of the Common Bench.[5] Under Henry V. there were four justices of the King's Bench and six of the Common Bench, in addition to the Chiefs.[6] Under Henry VI. and Edward IV. there were four justices of the King's Bench and seven[7] and at one time eight[8] of the Common Bench. The latter

---

[1] *Institutes*, vol. iv. p. 78.
[2] "Trial of Regicides," *State Trials*, vol. v. p. 993.
[3] Foss' *Judges*, vol. iii. p. 22.   [4] *Ibid.*, p. 195.
[5] *Ibid.*, vol. iv. pp. 21, 134.
[6] *Ibid.*, p. 190.   [7] *Ibid.*, p. 226.   [8] *Ibid.*, p. 390.

court had also this great advantage, that it sat always at Westminster, while the King's Bench, the Exchequer, and the Chancery were liable to follow the progresses of the King. And although it soon became the practice to dispense with the attendance of the judges and the barons, unless the King had some special need for their assistance, yet when he was located for an indefinite period at some provincial town, and had there established his Royal Court, the King's Bench and the Exchequer with their clerks, their secretaries, their treasure and their baggage moved from London in the wake of the Sovereign. Thus from 1277 to 1282 the Law Courts were at Shrewsbury,[1] while the King was fighting in Wales, and from 1298 to 1305 they were at York,[2] while the King was on his expeditions into Scotland. On the latter of these occasions a square chequer board with the necessary seats and fittings was erected in the yard of York Castle for the use of the barons and the accountants of the Exchequer.

The decadence of the smaller courts in the various counties and the scandals arising therefrom led to a new departure in the administration of justice, and in the reign of Edward III. (about 1327) Justices of the Peace for each county were first appointed. In or about 1350 they were ordered to hold Sessions quarterly to try breaches of the Statute of Labourers.[3] About 1359–60 [4] they were empowered to try crimes and misdemeanours

---

[1] Foss' *Judges*, vol. iii. p. 22.   [2] *Ibid.*, p. 23.
[3] 25 Edward III.   [4] 24 Edward III.

committed in their county, and by a Statute of Edward IV.[1] they were empowered to sit regularly in Quarter Sessions for general business.

The immediate reason for the permanent establishment of Quarter Sessions, as recited in the preamble to the Statute, appears to have been the misconduct of the sheriffs, who packed the juries, compelled the payment of excessive fees, and by various extortionate devices held unhappy suitors to ransom. And here again, the Anglo-Saxon system of self-government seems to have been recognised, by the removal of these trials from the Sheriff or officer of the Crown to the resident gentry and land-owners of the county.

The story of the Courts of Common Law from the closure of the Curia Regis to the end of the civil wars is a history rather of individual judges than of any substantial changes in legal procedure. The courts sat uninterruptedly through the whole period, for the sanguinary strife of political parties seems to have had no deterrent effect upon the course of litigation. With the exception of a wholesale removal of judges, many of whom were suspected of receiving bribes under Edward I., and of a batch of judges who were dismissed shortly before the deposition of Richard II. for alleged misconduct in their office, of whom several were afterwards reinstated, there was during this period but little interference with the judicial bench. During the Wars of the Roses each successful party appealed in turn for the support of

---

[1] 1 Edward IV. c. 2. Reeve's *History*, vol. iii. p. 9.

peaceful citizens by testifying to their respect for and
confidence in the judges of the several courts who had,
notwithstanding the distractions of the times, quietly and
courageously discharged their duties. Thus Sir Thomas
Billing, who was appointed Chief Justice of the King's
Bench by Edward IV. in 1465, was re-appointed by
Henry VI. on his return to power, and after the death of
King Henry remained Chief Justice under Edward IV.
Sir Edward Hussey, who was appointed to succeed Sir
Thomas Billing by Edward IV. in 1481, was re-appointed
by Edward V. in 1483, by Richard III. in the same year,
and by Henry VII. in 1486. The independence of the
judges during this period, with the courage of Sir Wil-
liam Gascoigne in the reign of Henry IV., and of Chief
Justice Markham in the reign of Edward IV. are among
the landmarks of English history. The tradition of Chief
Justice Gascoigne committing to prison the Prince of
Wales, afterwards Henry V., for a contempt committed in
the Court of King's Bench, has been investigated by Lord
Campbell, who gives the various authorities upon which
the story rests, and finds it to be substantially true.[1]
And Sir John Markham, though not exhibiting his independence in a form so attractive to the historian or
the public, undoubtedly suffered for his courage and his
integrity, and was for many generations held up as an
example to his fellow-men.

These judges, like their predecessors, administered the
law with care and, according to the feeling of the times,

---

[1] *Lives of Chief Justices*, vol. i. p. 125.

with mercy. In one special respect also they were far
in advance of the spirit of the age. For many generations, down even to the end of the seventeenth century,
every country in the known world had recourse to torture.
It was applied indiscriminately to extract confessions of
guilt or to obtain evidence incriminating suspected persons. During the early period of the Norman supremacy,
when disaffection to the ruling class was dominant, in
times of rebellion and of civil war, when charges of treason were scattered broadcast, and at other periods when,
owing to the general disturbance of the country, evidence
was rarely and with difficulty obtained against malefactors, great temptation must have been felt to extract the
necessary proofs by means of torture. It was practised
for that purpose in France, in Germany, in Spain, in
Italy. If an Englishman crossed the water to Normandy,
he was liable to its application, and the Pope permitted
it in his own dominions. And if it was true that no
English statute expressly authorised the use of torture, it
was equally true that no statute expressly forbade it.
But notwithstanding this universal practice of the continent of Europe and the absence of any express prohibition, the judges of England never had recourse to it.
Glanvil, writing in the reign of Henry II. on the laws
and customs of England, on the procedure of the duel and
the practice of the Great Assize, while treating in detail
of all such matters, makes no reference to the use of
torture as part of the judicial system. Fortescue, in the
reign of Henry VI., dealing with the laws and customs
of England as then established, praises those laws as

merciful and just, and condemns in strong and vigorous
language the resort which is had to the use of torture in
France, where he was then living, and points out with
good sense and much force the useless character of the
evidence thus obtained. At a later date Sir Edward Coke,
and under Charles I., Lord Chief Justice Richardson and
the whole bench of judges denounced its use, and declared,
in answer to questions from the Crown, that it was and
always had been unknown to the common law of England,
that the provisions of Magna Carta were inconsistent
with its ever having been recognised by the constitution
of the kingdom, and that no Englishman could by the
law of his country be put to the rack. And although
under the Tudors, under King James I., and possibly on
some occasions at an earlier date, torture was practised in
order to obtain evidence, yet it was done by extraordinary
tribunals, and not by the antient constitutional courts of
the country. Nor am I aware of any single instance,
even in the worst years of tyranny and prerogative, when
any man has been subjected to torture by order or assent
of the Court of Chancery or the Courts of Common Law,[1]

---

[1] The subject of torture as practised generally in Europe will
be found discussed with great keenness of investigation in a little
work entitled *Superstition and Force*, by H. C. Lea, Philadelphia,
1878. From the English point of view, see *Fortescue de Laudibus*,
etc., cap. 22; Countess of Shrewsbury's Case, 2 *State Trials*, p.
773; Peacham's Case, *ibid.*, p. 871; Felton's Case, 3 *State Trials*,
p. 371; Elizabeth Cellier's Case, 7 *State Trials*, p. 1205; the argu-
ments in Governor Picton's Case before Lord Ellenborough, 30
State Trials, p. 892; Stephen's *History of the Criminal Law*, vol. i.
p. 222; Lyttleton, *Henry II.*, vol. iii. p. 312; Jardine, 1837.

or when confessions obtained by the rack have been used for the conviction of accused persons.

During the period now under consideration the Bar, as an element of judicial life, and as a permanent institution of the country, first became fixed and ascertained. When the practice of advocacy, hired or voluntary, was first introduced into England it is impossible to determine. Serjeant Pulling, in the " Order of the Coif," [1] wishes to carry back the order of the serjeants to the time of King Alfred. Other writers of more moderate views have been content with ascribing it to a somewhat later period. That advocates were known in the Curia Regis under certain terms and conditions I do not doubt; but in regard of any definite period when they may be said to have been established, I prefer to stand on the clear and certain ground that the first official recognition of the counsel or advocate authorised to represent his client in court is to be found in the third year of King Edward I.,[2] when it was declared that, "if any Serjeant-counter do any deceit or beguile the court, he shall be imprisoned for a year and a day, and from henceforth not be heard to plead in the court for any man."

Under the Anglo-Saxons every litigant, whether in civil or criminal business, spoke for himself, except, as I think, women or children, who, not being able to come

---

[1] London, 1881: see the *Address of Lord Keeper Whitelock to the* 15 *Serjeants in* 1649, p. 231.

[2] *Statute of Westminster*, I. cap. 29: Foss' *Judges*, vol. iii. p. 47. Dugdale, in his *Chronica* Series, fol. 25, gives the names of the first serjeants-at-law under date A.D. 1276.

into court, were represented as best they might.[1] The
same right of representation accrued to women, children,
old men, and maimed persons, who were allowed to appear by their champions at the ordeal of battle, a privilege afterwards extended generally to litigants in civil
causes. As far, however, as is known, there was originally no limitation or restriction upon the litigant as to
whom he should select as his representative ; nor was exclusive audience in the courts, or admission to the lists as
champion, reserved for any class of the King's subjects.
There thus arose for the purposes of the duel a body of
bravos who, for sufficient payment, would undertake the
ordeal, and risk the chances of punishment in the event
of being vanquished. Accordingly some of the older
Corporations had in their midst a retained champion
who represented them, in defence of their rights, in any
litigation in which they might be involved. With the
growing discredit of the duel, to which the professional
champion greatly contributed, the extension of civil business and the complications thence arising, more careful
and exclusive study was given to the science of the law,
and a body of persons, mostly, no doubt, of clerical training, devoted themselves to this pursuit. As early as the
time of Henry II. we hear from Glanvil,[2] writing in or
about 1181, of the nomination of certain persons as attorneys " to win or lose " for the party nominating them,
but the passage does not appear to me to indicate any

---

[1] See, for an instance, *ante*, p. 16.
[2] *Glanvil*, by Beames, p. 275, book xi.

right or duty of advocacy. Such nomination also involved much delay, and the mandate required the King's
assent, in the absence of which the party was required
himself to be present in court. Some years later—about
A.D. 1207—ecclesiastics were forbidden to act as advocates in secular courts, and accordingly those of the
clergy who had adopted the law as a profession, and were
unwilling to be deprived of their means of livelihood,
assumed a coiffure or close-fitting head-dress of linen or
silk to hide their bald patches; and thus, according to Sir
Henry Spelman,[1] originated the Order of the Coif. The
fixture of a certain court for the trial of civil causes in
London also encouraged the calling or profession of advocacy, and led to the institution of the Inns of Court,
where students of the law could congregate as at a Uni-
versity, hear lectures on the Roman law and the laws of
their country, and prepare themselves for their future
duties. To these studies the great legal writers of the
period freely contributed; and although doubts have been
expressed whether all or any of these jurists are actually
responsible for the whole of the works attributed to them,
yet such criticism is speculative, and ought not in all
fairness to deprive these antient benefactors of the credit
of those volumes of the law to which their names have
for centuries been appended.

Ranulph de Glanvil had, in the twelfth century,
written our first legal treatise on the " Laws and Customs
of the Kingdom of England," and this had been extended

---

[1] P. 171; see 3 Dyer 301*b*.

and annotated, as is supposed, by Hubert Walter, his nephew and successor in the office of Chief Justiciar. Henry de Bracton, a justice if not Chief Justiciar under Henry III., wrote, on the laws and customs of England, a work comprising five large octavo volumes as published by the Commissioners of Public Records. The *Mirror of Justices*, ascribed to Andrew Horne, was written or annotated by him in the reign of Edward I. John de Britton, a justice of the King's Bench under Henry III. and Edward I., wrote, by command of the latter king, a work on the Common Law of England. Sir John Fortescue, Chief Justice of the King's Bench under Henry VI., wrote, during his enforced retirement in France, a treatise in praise and explanation of the laws of England for the instruction of his pupil, Prince Edward, eldest son of Henry VI., who lost his life at the battle of Tewkesbury ; and Sir Thomas Littleton, a justice of the Common Bench under Edward IV., wrote the celebrated work on the tenures of England, which was completed and re-edited by Sir Edward Coke in the reign of King James I. These great writers and profound jurists laid the foundation of English law as recognised and practised at the present day, and their works are still quoted in our courts as undoubted authorities.

The serjeants, who for some generations were the only recognised pleaders in the King's Courts, were part and parcel of the court itself. They held office under the Crown, were appointed by patent, and had a monopoly which was so far remunerative that they were required to give feasts, rings, and presents upon their appointment.

Their title, *Servientes Domini Regis ad legem*, Our Lord the King's servants at law, indicated the nature of their calling, and has stereotyped the functions of an English barrister at all times. And it is, I think, from a want of due appreciation of this attitude that foreign judicial writers have very signally failed to realize the actual position of an English barrister towards the judges, the clients, and the public.[1] The Bar, as represented in olden times by the serjeants, whether called narratores or counters, formed a well-recognised part of the judicial system. They could only plead in court after accomplishing certain studies and a certain period of probation. They took the oath of office before entering on the practice of their profession. They were liable to be sent to various circuits "to follow for the King," or, in other words, to do the King's business in the country. They had certain specified privileges, including a salary from the Crown, and from the time at least of Henry V., in accordance with the custom then existing, the judges of the Common Law Courts could be selected only from their ranks.[2] The serjeant's oath bound him to serve the *King and his people*, thus prescribing the divided allegiance which the Bar has always borne. His duties involved the avoidance of any deceit upon the court as represent-

---

[1] De Franqueville, in his *Système Judiciaire de la Grande Bretagne*, Paris, 1894, a work discussing our existing judicial system with great fairness, and giving evidence of much research, hardly does justice to the position of the English Bar in its relations to the Judicial Bench and the public.

[2] *Fortescue*, chap. l.

ing the King, and the giving of honest advice to the people as represented by the suitor. Thus was every serjeant made an assistant in the administration of justice, and there was required from him absolutely good faith towards the judge and the client, owing no more duty to the one than to the other. The education and the associations of the judge and of the serjeant were one and the same. Each was chosen from the same body of trained lawyers, each wore the same distinctive coif, and they addressed each other as " brothers " in public and in private.[1] And as the serjeants provided from their numbers the judges of the courts, so also the judges in their turn were replaced by the serjeants when the former were from any cause temporarily incapacitated for work. This double position of the sergeant, sometimes a judge, sometimes an advocate, is still continued in the case of leading counsel, who, as Recorders, try criminals in one town, and as counsel prosecute or defend them in another; who sit at times with the Common Law judges as Commissioners of Assize on one circuit, and practise as advocates on the next. Added to this, the custom—for the rules of the Bar are no more than customary rules—that separates the counsel from the client in the course of litigation by the intervention of an attorney or solicitor,

---

[1] " Every Serjeant wears in Court a white silk coif, which is a badge that they are graduates in law, and is the chief ensign of habit with which Serjeants-at-law are distinguished at their creation. Neither shall a Judge or a Serjeant-at-law take off the said coif though he be in the Royal presence and talking with the King's Majesty."—*Fortescue*, chap. 1.

is a custom of very remote origin, and is calculated to give the Bar an independence of judgment and of action which could not be guaranteed if by any means the counsel could be pecuniarily interested in the result of the litigation. And upon the same footing stands the equally immemorial custom which forbids a barrister to be the salaried advocate of a company or a corporation, and thus places him at the disposition of any of the people, who can have his services without his judgment being warped by a divided duty between them and their possible opponent. These rules, though customary alone, are old and settled like the customs of the Common Law, of which Montaigne has said that, beginning with trembling foot and placid mien, they have in time discovered an aspect so tyrannical and severe that they forbid us even to question them with an uplifted eyebrow.

Serjeants after a time becoming too few for the business to be transacted, counsellors at law were admitted to plead. The names of some eighty-eight of these counsellors, many of whom were afterwards serjeants and judges, have been extracted from the cases tried in the reign of Edward II.,[1] and they give the first instance of the employment of this class of advocate. The distinction between serjeants and counsel has existed ever since that date. There have always been the leading counsel, whether serjeant or king's counsel, holding his office by patent, and the junior counsel who, without any patent or official position, relies solely on his knowledge of law,

---

[1] Foss' *Judges*, vol. iii. p. 208.

and his skill in pleading and practice. This, almost the present classification of the Bar, appears to have definitely existed as far back as the time of Richard II., for that monarch's poll-tax of 1378, has the following assessments : [1]—

The Judges and chief Baron of the Exchequer . 100 sh.
Each Serjeant and " grant apprentice du loi " . 40 ,,
Other apprentices who pursue the law . . . 20 ,,
All other apprentices of less estate and attorneys 6sh. 8d.

Edward I., aptly called the English Justinian, while initiating beneficial reforms in the law, made little if any substantial alteration in the procedure of the high courts. He found it necessary, however, acting in the spirit of devolution which then animated the law reformers, to erect or reorganize various courts which, during his reign, came prominently forward. Among the most important was the HIGH COURT OF ADMIRALTY which, although its origin is usually attributed to Edward III., was an antient court though acting under somewhat different conditions in the reign of Edward I.[2]

The first Admiralty Ordinance, of which we have a record, was issued by Henry I., and dealt mainly with the subject of wrecks ;[3] Richard I., under whom were first published the sea laws of Oleron, so called from the island of that name where they were promulgated, speaks of the Court of Admiralty as being then a Court of Re-

---

[1] *Rot. Parl.*, iii. 58. Foss' *Judges*, vol. iv. p. 24.

[2] An Admiralty cause tried in this reign is given by Crompton, fol. 91, and accepted by Coke. *Inst.*, vol. iv. p. 140.

[3] Twiss' *Black Book of the Admiralty*, vol. i. p. xlvi.

cord.[1] John made an ordinance at Hastings, the premier Cinque Port, that all vessels should lower their sails on meeting the King's ships;[2] and Edward I. in council, tried and decided, in 1285,[3] a question of maritime law between the Cinque Ports and certain Gascony merchants according to the principles afterwards laid down in the Black Book. There appear during the following reigns to be records of decisions of various commanders, relating principally to the manning of the King's ships, and of punishments inflicted on various offenders. But it is doubtful how far the admiral of any particular fleet had judicial power beyond his own particular command.

The first Admiralty Jurisdiction in somewhat of the modern form, appears to have been committed to the Lord Warden and Bailiffs of the Cinque Ports. These important places provided the Navy of the West which was in effect the Navy of England, for that of the North was in the early days comparatively unimportant. The first Admiral of England was Gervase Alard, Admiral of the Navy of the Cinque Ports in the reign of Edward I. To him and to the Lord Warden of the Ports, questions of piracy and of maritime claims were submitted, a concurrent jurisdiction being exercised by the Chancellor [4] who, for many generations afterwards, notwithstanding the erection of a High Court of Admiralty, dealt with questions arising on the high seas involving the rights of foreign nations, or charges of piracy to which

---

[1] Twiss' *Black Book of the Admiralty,* p. xlvii.
[2] *Ibid.,* p. xlix. [3] *Ibid.,* p. lxx.; Rymer's *Fœdera,* 12, Edw. I.
[4] Crompton, fol. 54.

H

our ancestors seem to have been much addicted. Questions of charter—party, freight, or other contracts, were dealt with by the itinerant justices, who assumed jurisdiction over all such matters when the ships of the parties were within the territorial limits of a county.

When Edward III., after the battle of Sluys (A.D. 1340), obtained the sovereignty of the sea, he found it necessary to extend that sovereignty by erecting a court to keep the *Peace of the Seas,* as his Courts of Common Law kept the King's peace on land. And accordingly we find a memorandum issued by Edward III., requiring that the Justiciaries should be consulted as to the proper mode of proceeding, so as to secure the antient supremacy of the Crown and the power of the Admiral's office over the sea of England, so as " to maintain peace and justice amongst the people of every nation passing through the sea of England." [1]   The result of this enquiry was, that a High Court of Admiralty under the Lord High Admiral of England was established, and that in the reign of his successor, Richard II.,[2] laws were passed giving a distinct and statutory authority to the Court of the Admiral, which from that time forward has exercised its jurisdiction over all causes, matters, and persons maritime.[3] Exclusive power was however reserved to the Cinque Ports to try their own Admiralty cases in

---

[1] *Selden Society,* vol. 6, p. xxxv.; *Black Book,* Preface.

[2] Stat. 13 and 15, Richard II.

[3] A recent volume of the Selden Society (1894) gives a collection of pleas in the Admiralty from 1390 to 1404, and contains much interesting matter on the early history of the Admiralty.

Initial Letter of the Black Book of the Admiralty, described in page 99. It is illuminated in gold and colours, and is in the custody of the President of the Probate, Divorce and Admiralty Division of the High Court.

uis que some est
sait admiral pre
merement luy
fault ordonner
sub fautier desoubz
lui pour estre ses
lieutenants deput
ez z autres officiers
ses plus loyaulx
sages z discrets en
sa loy marinyz
anciens coustumes de lamer p en aueue perf
Frouuer par ainsi que par saide de dieu z leur bon
z droitture gouuernait soffice pourra estre gouu
re a shonneur z proussit du Royalme.

Initial Letter
from the Black Book of the Admiralty

their own local Court, a jurisdiction which still exists in
the Lord Warden, who exercises it in the person of his
Admiralty Judge.[1]

In order that the court thus constituted, with authority
to decide on international as well as on English rights,
should have before it a statement of definite principles
and a recognised practice to guide it in its deliberations,
there was prepared during the reign of Edward III. or
of Richard II. one of the oldest and most valuable of our
national muniments, the *Black Book of the Admiralty*.
This book, whose authenticity is vouched not only by its
internal evidence but by such eminent legal antiquaries
as Sir Leoline Jenkins, Prynne and Dr. Exton, was lost
in the beginning of the present century by the officials
in the Admiralty Registry, and Sir Travers Twiss, then
Queen's Advocate, was employed by the Government to
reconstruct it from a collection of the various copies
and extracts known to have been taken from the original
at Doctors' Commons. This work was successfully
accomplished, and what is an almost exact reproduction of the original was produced. A few years since,
not long after the completion of Sir Travers Twiss'
labours, the original was found to be still at Doctors'
Commons, and is now carefully preserved. It is a quarto
volume of about 260 pages in MS., written partly in
French and partly in Latin, and illuminated to a limited
extent, the first page having a coloured ship of war
very similar in design and equipment to that of the

---

[1] Crompton, 99; Jeake's *Charters of the Cinque Ports*.

gold coins of the Plantagenets and the seals of the Cinque Ports. It contains chapters (1) on the duties and privileges of the Lord High Admiral; (2) on how the Admiral should conduct his court; (3) on the crimes and punishments of the Admiralty, with a transcript of the laws of Oleron promulgated by Richard I.; (4) an inquisition taken at Queenborough in 1375, when forty-nine articles or Sea laws were agreed upon " by eighteen persons most famous for skill in sea-faring matters,"[1] to be given credit to as guides for the office of the Admiralty in England. This is followed by some chapters on the practice of certain foreign courts. There is also in another part of the book a treatise on the law and practice of the duello signed by Thomas, Duke of Norfolk, who was Lord High Admiral and Constable under Henry VIII., and died in 1535. The book thus commenced at some time during or after the reign of Edward III., was continued under Henry IV., Henry V., Henry VI., and Edward IV., who appointed the first judge of the Admiralty Court by royal patent, in the person of Dr. William Lacy[2] in 1482. A second book of apparently equal if not greater antiquity bound in wood with metal bosses, which, so far as it is perfect (the first half of the book having been cut away), begins in 1535, contains, among other things, the oaths to be taken by various Admiralty officials.

The Court appears originally to have sat at Orton Quay and other spots near London Bridge, until it was constituted a court for all England, when its sittings were

---

[1] *Exton's Dicæology*, p. 124.   [2] *Selden Society*, vol. vi. p. 65.

regularly held at Doctors' Commons. The trial of maritime criminals took place either by the Chancellor, or by the Admiralty Court, where they were tried sometimes by juries, sometimes by the judge alone.[1] The regular records of the Court begin about 1524, but intermittent records are to be found under the dates of Richard III. and Henry IV., and there are numerous documents relating to the judgments and the jurisdiction of the Court of Admiralty to be found scattered through the records of other courts and offices.

A reproduction in copper of the oldest known seal of the Court of Admiralty is given with the sixth volume of the Selden Society's publications. The ship on this seal resembles that in the Black Book, and is an almost exact reproduction of the seal of the Hundred of Tenterden, one of the limbs of the Cinque Ports, which bears the Plantagenet badge, the star of Bethlehem opposed to a crescent moon, and would probably have been granted during their dynasty. The impression is attached to an Admiralty warrant dated 1559; but the seal itself may, from its appearance, have been struck at any time from the reign of Edward III. to that of Henry VI.

The modern seal, used for appeals, is in silver, of the date of George IV. Under the royal arms of Great Britain and Hanover is a man-of-war in full sail, with the legend *Ab Edgare vindico*, which may, I think, be rendered, "From the time of King Edgar I claim the sovereignty of the sea."

---

[1] *Selden Society*, vol. vi. p. lxv.

Following somewhat on the same lines was the recognition or confirmation of the charters of the Cinque Ports. The constitution of these ports into a confederacy for the supply and maintenance of the Royal Navy was due to Edward the Confessor, who first appointed a Lord Warden with power and authority analogous to that exercised during the Roman occupation by the official known as the Count of the Saxon Shore. By his Royal Charter King Edward I. confirmed the charter or other grant of the Confessor and established on a firm footing the various courts and the special jurisdiction exercised by the barons of the Cinque Ports for many centuries. Their courts had civil, criminal, equity and admiralty jurisdiction, with no appeal beyond the Lord Warden in *Court of Shepway.*[1] They owned no subjection to the courts at Westminster whose writs of certiorari, mandamus, and habeas corpus did not run within their territory, and having a chancery and a chancellor of their own, they protested they were even beyond the control of the Lord Chancellor. The last Charter of the Cinque Ports is dated the 23rd December, 1668, and in it King Charles II. recites various charters that he has seen, including the charter dated the 6 Edward I., which is the earliest mentioned as then in existence. This Charter, however, recites and confirms the rights of the ports in respect of their courts and otherwise during the reigns of the

---

[1] The installation of Lord Palmerston as Lord Warden, published in 1862 by Edward Knocker, Town Clerk of Dover, gives an interesting account of the Antient Court of Shepway.

Confessor, of William the Conqueror, of Henry III., and of each succeeding monarch, until his own time.[1]

In an outbreak of lawlessness in the thirteenth century, men congregating together in large numbers, whose example the club-men of the seventeenth century seem to have followed, arming themselves with bastons or staves, beat and robbed unprotected cottagers and wayfarers. To cope with this disorder the King appointed certain judges of Trailbaston to visit the disturbed districts and execute speedy justice on these offenders. The result however was not satisfactory, and owing to numerous complaints, and probably to the too speedy execution of the judges' sentences, the scheme was after some years abandoned, and no further commissions of Trailbaston were issued. It is remarkable in regard to this title that it is not known accurately whether the term *Trailbaston* referred to the judge or to the malefactor. Coke[2] says, the commission was of Trailbaston, that justice might be dealt out as quickly as one could trail a club, and the judges were so named in respect of the speed of their procedure. On the other hand, the ordinance of 1305, which erected these courts, refers to " *transgressionibus nominatis trailbaston*," and a medieval ballad quoted by de Franqueville,[3] and edited by Wright, speaks of the *trailbastouns* being sent, some to prison and some to

---

[1] These Charters with extended annotations are printed *in extenso* in Jeakes' *Charters of the Cinque Ports*, published in 1728 at the desire, and mainly at the cost, of Chief Baron Gilbert. Before that date Jeakes' work was much consulted in MS.

[2] *Inst.*, vol. iv. p. 186.

[3] *Système Judiciaire de l'Angleterre*, vol. i. p. 154, note.

be hanged, and says, if chastisement had not been done
on *les ribaldes et bricouns*, no man could dare to live *en
messouns*. These courts were perhaps, in addition to
their novelty as courts of speedy dispatch, the earliest
instance of a special commission issued to try a special
class of offence. And as we hear no more of Trail-
bastons after the reign of Richard II., it may safely be
inferred that whatever were their errors of procedure
the courts of Trailbaston accomplished the object for
which they were instituted.

An official called *Clericus mercati hospitii regis*, the
clerk of the market at the King's gate, represented an
honourable office pertinent to the antient custom of holding markets in the suburbs of the King's Court. This
clerk, in the early times, witnessed the parties' verbal
contracts. At a later date he adjudicated on the prices
of corn, bread, wine, and other commodities, which had
been fixed by the justices of the peace at their assize.
He enquired as to all weights and measures, and saw that
they were correct according to the standard of the Exchequer at Westminster. He measured land according
to the standard, if any question of quantity arose, and he
had power to send bakers, brewers, and others, to the
pillory if in their dealings they offended against the
law. The King's clerk had a right to hold Courts for
the trial of weights and measures in every city, borough,
or town in the kingdom, subject to an appeal, if he were
guilty of extortion, to the Lord High Steward, who had
power to fine him for the first and second offences, and to
commit him to the Tower for the third.

An illuminated parchment, dated 12 Henry VII. (1497), was formerly nailed to an oak table in the Exchequer, but is now in private hands. It represents the King supported by angels over the heads of three Barons of the Exchequer. It gives in detail the various duties of a clerk of the market, with drawings of the several weights and measures. There are also representations of six ermined commissioners appointed to sit judicially on the assizes of bread, etc., including the Bishop of Llandaff, the Steward, and the Comptroller of the Household, and three other persons. It also gives a picture of a victim found guilty of false weights impounded in the pillory with his head through a post.[1] The clerk of the King's market exercised his jurisdiction at least as late as the time of Henry VIII., for we find that one of the articles of impeachment against Wolsey was that when the clerk had declared and stuck up the prices of goods to be sold in the market of St. Alban's, the Cardinal pulled down the notices of the King's clerk, stuck up notices issued by his own clerk of the market, and threatened to put the former in the stocks.[2]

The Court of Pypowders,[3] or *Curia pedis pulverizati*, was the court of the fair. · It was held before the steward or bailiff of the fair, who could hear on the spot all questions arising between parties at the fair,

[1] A drawing of this illumination is given in *Vetusta Monumenta*, vol. i. London, 1746. The antient punishment of pillory was to put the culprit's head through a pillar of wood.

[2] Coke, *Institute*, vol. iv. p. 272. Crompton, fol. 220–229.

[3] Crompton, fol. 229–230. Coke, *Institute*, vol. iv. p. 272.

provided the faults complained of occurred *in the fair*
and *in fair time,* which was strictly prescribed by
custom or statute. The dusty-footed frequenters of the
fair, coming hot and angry from their quarrels to the
Steward's Court, gave it the name of Pypowders, otherwise *pieds poudrés,* or the Court of the dusty feet. The
times and places of holding fairs were regulated by a
statute of Edward III., who also directed they were not
to be held in churchyards.

II.

The Chancellor—The Master of the Rolls—The Rolls House or
Domus Conversorum—Masters in Chancery—The Chancel-
lor's Marble Chair and Table—The Chancellor Sitting Alone
—Definite Subjects for his Adjudication—Equity and Com-
mon Law—Results of this Period—Robes of the Judges and
their Officers—The Judges' Scarlet—Court of Chancery—
Court of King's Bench—The Common Bench—The Exchequer
—Ordinance of 1635.

THE change of system which brought about the division
of the Curia into three courts, discharging separate and
independent functions, naturally exercised a corresponding influence on the position and the duties of the Chancellor. As the Chief Justiciar declined, the Chancellor
rose in importance, and from the reign of Henry III.,
when the former finally disappeared from the scene, the
Chancellor ceased to be the second person in the kingdom
and became the first. He was the King's confidential
adviser, the chief minister of the law, was called Lord
Chancellor of England, and took precedence of all other

judges and officials. He was still selected from among those having special relations with the Sovereign, and as such, was almost invariably an ecclesiastic. His position was thus, from an early date, distinct from that of the Common Law judges ; a distinction which became more pronounced from the fact that, while the Common Law judges were in the course of time invariably and necessarily serjeants-at-law before they took their seats as judges, no such qualification was required for the Chancellor or his deputy ; and from the creation of serjeants in the thirteenth century to the present day, no such qualification has ever been required, nor has there, in fact, ever been a Chancellor who was a serjeant-at-law, unless he obtained that degree long before and entirely apart from his appointment as Lord Chancellor. The most important, however, as the most antient of the distinctions between the Chancellor and the Common Law judges is to be found in the tenure of their respective offices. While the latter by custom, and now by law, hold their places so long as they conduct themselves well in their office, the Chancellor holds his office as a minister and not as a judge ; and as such he is and always has been appointed and removed at the pleasure of the Crown.

The Chancellor having secured for himself a position in which he could hold an independent court, his right to appoint deputies and assistants in case of need necessarily accrued. We hear of a Vice-Chancellor (*agens vice Cancellarii*) as early as Henry II. who, in 1177, sent Walter de Constantiis (*Vice-Cancellarcum· suum*) and Ranulph de Glanvil, one of his Justices, into Flanders on a diplomatic mission;[1] of another who was drowned, as before mentioned, in the time of Richard I., and of certain others mentioned by Lord Campbell. But such appointments were temporary and casual, and the recognised office of Vice-Chancellor of England did not arise till the reign of George III. (A.D. 1813), when, by virtue of an Act of Parliament,[2] Sir Thomas Plumer, the then Attorney General, was appointed the first Vice-Chancellor of England.

The Master or Keeper of the Rolls,[3] and of the State Papers connected with the suits and records, first, of the Chancery and afterwards of the entire kingdom, was an antient officer of this country. He first appears as an official in the reign of Edward I. (A.D. 1295),[4] who appointed Adam de Osgodby to this post. From that date to the Commonwealth there was an unbroken series of Chancery lawyers, mostly however ecclesiastics, filling the office of Keeper or Master of the Rolls. The Master sat usually at his house in the Rolls Garden, where he had a chapel, a residence, and certain conveniences for keeping the rolls. These were so called from their consisting of parchments and papers rolled up into bundles and so noted and put away. The Rolls House was formerly a house for converts from the Jewish

---

[1] Madox, vol. i. p. 77.

[2] 53 Geo. III., c. 24. Foss' *Judges*, vol. viii. p. 205.

[3] He did not receive the title of *Magister Rotulorum*, Master of the Rolls, until 2 Henry VII., c. 20 (A.D. 1487). Before that date he was always *Custos Rotulorum*, Keeper of the Rolls.

[4] Dugdale, *Origines Juridiciales*, fol. 32.

to the Christian religion. It was built and endowed by Henry III., and bore the name of *Domus Conversorum*. In the year 1290 the Jews were expatriated by Edward I., and there remained no longer any Jews in England to be converted or to enjoy King Henry's home and hospitality. The house was then given to William Burstall,[1] Keeper of the Rolls, to be occupied by him for life, or so long as he should remain in his office, and afterwards, in consideration of the moneys he had expended in its reparation,[2] it was ordered by Parliament that the said house should remain for ever annexed to the office of Keeper of the Rolls.[3] From this grant it has been assumed that the Master of the Rolls himself had some official or religious duty in regard to the conversion of Jews to Christianity, an assumption which gave rise to discussion when a very distinguished lawyer of the Jewish faith was recently appointed to that post. Although, however, the Master of the Rolls is *ex-officio* trustee of the Society for the conversion of the Jews, yet the practice is of modern date and no proselytizing duties are in any way incident to the tenure of the office.

Up to the reign of Henry VIII., the Master of the Rolls only sat to hear causes and make orders in the absence of the Chancellor, but, owing to the increase of business, Cardinal Wolsey as Chancellor appointed Cuthbert Tunstall his Master of the Rolls to be an independent judge, with power to sit daily, and to hear and adjudicate upon causes

---

[1] Coke, *4th Institute*, p. 95.   [2] 1 Richard II.

[3] The present Rolls House has no historical interest. It was built in 1717.

in equity. From that time forward the Master of the Rolls (sitting until after the Restoration, usually in the afternoon after the rising of the House of Commons) has regularly presided at the Rolls, and heard motions and causes.[1] Among other of his privileges he enjoyed the distinction that, until 1875,[2] he was, although a judge, not precluded by the tenure of his office from sitting in Parliament, and on many occasions the Master of the Rolls has not only sat in the House of Commons, but has occupied the distinguished position of Speaker.[3] His precedence among the judges was next after the Lord Chief Justice of the King's Bench, and before the Lord Chief Justice of the Common Pleas.

Subordinate to the Master of the Rolls, but occupying a very similar position, were the Masters in Chancery. Of those, of whom there were twelve, the Master of the Rolls was chief, and they together constituted a legal council to advise the Chancellor in matters of law and equity.[4] They were usually selected from such of the Chancery clerks as were best instructed in the practice of the office. They lived in the Chancery House, and, in addition to

---

[1] Crompton, fol. 42. Coke, 4*th Institute*, 96. Reeve's *History*, vol. iv. p. 369; Campbell's *Lives of the Chancellors*, vol. i. p. 506.

[2] Judicature Act 1875, sec. 5.

[3] Amongst others, Sir Thos. Phillips was Master of the Rolls and Speaker under James I.; William Lenthall, Speaker of the Long Parliament, was, during the whole of that period, Master of the Rolls; and Henry Powles was Master of the Rolls and Speaker in 1689. Sir John Romilly was M.P. for Devonport while he held the office of Master of the Rolls.

[4] " A Treatise of the Maisters of the Chauncerie." Hargraves, *Law Tracts*, p. 293.

their salaries and fees, were provided with their diet, wine and venison, and with gowns (one furred and one lined with taffetas), paid for by the Crown, and constituting the robes or livery of the office. They formed what was called "*concilium regis in cancellaria,*" the King's Council in Chancery, and being assumed to be more conversant with the law and practice of that Court than the Chancellor himself, they sat with him in his court and beside him on the woolsack in the House of Lords, of which one of the Masters was usually the Clerk, by right of his office. They were not, however, permitted to address the House, and one of the Masters having attempted to do so in 1576, they were after that date banished from the woolsack.[1] They were always ecclesiastics, and had a right, after certain services, to be presented to one of the Chancellor's livings, a right which they successfully asserted as against the Chancellor himself in the reign of Henry V.[2]

The Chancellor, from a remote period, at least as early as Edward II., sat in Westminster Hall. His place was at the upper end, where a flight of some six steps led to a marble table, opposite the centre of which was a marble chair affixed to the wall, "which marble chair," says Dugdale,[3] writing in 1666, " to this day remaineth over against the middle of the marble table." His seat of justice, however, was altered as circumstances required. He sat at times in the House of Lords and in Lincoln's Inn.

---

[1] Hargraves' *Law Tracts*, p. 283.   [2] Foss' *Judges*, vol. iv. p. 189.
[3] *Orig. Jud.*, fol. 87.

During the Commonwealth, Whitelock and his colleagues, Keepers of the Great Seal, frequently used the Middle Temple Hall, and for many years the marble table and chair were covered up, and the end of the Great Hall was divided between the Courts of Chancery and of the King's Bench, the former sitting on the right, and the latter on the left of the great window of the Hall.

And as his dignity and jurisdiction differed from those of the Common Law judges, so did also his method of dispensing justice. For while the judges sat in numbers, he and his deputies sat alone, except on such occasions as he summoned to his assistance one or two of the Common Law judges to sit with him on the trial of cases involving questions of Common Law. He was never as Chancellor decorated with the collar of SS, and his judgments were for many generations the outcome of his own orderly and instructed mind, guided, no doubt, by considerations of precedents and analogies, but doing equity as he thought right, and relieving suitors from the rigours of the Common Law. His equitable jurisdiction, however, is of somewhat doubtful origin, and I think it clear that at first he had no such jurisdiction, except in cases where no remedy could be obtained at law. A statute [1] of Edward III. gave the subject power to resort to the Chancellor for an original writ, when, according to existing forms at Common Law, justice would be otherwise denied him, a provision necessarily importing primarily a resort to the Courts of Common

[1] 36 Edw. III.

Law. By a statute of Henry VI.[1] it was provided that no man should be called to answer in Chancery, where there was a remedy at law. And although every Chancellor in succession in and after the reign of Henry II. heard causes and gave judgments, yet it does not appear, according to Lord Coke,[2] that any actual reports of cases decided by Chancellors sitting in Equity are to be found in the books before the reign of King Henry VI., after which date they are sufficiently numerous. Lord Campbell,[3] however, is of opinion that the existence of the Chancellor's equitable jurisdiction from the earliest period is clear and indisputable.

Notwithstanding the somewhat flexible rule of the Chancellor, there were certain definite grievances in respect of which the subject had always a right of appeal to his Court. These were,—

(1) For relief in all cases of fraud or deceit, for which there was no remedy at law.

(2) For relief against the effect of any accident by which a man was deprived of what would otherwise be his right, and to which the Common Law could not help him.

(3) In regard to breaches of trust by trustees and others, of which the law would not formerly take cognizance.

To these was afterwards added—

(4) The relief of mortgagors against rapacious

---

[1] 1 Henry VI.   [2] *Instit.*, vol. iv. p. 82.
[3] *Lives of the Chancellors*, vol. i. p. 7.

I

mortgagees, who took advantage of their position to foreclose their mortgages and ruin their unhappy debtors.

As the subject might always appeal to the clemency or equity of the Crown, so was the Chancellor's Court always open. He was not called upon to regulate his sittings by the duration of the terms which bound the Courts of Common Law, but he sat with equal authority in and out of term, in or out of vacation. He could at any time issue a writ of *habeas corpus* when a subject was imprisoned, and the Court of King's Bench was not sitting to grant his release, or to inquire into the cause of his committal. He granted, without regard to time or place, writs of prohibition to check the excesses of inferior courts, and injunctions to stay an impending injury or damage to the applicant. He could issue a writ, *ne exeat regno*, to prevent a would-be absconding debtor leaving the kingdom, and he habitually issued writs in furtherance of the process of the Common Law, or Ecclesiastical Courts, when the judgments of such Courts had, for certain reasons, become unenforceable without his aid. He could also, by right of his office, issue writs of *scire facias* to cancel letters patent granted by the king, when such patents could be shown to be erroneous or unjust. Thus, if the king granted two or more patents to the same effect to two or more persons, the first patentee had a right to call upon the Chancellor to cancel the other patents as improvidently issued; or when a patent was granted on a false statement of facts, and it thus appeared to have been obtained by fraud, or when the king had granted a patent which he had by law no power to grant, then also, *ex debito justitiæ* (for the sake of justice and right), the letters patent were cancelled. This power, which dates back to a very early period, has been suggested as the origin of the name *cancellarius*, or canceller of the king's patents. For it is said, that upon the patent being shown to be bad in law, the Chancellor took the parchment and cancelled it by drawing lines across it like bars of a casement, or, as Coke says,[1] "like a lettice." An anecdote is told of Lord Chancellor Gardiner, in the reign of Queen Mary, who in sight of the House of Lords cutting away from a Bill certain clauses which had been thrown out by the Commons, and not insisted on by the Lords, made use of the expression, "Now do I rightly the office of a Chancellor."[2] One would hardly accuse Gardiner of a pun, but his words can scarcely be said to give much authority to the contention.

Thus these two streams of Equity and Common Law, flowing from the same fountain head, have been seen to permeate the judicial fields from the Anglo-Saxons to the Tudors. In the course of time they widened their banks and the current flowed over more expanded ground, but their course had continued to be parallel and not intersecting. If the Chancellor had obtained precedence over the Chief Justice, it was because, in the ordinary course of events, the man who is at once a lawyer, a priest and

---

[1] *4th Institute*, p. 88.

[2] Lord's *Journal*, vol. i. p. 484. Campbell's *Lives of the Chancellors*, vol. i. p. 2.

a statesman would naturally supersede the man whose special qualifications were those of a lawyer alone. But the Chancellor's office and his position were gradually magnified by the greater duties cast upon him, and it will be found at a later period when the Chancellor became the would-be director, if not the rival of the monarch, and claimed not only to modify the rigours of the Common Law, but to inquire into the decisions of the King's Bench and Common Pleas, and to set aside their judgments in respect of matters specially within their cognizance, that the king and the people made common cause to destroy the Chancellor who had interfered with the action of the popular courts, which had always been regarded as component parts of the antient laws and customs of the country. No doubt the law they gave effect to was capricious ; but, unlike that of their neighbours, it was not bloodthirsty, and it recognised the right of the commonalty to come freely to their open sittings and to take part as jurors and assessors in the administration of justice.

This third period had accordingly seen the Curia Regis finally abolished and the Common Law Courts of the King's Bench and the Common Pleas instituted in its place. The parliamentary protests [1] against the realm being governed by men of the Church with a very undue proportion of laymen bore its fruit in the Common Law, if not in Chancery, and a race of lawyers now administered justice in the highest places instead of ecclesiastics or nobles, some fully, but most of them

---

[1] Especially in 45 Edward III. ; see Coke, *4th Inst.*, p. 78.

imperfectly instructed in the laws and customs of England. It propounded the irremovability of the King's judges, except for misconduct in their office, and saw it adopted in a general if not perhaps a universal practice, though no statute or ordinance was passed to that effect. It witnessed the final and complete establishment in the Common Law Courts of trial by jury as a substitute for all other modes of trial for civil and criminal pleas, and the death by non-user of the ordeal of fire and water, for, like the ordeal of battle, no statute or ordinance forbade the courts to have recourse to the triple ordeal or any other of the so-called judgments of God. It saw for the first time the administration of the counties by Justices of the Peace and the foundation of Courts of Quarter Session. It witnessed the elevation of the Chancellor to the position of an independent judge with a staff of trained lawyers as his council and his assistants in his office. It welcomed the perfect enrolment of decrees in all judicial proceedings, and the establishment and regulation of the Bar as a part of the judicial system. The law itself, with its antient customs and recent statutes, was then for the first time discussed and displayed by great writers and jurists for the instruction of students in that learned profession, and for the satisfaction of that growing class of Englishmen to whom its immemorial customs and sinuous ways were becoming day by day subjects of greater interest and of more serious consideration.

It remains to say a few words on the robes of the judges and the mode in which they sat in their various courts. Whether the Chief Justiciar, the Chancellor, the

barons, and the other judges of the Curia Regis wore
any, and if any, what special robes, while administering
justice, it is impossible to say. I think it probable that
they had no special costume, each wearing the dress
applicable to his station in life. Grimbald's seal of the
time of Henry II., which gives, as is supposed, the first
example of judicial costume, depicts the judge in a robe of
some soft material fastened at the waist and open in front
from the knees downwards, having therefore no special
features to distinguish it from the robes of an ecclesiastic
or person of importance of that date.[1] From the institution of the courts of Common Law, however, we have some
certain records of the costume and appearance of the
judges. It was the custom of this period, a custom which
in fact continued to the time of the Stuarts, to provide
the judges, in addition to their salary, with diet and with
robes for use during their term of office. That the first
judicial colour was scarlet admits I think of little doubt.
It was the judicial colour throughout Europe in the
Middle Ages. The magistrates of Venice composing the
Council of Ten wore scarlet robes. The judges who tried
Savonarola, in 1495, appear from an old painting in
Florence to have been clothed in scarlet. And the dress
of such of the higher orders of the clergy as would have
occupied the position of judges in England was, in the
thirteenth and fourteenth centuries, usually scarlet. Dur-

---

[1] An exemplification of this seal is given in Dugdale's *Orig.*,
fol. 100, and in Planché's *History of Costumes*, p. 426; Foss'
Judges, vol. i. p. 257, doubts whether Grimbald was ever a
Justice of the Curia, and thinks he was a Sheriff.

ing these centuries the wealth and luxury of the priests were common subjects of invective among the reformers, whose disciples lampooned them freely in the songs and poems of the time, the scarlet robes of the clergy being particular objects of aversion. Examples of this are to be found in the well-known *Ploughman's Complaint*,[1] written about 1394, and many similar passages are to be found in other writings published during that period in hostility to the clergy, the monks and the friars.

In the time of Edward III. the judges of both benches and the barons of the Exchequer had the same judicial dress with no distinction between the chiefs and the puisnes.[2] The cloth given them is described as *pannum curcum* or *curtum*.[3] If the latter, it would mean short cloth as distinguished from long cloth, the size of which was then regulated by statute. *Curcum* is not easy to translate, but I think it may be derived from *curcuma*, a plant which gives a saffron dye, which treated with alkali produces a red colour. This is to some extent

[1] See *Political Poems and Songs from Edward III. to Richard III.*, by T. Wright; London, 1859.

> " With cloth of gold both new and redde
> With glitterande gold as grene as gall." (p. 308.)

> . . . . .

> " Of scarlet and grene gaie gounes
> That mote be shape of the newe." (p. 332.)

[2] Dugdale, *Orig.*, fol. 98. Foss' *Judges*, vol. iii. p. 359.

[3] *Originalia Roll*, 21 Edward III. rot. 66. It must be borne in mind that *c* and *t* are so much alike in the writing of this period that it is frequently very difficult to distinguish one letter from the other.

borne out by a reference in Dyer,[1] who, describing the
costumes of the judges and others at the trial by battle in
Tothill before referred to,[2] says, that in a battle waged in
the 29 Edward III. (A.D. 1355) the several "parties
appeared arrayed as here," special reference being made
to the judges in their scarlet robes. Unless this suggestion is well founded there cannot be produced any
record or order showing that the judges' robes were
scarlet, otherwise than by custom, until the order of 1635
hereafter mentioned. With this cloth they had fine
linen silk for the summer, and miniver and other furs
for the winter. Under Richard II. the judges had green
cloth for the puisnes and the chief baron, with an addition of green taffetas for the two chief justices for their
summer robes.[3] In the time of Henry VI. they had two
sets of robes, one with fur at Christmas and one with
linen at Pentecost.[4] The summer robe was also of green
cloth or taffetas, as under Richard II., and the winter
robe was violet. On arriving, however, at the period of
Henry VI. and Edward IV., we have precise information that the ordinary costume of the judges of the
Common Law Courts of both benches was scarlet cloth.
This is derived from a valuable illuminated MS. now in
the library of the Inner Temple, and undoubtedly of the
date of Henry VI. or Edward IV. This MS. formerly
belonged to Mr. Selby Lowndes, to whom it descended

---

[1] Vol. iii., p. 301.   [2] *Ante*, p. 64.
[3] Dugdale, *Orig.*, fol. 99.   Foss' *Judges*, vol. iv. p. 19.
[4] *Ibid.*, p. 226.

from William Fleetwood, Recorder of London in the time of Queen Elizabeth, and formed portion of a MS. copy of an abridgment or digest of the laws which internal evidence shows to have been of the fifteenth century. It was reproduced by the Society of Antiquaries in 1860,[1] and gives an authoritative record of the costumes of the period worn in the Courts of Chancery, of King's Bench, of Common Bench, and of Exchequer. This information was not available either to Dugdale, who wrote in 1666, or to Foss, who wrote in 1851.[2]

Over the heads of the judges in each of the courts appear the arms of Edward the Confessor, five doves or martins surrounding a patonce cross, thus indicating that even at that period, four centuries after the death of the Confessor, the spirit of his just and equal laws was still supposed to inspire the administration of justice. These arms are accompanied by those of the reigning monarch, the emblems of France and England having been borne equally by Henry VI. and Edward IV., and by the arms of England, three golden lions passant on a field of red. It also appears that judges, clerks and serjeants are closely shaved, and that serjeants, counsel and certain officers of the court, but not the judges, wore parti-coloured garments. These were liveries, and were worn indifferently by menial servants and by squires and gentry who attached themselves to certain great families. From

[1] *Archæologia*, vol. xxxix. p. 357.
[2] A coloured drawing of Judges in their robes in the time of Queen Elizabeth given in Green's *Short History*, etc., vol. iv. p. 996, seems to me to be fanciful and misleading.

Edward III. to Henry VIII. numerous statutes were
passed to restrict the wearing of these parti-coloured
suits, but from all such statutes serjeants-at-law were
excluded, and they accordingly continued to wear these
gowns till the death of Queen Anne, when, according to
the late Chief Baron Pollock, the whole bar went into
mourning from which it has never emerged.

The first of these illuminations depicts the Court of
Chancery. The principal figure on the bench is supposed
to be the Chancellor,[1] who is robed in scarlet, with a
red velvet turban or cap commonly used at this period.
At his side is the Master of the Rolls, a tonsured ecclesiastic also in scarlet with no coif, holding a deed with
a large seal as to which he appears to be delivering
his judgment. On either side of the court are two
tonsured ecclesiastics in mustard-coloured robes, also
without coifs, making in all six persons on the judgment
seat. The latter are obviously Masters in Chancery,
whose duty it was to sit with the Chancellor, and who
had probably not yet received their solatium in the gift
of one of the Chancellor's livings. At the green table
under the Chancellor are the clerks making up the rolls,
while an officer of the Chancery is affixing the Great Seal
to a patent. Various writs already tested lie on the
table. Three serjeants in parti-coloured robes and coifs
and two barristers appear to be addressing the court,
and five clerks or reporters in the back row are leisurely

---

[1] He is thought to represent Richard Neville, Earl of Salisbury
(A.D. 1454), one of the very few laymen who held the post of
Chancellor during the early period.

Court of Chancery.

THE COURT OF CHANCERY, TEMP. HENRY VI.

The Chancellor, the Master of the Rolls, and four Masters in Chancery on the Bench.

From an illuminated MS. in the Inner Temple.

See page 122.

taking notes. The faces in this as in the other illuminations appear to be portraits, but it is fruitless to attempt any identification of the parties represented.

In the King's Bench are five judges [1] in scarlet, wearing coifs. To the right of the judges a jury is being sworn by an usher clad in a parti-coloured robe. Facing the judges a prisoner, chained by the feet, is holding up his affidavit hand and pleading to an indictment. He is in custody of a gaoler in a mustard-coloured jacket with a short sword and a long staff, and is supported on either side by a serjeant retained for his defence. Two tipstaffs, one in blue and one in mustard colour, armed with staves, have charge of a gang of prisoners of woe-begone aspect, each chained by one leg to the floor. Clerks at the table are making up the rolls.

In the Common Bench are seven [2] judges in scarlet with coifs. Under these are the officers of the court, and facing them is a defendant in his shirt with bare legs in custody of the tipstaff. Five serjeants appear in particoloured gowns or coifs. There are no counsel and there is no jury. All the officers, except the gaoler, are in parti-coloured robes, the latter is dressed like his fellow in the King's Bench.

In the Exchequer the Chief Baron appears in a scarlet

---

[1] If the date of these illuminations is correctly assumed at or about 1450, then Sir John Fortescue would have been Chief Justice of the King's Bench, as he occupied that post from 1442 to 1461.

[2] There were seven judges in the Common Pleas at the beginning and at the end of this reign. Foss, vol. iv. p. 231.

gown and in a turban somewhat similar to that of the Chancellor. With him on the bench are four barons in mustard-coloured robes, two with turbans of saffron on their heads and two wearing a kind of yellow coif, and holding their turbans in their hands. Under them, seated at a green table, without, however any chess-board squares, are the officials of the Exchequer, one of whom, a teller in a mustard robe, is counting the golden nobles produced by the accountant. A man stands near the table holding up a bag of silver pieces, and chests of treasure are on the floor. At one end of the court is a lock-up or cage for defaulters, of whom two are seen through the bars. Three serjeants in coifs, and two counsel in parti-coloured robes appear to be taking part in the proceedings.[1] In each court the judges sit on a raised bench far above the heads of the officers and the general public. And it is said that on the rare occasions in which the King in person attended the court, a seat was provided for him above the heads of the judges, who proceeded to hear motions and make orders as in his absence. Their hours according to Fortescue were, in the fifteenth century, from 8 to 11 a.m., after which hour the courts were closed, the judges retired to study the law and to prepare

---

[1] In a sketch of the Court of Exchequer in Ireland, published in the *Gentleman's Magazine*, vol. xliii. p. 3, under date *Henricus dei gra.*, which is believed to be Henry IV., a person, supposed to be either the Chief Baron or the Chancellor of the Exchequer, is attired similarly to the barons in the English illuminations, with the same description of turban. The table has red and white squares and the teller or treasurer is counting gold nobles from an accountant's bag.

Court of Exchequer

Face page 124.

THE COURT OF EXCHEQUER, TEMP. HENRY VI.

The Chief Baron and four Barons of the Exchequer on the Bench.

From an illuminated MS. in the Inner Temple.

See page 123.

themselves for the work of the morrow, and the suitors went to St. Paul's to consult the serjeants whom they found each beside his own pillar in the nave, or to the Inns of Court to see those of their counsel who were not yet called to the degree of the coif.

An ordinance [1] made by the judges on the 4th June, 1635, finally settled the colours and the changes of the judges' robes, and its directions were with slight modifications still observed by the judges until they left Westminster Hall for their new habitation in the Strand. By that ordinance the black and the violet gowns with various furs are to be worn at certain specified dates, but in the Criminal Courts, when the judges are trying prisoners or charging the Grand Jury, on all Sundays, Saints' days and holidays, when they go officially to St. Paul's, to Westminster Abbey, or to any other church, when they swear in the Lord Mayor of London, or dine with the High Sheriff, or when they attend the Sovereign in the House of Lords, they are to wear their scarlet gowns, thus recognising scarlet as the antient and honourable colour and badge of their high office. The green robe introduced by Richard II. seems by the seventeenth century to have gone altogether out of use.

The judges sat in Westminster Hall, which, after having been flooded and burned in 1263, and again burned in 1299, was repaired by Edward III., and finally reconstructed into somewhat of its present condition by the munificence of Richard II. The walls were raised two

---

[1] Dugdale's *Orig.*, fol. 101.

feet and re-cased, new windows were inserted, and a porch and towers were erected at the north end. Buttresses were built to strengthen the walls, and the magnificent chestnut roof now existing was then added. The hall itself was decorated, and the niches filled with statues of which three only have been preserved, and are now in the custody of the Architectural Museum. William of Wykeham, founder of Winchester College and of New College, Oxford, was the Chancellor who undertook the restoration, and Geoffry Chaucer the poet, himself bred to the law at the Inner Temple, acted as clerk of the works.

CHAPTER IV.

THE COURTS OF THE FOREST.

THE cruelty and the oppression of the Forest Laws, the
vast area over which they exercised their sway, and the
hatred engendered by the fierceness of their administration played so important a part in the early history of
our country that no sketch of English Courts of Justice
should fail to give some account of the inception and
progress of the Forest Courts.

Hunting and sporting have ever formed part of the
recreation if not the business of mankind, and from the

most remote periods rulers and monarchs have claimed
them as royal pastimes, and have arrogated to themselves
the right of controlling them by their edicts and their
ordinances. Much doubt has arisen how and when laws
regulating the forests of England or declaring the rights
of the Sovereign and the privilege of the people originated. Without entering into a discussion which would
perhaps be of purely antiquarian interest, it may suffice
to say that, so far as I have been able to ascertain, the
first ordinance or edict on this subject is to be found in
the reign of Canute (A.D. 1016). In what is termed the
"Dooms," otherwise the Laws of Canute, under cap. 81,
the following passage occurs:

> "I will that every one be entitled to his hunting
> in wood and in field in his own possession. And let
> every one forego my hunting: take notice where I
> will have it untrespassed on under penalty of full
> ' wite ' " (fine).[1]

The accuracy of this passage is however seriously im-
pugned by modern writers, and Sir Edward Coke in referring to it expresses a doubt whether this or a supposed
copy in somewhat similar language, but substituting the
word *plain* for *wood*, represents the real ordinance, or
whether in fact they are not both the products of writers
of a later date, who have ascribed to Canute what they
believe from tradition and not from knowledge to have

---

[1] " Dooms of Cnut," *Ancient Laws and Institutes,* vol. i. p. 421.
Manwood, *Treatise of the Laws of the Forest*; London, 1598. *Über
Pseudo-Cnuts Constitutiones de Foresta von Liebermann*; Halle, A. S.
Max Niemeyer, 1894.

been the law in his day. The question is, however, fairly dealt with by the investigation and report of the Commissioners of Public Records, who in 1840, under the orders of the late King William IV., printed the antient laws and institutes of England secular and ecclesiastical, and are satisfied that the Ordinance or Doom, as given above, was in substance issued by the Danish King. These Dooms were followed by *Constitutiones de Foresta*[1] (Constitutions of the Forest) promulgated by the same monarch. By them he appointed from the Thanes four chiefs of each forest called *primarii* who were to do justice,[2] under whom were four *Mediocris*, Medial Thanes, or "*yoongmen*," who undertook the care of vert and venison but did not meddle with the admɪnstration of justice.[3] Subordinate to each of these, again, were two smaller men, called *Tithing men*, to whom were committed the nightly care of the vert and venison and other servile duties, but who, if theretofore slaves, became free on being appointed to this office in the forest.[4] All complaints against the "yoongmen" and the tithing men were heard and disposed of by the primarii, and complaints against these latter were heard and dealt with by the King in person.[5]

Four times a year forest causes were to be tried, and the triple ordeal was to be practised; but the ordeal of fire was not to be had recourse to, unless the truth could

---

[1] *Ancient Laws and Institutes*, vol. i. p. 426. See also Hallam's *Middle Ages*, vol. ii. p. 361, as to these divisions of the people.

[2] Sec. 1.   [3] Secs. 2, 3.   [4] Secs. 4, 5.   [5] Sec. 10.

not otherwise be ascertained.[1] If any man used violence towards a Primarius of the forest, he was, if a freeman, to lose his freedom and all his goods ; if a villain, to lose his right hand ; and if either repeated the offence, the penalty was death.[2] If any were caught offending in the forest, he was to pay a penalty according to the nature and the gravity of the offence.[3] A distinction however was drawn between offences against the venison and those against the vert, the latter being regarded as of small account ; also as between offences against beasts of the forest and royal beasts, and the penalty was varied as it affected freemen or slaves, masters or servants, known or unknown people.[4] A scale of fines was also tabulated for the punishment of those who hunted beasts or stags, and it was provided that if a freeman hunted a royal stag he should be imprisoned for a year ; if he was not a freeman, then for two years ; but if he were a slave, then to be outlawed.[5] If, however, he killed a royal stag, then the freeman lost his freedom, the unfreeman or ceorl lost his liberty, and the slave lost his life.[6] Bishops, abbots and barons were not to be indicted for venison unless they killed royal beasts, when they were subject to a fine at the King's pleasure.[7] Then followed an enumeration of beasts of the forest which might be killed without penalty, and it was expressly declared that a wild boar (aper), though a beast of the forest, had never been held to be an

---

[1] Sec. 11.   [2] Secs. 15, 16.   [3] Sec. 20.   [4] Sec. 21.
[5] Sec. 24.   [6] Sec. 25.   [7] Sec. 26.

animal of venison.[1] Greyhounds were not to be kept by the " yoongmen " unless *genuiscissio* (hamstringing) had been performed in the presence of a primarius, or unless they were kept ten miles from a forest. If kept within from ten to seven miles of the limit, the owner paid one solidus per mile ; if within seven miles, the dog was forfeited and the owner paid ten solidi.[2] But *velteres* or *langeran* (a small breed of harriers, hunting by scent) and *ramhundts* (lap-dogs) could be kept as being of no danger to the deer.[3]

There is some reason to suppose that the Confessor issued or gave his sanction to a Forest Law, probably that of Canute, but no trustworthy evidence is at this time available, although there is a record in Camden's *History of Britain*, of his having appointed a guardian of the forest of the hundred of Chelmer and Dauncing, in Essex.[4] During the reign of the Confessor, therefore the Game Laws were, according to the rude sentiment of the

---

[1] Sec. 27. [2] Sec. 31. [3] Sec. 32, Manwood, fol. 8.
[4] Camden, fol. 310. The text is set out in Crompton, fol. 147, who speaks of the original being in the Exchequer. If *genuine*, it is curious, among other reasons, for indicating the beasts and the vermin that passed under the grant. It is as follows:—

> " Iche Edward King
>   Have geven of my Forrest the keeping
>   Of the hundred of Chelmer and Dauncing
>   To Randolph Peperking and to his Kynlyng,
>   With Hart and Hinde, Doe and Bucke,
>   Hare and Foxe, Cat and Brocke,
>   Wyldfowle with his flocke,
>   Partridge, Fezant Hen and Fezant Cocke,
>   With greene and wilde Stub and Stocke.

period, neither cruel nor irksome. Every man was at liberty to hunt on his own land. Penalties for trespass were moderate ; and, so far as is known, the administration of the forest law was not a subject of complaint from any class of the community. Under the Conqueror, however, the position of affairs was grievously altered. Absolute and exclusive right was claimed for the King in all existing forests. This claim was pushed to the extent of prohibiting the presence in any forest of any members of the community, except those licensed by the King or his officers. And looking upon the hunting of big game as a royal prerogative, to which all private rights must give way, he proceeded to create the New Forest under circumstances which will ever attach a blot to his name and reputation. According to Camden, the Conqueror caused

> To keepen and two yeoman by all their might,
> Both by day and eke by night,
> And hounds for to hould
> Good, swift and boulde.
> Foure greyhounds and six Raches,
> For Hare and Foxe and Wyld Cattes;
> And, therefore, yche made him my Booke;
> Witnesse the Bishop of Wolftone,
> And booke y learned many one,
> And Sweyne of Essex our brother,
> And tekyn him many other ;
> And our steward Howelyn
> That besought me for him.

*　　*　　*　　*　　*

Cel graunt fuit signe evesque crosses de or : car avant venus des Normans en Englit : les charters fuèr signez ave crosses d'ore et auters signes et apres lour ven, fuit use de sealer ave cere : et totum fuis escrie."

towns, villages, and sacred edifices over some 17,000 acres
of a thriving part of England to be devastated, and their
occupants to be scattered far and wide, in order to trans-
form the antient wood of Yten into the New Forest.
Churches and buildings were thrown down, thirty-six
ecclesiastical houses were rooted up, and the people
exterminated. Fiercer than a tempest or a whirlwind,
his edict swept over the land, turning a fruitful and
populated plain into a howling wilderness. "He loved
the high game" it was said, "as if he were their father";
and for their sakes he denuded the land of both God and
man, and made it a home and a sanctuary for wild beasts.[1]
This act of sacrilege and spoliation roused against him the
hatred of all England, noble, cleric and ceorl, and was the
precursor or the proximate cause of those Forest Laws
and Courts which, for centuries, held an unenviable notoriety in Europe, and were the cause of endless disputes
between the Crown and the subject. Nor did the clergy
of the period fail to call attention to the consequences of
his crime. Richard, his second son, and William Rufus,
his son and successor, both died in the New Forest; the
former from a fever produced by the pestilential air of
the woods, and the latter from the arrow of Sir Walter
Tyrrell. The Conqueror's end was not less suggestive,
for he met his death through his horse falling among the

---

[1] Lappenberg: *England under the Anglo-Norman Kings*, p. 214.
Historical Inquiries Concerning Forests, etc. P. Lewis, London,
1811, goes with great detail into the history of the New Forest,
and gives names of hundreds, villages and churches in the time
of the Confessor.

burning ruins of a religious house, which he had fired after
the capture of Mantes.   And so strong and permanent
was the effect of this crime of devastation that, though
succeeding monarchs, in the exercise of their real or
assumed prerogative, added to and extended the borders
of existing forests, no one, until the reign of Henry VIII.,
ever made the attempt to construct a forest where none
had formerly stood.   And when this latter monarch
attempted, but with small success, to create a forest at
Hampton Court, he proceeded by way of Parliament,[1]
obtaining an Act to authorize his so doing, after agreeing
with and compensating the owners of lands that he proposed to take.

That the Conqueror issued an Ordinance of the Forest,
as stated in the Anglo-Saxon Chronicle, admits of little
doubt, though the text of no such document is extant.
Nor is it doubtful that such law was cruel, unjust, and
oppressive.   It was formerly the habit in granting charters which were renewed from reign to reign, sometimes
with modifications, and sometimes without, to recite in
the later charter the text of the former, which was then
lost or destroyed as of little value.   The Charters of the
Cinque Ports,[2] commencing with the Confessor and ending
with Charles II., are an instance of this practice; and we
are thus enabled, by consideration of the recitals in the
repealing Acts of Henry III. and Edward I., to arrive
at the substance of the ordinance of the Conqueror.

---

[1] *Co. Inst.*, vol. iv. p. 300, 31.   Henry VIII. cap. 5.
[2] Jeake's *Charters of the Cinque Ports*; London, 1728.

In the Laws and Customs of King William, setting out his intended mode of governing England, the Conqueror who, inspired by his clergy, objected to capital punishment, except for offences touching his own person and authority, declared that no one should henceforth be killed or hanged for any fault, but that his eyes should be put out, and his foot, hand or other limb be cut off, so that his dismembered body might remain so long as he lived an evidence of his guilt.[1] This statute or ordinance, it will be observed, makes no special reference to the forest; nor does this or any other ordinance of the Conqueror, so far as is known, declare in terms how offenders in the forest are to be punished. But judging from the contents of later charters which declare that this punishment shall not be inflicted on any man for offences in the forest, it would appear that the character of such offence (*quantitatem delicti*) was held to be in the highest degree penal, and that life and limb were, in fact, freely taken by the Conqueror and his sons from those unhappy persons who were by accident or intention offenders against the Laws of the Forest. This agrees with the accounts of the early historians, and with the traditions which have been handed down to us from the earliest ages of the Norman occupation. Thus, therefore, not only were the landowners of England held liable to be

---

[1] "Interdico etiam ne quis occidatur aut suspendatur pro aliqua culpa, sed eruantur oculi, et abscidantur pedes, vel testiculi vel manus, ita quod truncus remaneat vivus in signum prodicionis et nequicice suæ: secundum enim quantitatem delicti debet pena maleficis infligi." *Ancient Laws, etc.*, vol. i. p. 494.

despoiled of their lands at the King's pleasure, but the
freeman and the peasant were excluded from thousands
of acres of fertile soil. They gazed upon desolate
pastures where their cattle were forbidden to feed ; upon
fruits, vegetables, and herbs which they dared not gather ;
upon well-stocked rivers which they were unable to fish ;
and they lived under a constant fear of fine, imprisonment, and mutilation. Their lives and their properties
were subject to increasing exactions, and themselves were
obnoxious to the wanton charges of the officers of the
forest, who made their presentments as accusers, and
then tried them as judges. For, as the common people
were kept out of the woods, so was the Common Law
kept out of the courts, which had their laws to themselves
and their own executive to enforce them.

The exact extent of the forest land under the Norman
kings is difficult if not impossible of ascertainment. No
forest map contemporaneous or subsequent is known to
exist, and information on the subject is only to be obtained from a laborious search among old records, fines
and transfers of land. In order to give at a glance some
idea of the quantity of forest land at this period, I have
sketched very roughly a map of England, showing in
black the large tracts subject to the Forest laws. Necessarily it is little more than an estimate. It does not
include the smaller forests, chases, parks and warrens
which existed in all parts of the country and were subject to this oppressive jurisdiction. Nor is it to be regarded as more than approximately delineating the limits
of the several forests. Of these, including the New

A Sketch Map of England, about the time of Magna Carta, showing roughly, in black, the forest land of England. Wales was not then subject to the English crown.

See page 137.

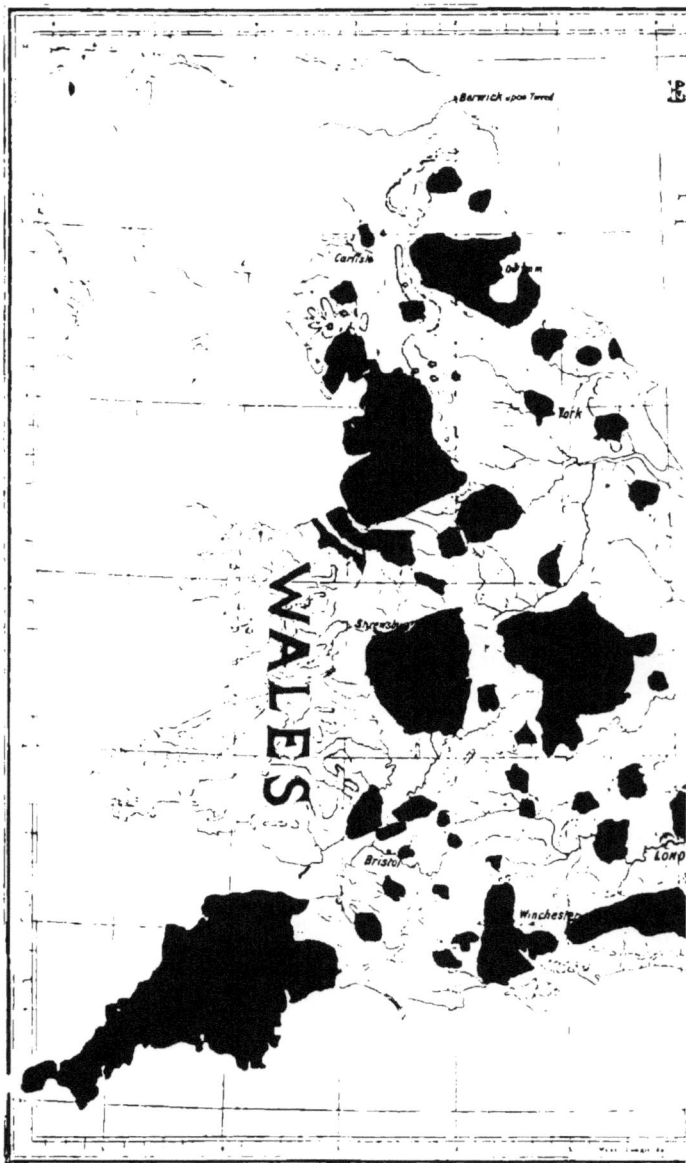

Forest, there were in all sixty-nine,[1] but the actual woodland area only comprised to a small extent the quantity of lands subject to the Forest as contrasted with those subject to the Common Law. From the best information that can be obtained it would appear that considerably more than one-third of the whole of England was before the signing of Magna Carta subject to the Forest law, and under the jurisdiction of the Chief Justice of the Forest. There was hardly a county in England where some forest or chase did not exist, and apart from various woods or forests whole counties were in many instances subject to the Forest Laws. Mr. Pearson,[2] who has very carefully inquired into the subject, has given a list of counties, forests and chases, subject to the Forest law when forest rights were extended to their utmost limit, vouching his accuracy in each instance by referring to entries in original and in many cases contemporaneous documents, and I have availed myself of much of the information which he has collected in the map that I have prepared. From this it appears that the entire counties of Cornwall, Devon, Essex, Rutland, Leicester, Northampton, Huntingdon and Lancaster, were then subject to Forest law. A huge area of forest land swept across the Midlands from the Wash on the east to Wales on the west. A vast tract of forest land stretched from Stafford to Worcester, and from the Wrekin to the Trent, including woods in the counties of Stafford, Worcester

---

[1] Manwood, fol. 70.

[2] *Historical Maps of England during the first Thirteen Centuries*; London, 1869.

and Salop. A dense forest with occasional clearings stretched from the Tyne to the Tees. The county of York, which suffered much from the Conqueror's devastation, is known to have contained numerous forests, and the Record Society of the North Riding are of opinion that at least the whole of the eastern division of the Riding was formerly under the Forest law.[1] Many of the Yorkshire forests are now untraceable, but similar inquiries to those lately undertaken into the history and customs of the Forest of Pickering may in time bring to light many forgotten features of the county. The New Forest inclosed a great part of the county of Hants, and the wood of Andred afforested long districts in the north of Sussex, in Surrey, and in Kent. The forests of Epping and Hainault bordered on London, and afforested the whole of Essex and a portion of Middlesex. This then was the vast territory subject to the exceptional treatment of the Forest law ; a law which gave rise to armed resistance, which was a stimulating element in the struggle that brought about the great charter of our liberties, and which was from time to time, as the Crown or the people had the upper hand, enforced or minimised by charters and confirmations, by ordinances and assises.

Before proceeding further it will be well to consider what was the nature and legal definition of a FOREST and its dependencies, what were the beasts and birds which came within the protection of its laws and what were the offences *contra pacem foresti*, against the peace

----

[1] *North Riding Record Society*, vol. i., N.S. (1894).

of the forest and the quietude of the beasts that roamed therein. "And seeing," says Lord Coke, with a quaint touch of humour, "that we are to treat of matters of game and hunting, let us (to the end that we may proceed the more cheerfully) recreate ourselves with the excellent description of Dido's doe of the forest with a deadly arrow sticken in her." To which the old editor appends a note, "like to an evil conscience in the false and furious officer of the Forest," adding, as if in fear of the Star Chamber, "if any such there be." [1] A forest, in the old English a *buck-holt* or deer park, now said to be derived from *foris*, out of doors, is described by an Elizabethan authority, as "a safe abiding place for wild beasts who belong to the woods, not however to all woods, but to those which are suitable for such purpose ; and thus in the word forest the letter *e* is changed into the letter *o*, as if one said *foresta*, or *ferarum statio*. And a forest is not to be found in every county, but only in woody places where are great covers and fruitful pastures." [2] The antiquity and locality of these old

---

[1] *4th Inst.*, p. 288. The passage is thus rendered by Dryden, *Æneid*, Bk. IV. :—

> "So, when the watchful shepherd from the blind,
> Wounds with a random shaft the careless hind,
> Distracted with her pain, she flies the woods,
> Bounds o'er the lawn, and seeks the silent floods
> With fruitless care ; for still the fatal dart
> Sticks in her side, and rankles in her heart."

[2] *L'authoritie et jurisdiction des Courts de la majestie de la Roygne, per R. Crompton, del milieu Temple, Esquire, Apprentice del Ley ;* London, 1594. Black letter, fol. 146. The learned author quotes this passage, which I have translated, from Treherne.

forests are now beyond recall. It was said of our Courts
of Justice in the time of Edward IV., that they were all
so old that no one could tell which was the oldest, and
similarly of the forests Lord Coke says,[1] " the forests in
England (being in number sixty-nine), except the New
Forest in Hampshire, erected by William the Conqueror,
as a Conqueror, and Hampton Court Forest by Henry
VIII., by authority of Parliament, are so antient as no
record or history doth make any mention of their erec-
tions or beginnings." And, indeed, according to the
oldest description of our island it appears to have been
originally one huge forest containing a considerable area
of cultivated land, which increased in size and fertility
generation by generation, until in the present day the
face of nature is entirely changed, and we dwell in a
luxuriant pasture, dotted only here and there with the
remains of a primæval forest. A forest accordingly was
the personal and peculiar privilege of the King,[2] to
whom alone pertained the right of appointing a Justice
Seat or a Chief Justice, the existence of which was the
insignia of a royal domain. Being his in such ample
possession, he could grant to any person the whole or
any portion of his forest, either absolutely or with such
restrictions and limitations as he might think fit.

A forest, however, in the hands of a subject became a
CHASE which, except by special order of the King, was
subject to the jurisdiction of the Common Law [3] and its
judges, and was not under the Forest Law. It had no

---

[1] 4th Inst., p. 318.   [2] Manwood, fol. 72.   [3] Coke, 4th Inst., p. 314.

Court of its own, and matters affecting the chase and its owner's rights were disposed of in the Court of the Hundred or of the County and not by the judges of the Forest. No one therefore was the owner of a forest but the King, who provided for its administration and appointed its officers.

A PARK, unlike a chase which was always open, was an enclosed space for game or beasts, and might be held either by a grant from the King, or by prescription, which presumed the existence of a grant issued at some long antecedent period, but then lost or mislaid. It was, however, held subject to this condition, that if the wall or paling by which it was surrounded were broken down so that the beasts could pass through, the park, if in a forest, was forfeited to the Crown and could only be resumed by a new grant from the King after such payment as could be obtained from the owner of the land.[1]

A WARREN which might, like a park, be constituted either by a grant from the King or by prescription, was land devoted to hold pheasants, partridges, rabbits and hares, but no wild beasts or vermin. This was also subject to the Common Law, having no court of its own.

The right of showing a title by prescription, or by ownership beyond the memory of man, was always recognised from the earliest date, but subject to this no one could have a park, a chase, or a warren, *even on his own freehold land* except by grant of the King. For the privilege of making chases, parks and warrens

---

[1] Crompton, fols. 150–157.

pertained solely to the King, and any infraction of this privilege was followed by the forfeiture of the land so afforested or parked, together with grievous pains and penalties.

The BEASTS OF THE FOREST were divided into two classes, those fit and those unfit for human food, the former of which were called by the generic name of VENISON, or venatio. These included the hart and the hind and their progeny, hares, male and female, rabbits, *sanglier*, viz. wild boars and their progeny, and wild bulls. Of the latter class (not being venison) were wolves, male and female, foxes, martens, wild cats, squirrels, and wild bears. Fortescue, however, writing in the fifteenth century, says there were no wolves, or bears, or lions in England at that time, so that the sheep could lie out at night in their folds without shepherds.[1] Crompton,[2] writing in the sixteenth century, says there were no wild bears in the time of Edward III., and Coke does not mention them at all. Wild elks are also mentioned in a statute of Henry VIII.[3] though not by Coke. Wild goats, though beasts of the chase, are said by Coke not to be beasts of the forest[4]; nor otters,[5] which being amphibious were not easily classified. Crompton however declares that wild goats were beasts of the forest, and gives an instance where a man was indicted under the Forest law for a wild goat, and the indictment was held good.[6]

---

[1] *Fortescue de Laudibus, etc.*, ch. 29.   [2] Fol. 171.
[3] 33 Henry VIII.   [4] *4th Inst.*, p. 317.   [5] *Ibid.*, p. 316.
[6] Fols. 157, 178, 198. The term used is *capreolus*, which is said sometimes to be a roebuck, and sometimes to be a wild goat.

Of BIRDS, the hawk with its progeny seems to have been the only privileged bird, and even that was not privileged at Common Law, but was made a bird of the forest and subject to its laws by operation of the statute.[1] A protection was also granted to herons by reason I suppose of their providing sport for the hawks.

The soil of the forest and its produce was known as VERT (green), and was of three sorts: (1) *Hautboys*, or trees, such as oaks, beeches, etc., which served for shelter and browse for the beasts, and trees which provided food for man and beast, such as apples, pears, nuts, and the like ; (2) *Arborescentes*, or shrubs, which provided food and shelter, such as blackthorn, hawthorn, etc. ; and (3) *herbæ*, herbage, such as gorse, heather, and the like, used for shelter for the smaller game.

Round each of the King's forests was a belt of land of varying width, called the *purlieu*. It was not the land of the King but was that of his tenants or of other landowners. Upon this land the guardians of the forest had a right at all times to enter to drive back into the forest any game that might have escaped therefrom. In this land, according to the Common Law as laid down by Coke,[2] every owner had the right to hunt at his pleasure, a right also declared in various charters, but one which the Norman kings disregarded, holding that such external hunting disturbed the peaceful occupation of the forest by the big game located therein. In addition to the purlieu appurtenant to the forests existing at the Con-

---

[1] Crompton, fol. 171.   [2] *4th Inst.*, p. 303.

quest, when lands afforested by Henry II., by Richard I., or by John, were disafforested by Henry III., those lands did not revest absolutely in their former owners, but became the purlieu of the forest of which they had recently formed part, and the *purlieu man*, as he is called in the old reports, was subject to all the various exactions and restrictions attaching to an original purlieu.[1]

In order that the epithets bestowed upon the courts and the customs of the forest may not seem to have been mere words of abuse or disloyalty, it will be right to mention some, though by no means all, of the interdictions and impositions put upon the country by the kings and their lessees. These were not all imposed simultaneously, having been added to from time to time, but they represent in substance the condition of the Forest Laws from Richard I. to Henry VII. And although, as already explained, no one could have a forest and a judge of the forest, except the King and his direct donee, yet other lords of chases, of parks, and of warrens, were not slow to adopt the practice of the Crown, charging fees and fines and exacting services, alleging such quasi-forest rights to be reasonable customs at Common Law, acquired by prescription and by constant use beyond the memory of man.

No man was entitled to hunt in the forest without the King's licence, which was rarely granted, and when granted was subject to heavy payment.

A special warrant, to be obtained only from the king or his officers, was required for a man to pasture his goats,

---

[1] Coke, 4th *Inst.*, p. 303. Crompton, fol. 153.

his sheep, or his swine, within the limits of the forest, or to cut heath, whins, or turf.[1]

No brewer or baker could brew or bake[2] within the forest, and if any white tanner or bleacher were found in the forest he was removed and fined, " because they are the common dressers of the skins of stolen deer." [3]

When a forest was bounded on any side by a river, no one could fish that river without warrant.[4]

No man could build a house within the limits of a forest, though on his own freehold, nor even a hedge four feet high.[5]

No man, woman, or child, without warrant from the King or his officers, could pick nuts in a forest, nor take honey from a hollow tree without being liable to fine and imprisonment.[6]

If a man cut wood in a forest, and carried it away in a cart, the cart and horses were forfeited, and the man was fined ; or if he carried boughs on a horse, the horse was forfeited, and the man was fined.[7]

If a man had a horse pasturing in the forest, either with licence or without, and he came by night to take out his horse, he was liable to be imprisoned, and then to be bound over in sureties to be of good behaviour for the future, as it was declared to be against the laws of the forest that any one should *under any circumstances* enter a forest by night and thereby disturb the peace of the beasts.[8]

---

[1] Crompton, fol. 196. [2] *Ibid.*, fol. 195. [3] *Ibid.*, fol. 190.
[4] *Ibid.*, fol. 199. [5] *Ibid.*, fol. 189. [6] *Ibid.*, fol. 183.
[7] *Ibid.*, fol. 190. [8] *Ibid.*, fol. 189.

L

A like punishment was due to any man against whom it could be said that he entered a forest with intent to chase the game, although in fact he did nothing. And a man might be indicted and punished as a common malefactor of venison, though he was not guilty of any overt act.[1]

If a hue and cry after malefactors were raised by the foresters or other officers of the forest, and it were not pursued and followed with effect, the whole township was fined.[2]

The lord of a forest could enter any man's woods within the purlieu of the forest and cut down his brushwood for the deer in winter.[3] He had also this prerogative, that at such times as he should be disposed to hunt within the forest, every man must be ready to hold a greyhound for the taking of wild beasts, in such places as might be appointed, or in default to be fined.[4]

An habitual method of extortion by the officers of the forest was to allege that certain duties or services had to be performed, according to the custom of the forest, by certain persons, and then to take money for the release of these services. The moneys so paid were called *quittances*, and they were exacted in release of the following among other alleged obligations of the denizens of the forest:—

Escapes.[5] When cattle had accidentally wandered into the forest and were alleged by the officers to have become

---

[1] Crompton, fol. 191.　　[2] *Ibid.*, fol. 190.　　[3] *Ibid.*, fol. 193.
[4] *Ibid.*, fol. 197.　　　　[5] *Ibid.*, fol. 197.

forfeited by reason of their trespass, for the owners to be free of such forfeiture.

Footegeld.[1] When a freeholder had dogs for his own protection, not lawed as required in the case of mastiffs.

Tristris.[2] To be free of holding greyhounds when the lord was hunting.

Allgelds.[3] To be free of the alleged duties of gathering sheaves of corn, collecting lambs, shearing sheep, and carrying wood for the use of the foresters and at their order. This was an illegal exaction for which certain foresters of Yorkshire were convicted and fined.

Woodgeld.[4] To be free of the alleged duty of gathering wood for the use of the officers of the forest.

Horngeld.[5] To be free of gathering up the horns of beasts.

Buckstall.[6] To be free of making a corall for the beasts and rounding them up.

Chimagium.[7] To be free of paying toll for passing through the forest.

Scoto.[8] To be free of providing meat and drink for the officers of the forest when required by them to do so. This was also declared an illegal exaction by 25 Edward III. c. 7, but it appears nevertheless to have been continued by the foresters like the claim for gathering corn and wool. Certain forests also had customs of their own, and among others the forest of Halifax had what was

[1] Crompton, fol. 194.
[2] Coke, 4th Inst., p. 305.
[3] Crompton, fol. 194.
[4] Coke, 4th Inst., p. 305.
[5] *Ibid.*, p. 305.
[6] *Ibid.*, p. 306.
[7] *Ibid.*, p. 306.
[8] *Ibid.*, p. 306.

termed the gibbet right, viz. the power to hang any thief found in the forest, a right which found its declaration in the seal of the forest so late as the year 1662.[1]

To enforce the King's prerogative, and to secure the due payment of all rents and dues, judges of the forest were appointed by the Normans, superseding the former judges and keepers, with power to hold courts, to try offenders against the laws of the forest, to settle the limits of the forest and the purlieu, and to hear and determine claims made by those of the King's subjects who alleged that their rights had been invaded. Two of these officers, one for lands North, and one for lands South of the Trent, were accordingly nominated. Each was called a CHIEF JUSTICE OF THE FOREST, and being a high officer of state, was, until the reign of Henry VIII., appointed by the King's writ.[2] Subordinate to the Chief Justice, and holding quasi-judicial courts, were the *Verderers* (viridarii), who were chief officers of the forest. Their duties were primarily in regard to the vert, but they also held Courts of Inquiry, made presentments to the Chief Justice, and issued attachments or committals to prison in default of bail in all cases of transgression in the forest, either by hunting or stealing game, or by taking of vert, or otherwise. Of these Verderers there were commonly four in each forest. They were elected like coroners, by the freeholders of the forest and the purlieu, on a writ issued by the King.[3]

---

[1] This seal, of which an example is attached to a grant now in the British Museum, is reproduced as an illustration.

[2] Coke, *4th Institute*, p. 290.   [3] *Crompton*, fol. 160. 4 Edward IV.

1

2

3

SEALS OF THE FOREST.

Face page 148.

1. *The Seal of Henry Ratcliff, Earl of Sussex, Chief Justice of all the Forests, Chaces, and Warrens of Queen Mary, "citra Trentram,"* circ., 1553. (Brit. Mus., xxxvi. 161.)

2. *The Seal of Sir Giles Dawbney, Knt., and Sir Reginald Bray, Knt., Justices in Eyre, "citra Trentham,"* 12 *Henry VII.* (1497). (Brit. Mus., add. ch. 22,399.)

3. *The Seal of Sir Thomas Lovell, Knt., Justice in Eyre, "citra Trentam,"* 4 *Henry VIII.* (1513). (Brit. Mus., add. ch. 8,404.)

4. *Seal of the Corporation of Halifax, W. R. Yorks, illustrating the " Gibbet Law " of the Forest of Hardwick, co-extensive with the parish of Halifax,* 1662. (Brit. Mus., xlix. 136.)

The *Agistators*, or agisters, who managed the agistment, or hiring out of portions of the forest for the feeding of cattle, were also usually four in number.[1]

Forestarii, the foresters or woodwards, were charged with watching the forest and attaching and presenting all who interfered with the King's beasts or his birds, or who trespassed on his vert. They were appointed by patent, and had no judicial or quasi-judicial position; but, owing to their duties as gamekeepers and informers, they were special objects of aversion by the English commonalty. Their number seems to have been unlimited either by custom or by ordinance. These Verderers and foresters held their offices under the Crown, and were paid, not by salary, but by fees, fines, and services, which they were authorized by custom, or otherwise, to levy on or exact from the woodland population. That they did levy fees and fines and exact services to an extortionate extent, and hold accused persons unreasonably to ransom, appears sufficiently from the declaration that when a Verderer or a Forester is found guilty of such an offence, either by the Swanimote or the King's Justices, he shall suffer fine and imprisonment, with full restitution to the party injured.[2]

The *Regarders* were appointed as surveyors over the other ministers of the forest. The office was created by Henry II., and was in the gift of the King. Not more than twelve of these could however be appointed for any forest. Their chief duty was to survey the forests, and to

---

[1] Coke, *4th Institute*, p. 293.   [2] Crompton, fol. 155.

take care that all encroachments, assarts and crimes of vert or venison were duly presented to the Chief Justice.[1]

The Verderers held every forty days a court, called a WOODMOTE, at which presentments were made, the Foresters made their charges, and the accused were either released or held to bail; if taken in the fact, by recognizance of sureties; if only charged on suspicion, by recognizance of their goods. This, however, was only a Court of Inquiry and Report, and when cases were thought to be serious they were sent forward.

The principal court of the Verderers was called the SWANIMOTE or Court of the Ministers of the Forest, from the Saxon word *swain*, a minister, and *mote*, or gemote, a Court. In it the Verderers were the judges, the court being summoned and presided over by the Steward of the Forest. At this court, which had a qualified judicial power, viz. to convict and attach offenders, and to send them for trial before the Chief Justice, but not to punish them, the foresters made their presentments and charges, and brought to trial offenders whom they had attached. The freeholders also, and others within the limits of the forest, were bound by law to attend these courts, and to serve on inquests and juries when their attendance was required. The Verderers sat in Swanimote, according to custom and ordinance, thrice in every year, the

---

[1] Various forms of enquiry of and direction to the Regarders, and form of questions to be put to the Swanimote of the Forest of Sherwood, in the reigns of Edward III. and of Henry VIII., are set out in Crompton, fols. 171, 181, 201.

first time fifteen days before Michaelmas, the second about the feast of St. Martin, and the third before the feast of St. John the Baptist. And their court was appurtenant to a Forest and to no other place; in the same way, as we shall hereafter see, that a Clerk's Court was appurtenant to a market, and a Court of Pypowder to a fair. It appears, however, that although they had no power of inflicting punishments, yet when a verdict as to a trespass in vert or venison was found by the Verderers and returned to the Chief Justice, the latter proceeded at once to pass sentence on the convict, and would not allow the propriety of the Verderer's verdict to be in any way impeached.[1]

A court was also held once in every three years for the SURVEY OF DOGS. By Norman custom, any man who was entitled to live in a forest, was also permitted for his protection to keep mastiffs; but to prevent the mastiff following his natural inclination and hunting the big game, he was, under the rule of the Conqueror and his sons, expeditated, *i.e.* the claws and the ball of each forefoot were cut out, so that the mutilated beast could serve at the best but as a poor protection against the beasts and the thieves of the forest.[2] And once in every three years the Regarders of the Forest examined all dogs, and reported those whose feet were not duly lawed. This cruelty to dumb and faithful beasts was to some

---

[1] Coke, *4th Institute*, p. 290.

[2] Lord Coke says the word mastiff is derived from the words *maes* and *teef*, because he was a dog whose presence amazed the thief. *4th Institute*, p. 308.

extent mitigated by the Statute of 9 Henry III. (Carta de Foresta), by which it was declared [1] that the expedition or lawing of dogs should for the future consist only of cutting the claws to the flesh of the forepaw and not interfering with the ball of the foot.

Causes being thus prepared, they went before the COURT OF THE CHIEF JUSTICE who, however, sat only once in three years. Before his arrival it was the duty of the guardian to perambulate the forest and to ascertain who had made encroachments in the forest called *purprestures*, and who had grubbed and brought into cultivation any land in or adjoining the forest, called *assarts*, without the King's licence. These offenders were summoned and presented before the Chief Justice, who also decided, not according to Common but according to Forest law, what punishments were to be inflicted and what penalties paid. He also settled, by the same law, any claims to franchises, parks, warrens and vineyards in the forest, as also all claims of the Hundred, all claims to the goods of felons found in the forest, and any other question that might arise between the King and his subjects, or between any private persons within the limits of the forest. He also passed sentence on transgressors who had been tried and convicted by the Verderers, and in other respects performed all the duties of a Justice in Eyre. [2] Forty days' notice was given of the holding of the Chief Justice's Court and the Sheriff or Vicomte of the county duly summoned [3] all archbishops, bishops,

---

[1] Sec. 6.   [2] Coke, *4th Institute*, p. 290.
[3] Crompton, fol. 149. A form of summons is set out.

abbots, barons, and freemen, who had holdings within
the limits of the forest, together with four men and
a foreman (*prepositus*), from every village within the
bounds, and twelve good and lawful men of every
borough within the said bounds, who were accustomed
to be summoned, to attend the court and try the pleas
of the forest. Notice was also given to all persons
attached for vert or venison, or who claimed any fran-
chise in the forest, to attend in person and make their
defences or claims at a certain time and place; and at
such time and place, once in every three years, all
persons having claims to franchises in the forest were
compelled to appear in person or by attorney, and make
their claims, or their rights would be declared forfeit, and
their lands, franchises, and rights would be seized into
the hands of the King.[1]

The jurisdiction of the Chief Justice of the Forest was
however, strictly limited to the forest, and to what were
called the pleas of the forest, viz., questions as to trespass,
hunting, encroachments and the like. If a felony or a
misdemeanour (called *transgressio*) were committed in the
forest, the Common Law judges had the trial of it, and it
accordingly went to the County Court or to the judges of
assize when they came their circuits. In the same way
if a Verderer were dismissed on a false charge and the
forest judge would not reinstate him, he had a right to
appeal to the Chancellor for a writ to enquire into his loss
of office, and to reinstate him if his removal were obtained

---

[1] Crompton, fol. 153.

by falsehood or by fraud.[1] At a later period the Chief
Justice of the Forest, if a difficult question of law arose
before him, could send it for the opinion of the judges of
the King's Bench.[2] The Common Law judges, however,
had no power to grant bail in forest cases,[3] as that was a
matter peculiarly within the province of the Chief Justice
and the officers of the forest, and the accused had therefore to get himself admitted to bail by the Verderers or by
the Swanimote, or to remain in prison till the Chief Justice
came on his triennial visit. Rents and fines thus enforced,
or voluntarily paid to the officers, were handed over to the
sheriff of the county in which the forest was situate, who
paid them into the royal chest each Michaelmas when he
carried in his balance and settled his accounts with the
Crown in the Exchequer.[4]

Courts thus constituted, with officers dependent, not
upon a salary but upon the income they could secure from
alleged transgressors, afforded many opportunities for
oppression and extortion, while the long periods that
lapsed between the sittings of the Chief Justice, during
which time many of the offenders of the forest were kept
in prison, or grievously afflicted in their estates by the
difficulty of finding sureties, made the position of the
denizens of a forest almost insupportable. And so matters
continued under the Conqueror and William Rufus, and
also under Henry I: for although that King gave a
Charter of Liberties to his subjects at his coronation, yet

---

[1] Crompton, fol. 196.   [2] *Ibid.*, fol. 160.   [3] *Ibid.*, fol. 156.
[4] Hall's *Antiquities of the Exchequer*, p. 141.

in regard to his forests his only declaration was, that by the common consent of his Barons he held them as his father held them.[1] His further general declaration that he would observe the laws of the Confessor, may perhaps have for a time quieted their apprehension in this respect. But like his father he loved the high game, and had a private menagerie in his park at Woodstock, comprising wild beasts from foreign parts, such as lions, leopards, lynxes, camels and porcupine.[2] And in order that he might feast his eyes on big game also, when in Normandy, he had a similar menagerie constructed at Caen, near the church where his father was buried.

Stephen hunted and held pleas of the forest at Brampton near Huntingdon, in the first year of his reign,[3] but afterwards spent his time in domestic brawls, and accordingly the first Statute of the forest after the Conquest is to be found A.D. 1184, issued by Henry II., called Assisa de Foresta.[4] This somewhat modified the severity of the law, but otherwise it provided that if any one transgressed and was convicted, he should suffer the full penalty that was inflicted in the time of Henry I. A clause,[5] illustrative of the period, and of the King's determination that all Englishmen whether eccleciastics or laymen should be equally subject to the law, provided that no cleric should transgress in the matter of the King's venison or hunt in

---

[1] Stubbs' *Charters*, p. 93.

[2] Lappenberg, *Anglo-Norman Kings*, p. 355. *Gesta Stephani*, p. 87. William of Malmesbury, p. 638.

[3] Madox, *History of the Exchequer*, vol. i. p. 13.

[4] Stubbs' *Charters*, p. 150.   [5] Cl. 9.

his forests, and all foresters were warned that if they found any clergy so transgressing they should not hesitate to lay hands on them, hold them, and attach them in prison, for which his ordinance would be a sufficient warrant. It was further declared, by sec. 12, that if any one were convicted of transgressing in the forest, sureties for good behaviour should be taken after the first and second offences; but after the third offence nothing short of the body of the offender would satisfy justice. By clause 13, every boy of the age of twelve years, within the forest, and every cleric holding by a lay tenure, was required to swear *pacem venationis* (the peace of the venison) viz., to obey the laws of the forest. By clause 14, the lawing of mastiffs was to take place whenever they were within the peace of the forest. By clause 15, no tanner or bleacher was to live in the forest; and by clause 16, any one was rendered liable to imprisonment for a year, to be followed by the giving of sureties for good conduct, who hunted by night either in the forest or in any other place where wild beasts were accustomed to roam. His Chief Justices of the forest were Alan de Nevil and Thomas Fitz-Bernard.[1]

Over how long a period life was taken and mutilation practised as a punishment for forest offences does not clearly appear. I am disposed, however, to believe that it ceased during or soon after the time of Henry II. In the early part of this reign there appear amongst the returns to the Exchequer, small sums, being the value of the goods

---

[1] Madox, vol. i. pp. 125, 135.

of persons who suffered by judgment of the water for forest offences.[1] But they do not appear to extend beyond this period, and although the declaration by statute, that no one should lose life or limb for such offences, was not actually published until A.D. 1217, yet the reign of Henry II. was one of mercy, as compared with that of his predecessors. And if it be urged that, had the taking of life and limb ceased about that time, there would have been no need for the express stipulation in the Carta de Foresta, that such punishment was not according to law, I would reply that the continued exaction and extortion of the officers of the forest would fully justify the action of the barons who might reasonably suspect that, unless for some such charter as that promised by John and granted by Henry III., a temporary suspension of their opposition might induce in tyrannical rulers or grasping servants a recurrence of the old and hateful proceedings.

The fines, however, during this period, were frequent and excessive. From a list of amercements paid into the Exchequer during the reign of king Henry II., collected by Madox from the pipe roll,[2] it appears that in the 22nd year of this sovereign, Henry de Brus and 70 others were fined in sums rising to £100 each, in regard of forest offences in Yorkshire; Henry de Nonart and 50 others were fined 30 marks for similar offences in Devonshire; Robert Carter and 30 others, 10 marks for the same in Shropshire; about 60 persons for Northamptonshire; 30 persons, in 50 marks, for Herefordshire;

---

[1] Madox. vol. ii. p. 131.   [2] *Ibid.*, vol. i. p. 541.

60 persons, in 50 marks, for Nottinghamshire; 40 persons in £50 and under, for Worcestershire; 40 persons, in 50 marks, for Wiltshire; 50 persons, in 50 marks, for Essex; 40 persons for Hampshire, and similarly for other counties. In Northumberland also, men were fined 22*s.* 4*d.* each, for not cutting the feet of their dogs.[1]

Richard I. and John, both of whom like their Norman relations, were great hunters, pressed the laws and gradually enlarged the borders of their forests. And thus it occurred that clauses for the amelioration of the laws and customs of the forests found their way into Magna Carta.[2] " All forests which were afforested in our time," it was declared, " shall be forthwith disafforested." " All bad customs of forests and warrens, and of foresters and warreners, sheriffs and their servants, shall be forthwith enquired into in each county by twelve sworn knights of the county, to be chosen by the good and lawful men of the county, who are to report within forty days." To effect this enquiry, an order was issued by the King on the same day to elect twelve knights[3] of the shire and to make the neccessary enquiry into " *pravis consuetudinibus,*" the wicked customs. But it seems easier to persuade a king to sign a charter against his will, than to induce him and his successors to carry it loyally into effect. No forest charter was ever granted

---

[1] Madox, vol. i. p. 559.

[2] Stubbs' *Charters*, p. 294.

[3] By the report of these knights, after their perambulation, the County of Lancaster was in great part disafforested (Pearson's *Historical Maps*).

by king John,[1] and although Henry III. issued the famous Carta de Foresta with a view of carrying out the promises of his father, yet, as Lord Coke observes, this very charter on which the lives and liberties of the woodland population depended, was confirmed, and re-enacted, and ordered to be put in execution, no less than thirty times between the death of John and that of Henry V.[2]

Carta de Foresta,[3] the Great Charter of the woodland population, nobles, barons, freemen, and slaves, loyally granted by Henry III. (A.D. 1217), in the third year of his reign, contained the following among other provisions. All forest lands made by Henry II. were to be viewed, and if he had made forests to any one's hurt, they were to be disafforested.[4] All forests made by King Richard and by King John were to be disafforested.[5] The lawing of dogs was to be by cutting their claws only.[6] The Court of Swanimote was only to be held thrice yearly,[7] a practice having apparently crept in of holding it oftener. No one was to lose life or limb for venison; but if he were caught and convicted of taking venison, he was to be heavily fined (grievously payned), if he had the money to pay his fine. If he had not the money, he was to lie in prison for a year and a day, and if by a year and a day he could find sureties, he should go out of prison; but if not, he should abjure

---

[1] Hugh de Neville was Chief Justice of the forests under King John. Dugdale, *Orig.*, fol. 9.

[2] *4th Inst.*, p. 303.

[3] *The Great Abbrydgement*, fol. 117. Stubbs' *Charters*, p. 347.

[4] Clause 1.   [5] Clause 3.   [6] Clause 5.   [7] Clause 8.

the realm of England.[1] Clause 11 provided that every
archbishop, bishop, earl, or baron, coming up by the
King's command, if he passed through a forest, might
take a beast or two, and the same in returning. But he
was to do so in sight of the Forester if he were present;
if he was absent, he was " to blow for him, lest it should
seem to be done by stealth." This right to hunt on
the way to and from attendance on the King was, at
a later date, extended to all lords of Parliament and
knights of the shire on their way to and from the meeting
of Parliament.[2]

Edward I., in 1297,[3] confirmed " the Charter, made by
the common consent of all the realm in the time of
Henry III., to be kept in every point without breach."
In the *Ordinatio Forestæ* (A.D. 1305)[4] he expressed his
sympathy with the sufferers under the Forest Laws, and
he also made some further inquiries as to purprestures,
or alleged encroachments.[5]

No reference is made in these later Charters to the
clause in the Assisa de Foresta relating to the clergy.
That all orders of the clergy were hunters, and that the
inferior orders probably produced many a Friar Tuck, is,
I think, established by the clauses I have extracted, and
by the reports of many old cases in which the clergy are
concerned. There seems always, however, to have been
some scruple of conscience with the reverend gentlemen,
by reason of the early canons which categorically forbade

---

[1] Clause 10.   [2] Crompton, fol. 168.   Coke, *4th Inst.*, 305.
[3] *Confirmatio Cartarum*, Nov., 1297.   Stubbs' *Charters*, p. 486.
[4] 33 Edward I., Stat. 5.   [5] *Britton*, by Kelham, p. 101.

it. Thus, by the *Liber Pœnitentialis* of Theodore,[1] a clericus who hunted, was ordered to do penance for a year ; a deacon, for two years ; a priest, for three years. By the *Liber Pœnitentialis* of Egbert,[2] a cleric who hunted was to abstain from meat for twelve months ; a deacon, for two years ; a priest, for three years ; a bishop, for seven years. By the canons of King Edgar [3] (cl. 64), it is said : " We enjoin that a priest be not a hunter, nor a hawker, nor a dicer, but apply to his books as becomes his order." Lord Coke, however, who, besides being a great lawyer, was also a considerable theologian, justifies the hunting of the clergy on what seems to us now to be a ground somewhat inconsistent with the canon. "Albeit," he says, "spiritual persons are prohibited by the Canon Law to hunt, yet, by the Common Law, of the land they may for their recreation, *to make them the fitter for the performance of their duty and office, use the recreation of hunting. . . .* And at this day, and time out of mind the king hath had, after the death of every archbishop or bishop, *mutam suam canum*, his kennel of hounds, or a composition for the same." [4] But, as he afterwards adds, if the Common Law gives a priest the right to hunt, no Canon Law can be heard against it.

Edward III. added to the forest penalties by making it a felony, with benefit of clergy, to steal in the forest any man's long-winged hawk, or to find and conceal one.[5] The former was a stealing at Common Law, but the

---

[1] C. xxxii. sec. 4. [2] *Ancient Laws and Institutes*, vol. ii. p. 215.
[3] *Ibid.*, vol. ii. p. 259. [4] *4th Inst.*, p. 308. [5] 57 Edward III.

latter was a new crime created by the statute, contrary to the clear and well-approved doctrine that there is no legal ownership in wild game, which becomes the property of the finder or the killer on his own ground.

Richard II., in a law of the Forest,[1] had a curious reference to *gentlemen's game*. He instituted a property qualification whereby no layman, not having land of the value of forty shillings per annum, nor any clerk not having £10 per annum revenue, should have or keep any greyhounds, etc., to destroy deer, etc., *or any other gentleman's game*, under a penalty of a year's imprisonment, followed by giving of sureties for good behaviour.

In 1376, during the reign of Henry IV., the commoners of Hertfordshire appealed against the evil customs of the officers of the Forest of Ewyastone, who confiscated their beasts that wandered into the forest. To this the king replied that the good old laws of the forest were to be observed, and the contrary to be forbidden by a writ under the Privy Seal. A truly royal answer, says Coke, and worthy of the Plantagenet.[2]

During the wars of the roses no forest legislation took place. The woods became the home of runaways and outlaws, and foresters and commoners did much as they liked till the restoration of peace under Henry VII., one of whose first acts after ascending the throne was to deal with these laws. By this time, however, the hunting of big game, which after all is typical rather of the

---

[1] 13 Richard II., c. 13.　　　[2] Coke, *4th Inst.*, p. 318.

unlettered savage than of the educated Christian, had given place to other pursuits. Archery had taken its place as a popular recreation, without disappearing altogether as a science of military warfare. Jousts, tournaments, and fighting at the barriers, demanding strength of limb, courage, and dash, were recreations of the gentry, while quarter-staff, wrestling, football, and bear-baiting, had taken their place as amusements of the people. Kings and " gentlemen " still hunted the deer ; but the big game, the bear, the wild bull, the wild boar, and the elk, except in special preserves, had disappeared, and the pressure of the forest laws was lifted from the people as the reason for their existence gradually died out. By the beginning of the seventeenth century, the " high game " of the Conqueror was a memory of the past, and in the course of that period M. de Beaumont, in his dispatches to Louis XIV., while speaking of the savagery of the English in regard of their civil wars and their cruel punishments, ascribes it to the absence of wild beasts from the country. In this, he suggests, they have the disadvantage of the inhabitants of other countries, who, by the pursuit of wild beasts, can give vent to their evil passions ; while the English, having exterminated all their wild beasts, can only indulge their savage instincts by pursuing and slaying one another.

Henry VII., however,[1] who could hardly be regarded as a sportsman, legislated against the killing of game by means of a stalking-horse, a most unsportsmanlike pro-

---

[1] 1 Henry VII., c. 7 ; 19 Henry VII., c. 11.

ceeding, which well deserved to be forbidden, and he empowered justices of the peace for the first time to hear and determine many matters connected with the forests and their game.

Henry VIII., as before stated, tried to create a forest at Hampton Court by authority of Parliament. Philip and Mary had a Forest Law, but more for the purpose of preventing the meeting of conspirators than to preserve sport,[1] and references to justices of the peace trying forest cases occur again. Elizabeth [2] and James [3] had statutes as to foresting, and again justices of the peace are given jurisdiction. These two monarchs also themselves made ravages on the royal forests: Elizabeth, to find timber for her ships, and James, to provide timber for sale. The latter also increased the property qualification for would-be hunters.[4] But the forest laws had then almost ceased to operate, for Manwood, in the preface to his work on the forests, gives as his chief reason for embarking on the investigation, that so few know the laws of the forests, and yet so many fall into danger thereof, "as they are grown clean out of knowledge in most places in England."

Sir Edward Coke, writing his *Institutes* in the reign of Charles I., and discoursing learnedly and sportingly on the pursuit of game, speaks of the Chief Justice of the Forest as a great official, whose authority and dignity were then known and recognised. But the duties of this

---

[1] Crompton, fol. 158.   [3] 1 Jac. I., c. 27.
[2] 23 Elizabeth, c. 10.   [4] 3 Jac. I., c. 13.

great official had almost become nominal until King Charles I., in one of his inspirations of madness, revived this most odious of all jurisdictions, and sent out his Chief Justices of the Forest to make raids on the forests and the freeholders. Proceedings for incroachment by building on and cultivating what was alleged to be forest land in the forests of Dean and Waltham, were instituted and tried at the Justice Seat before the Chief Justice of the Forest. Verdicts were found for the Crown and fines of £12,000, £35,000, and £98,000, which it was found impossible to collect, were inflicted, farms and ironworks long in use were confiscated to the king,[1] and a territory of many thousands of acres was declared to be beyond the protection of the Common Law, and subject only to that of the Forest.

This, however, was followed by an Act of 1640,[2] by which it was declared that all forests should be held to be disafforested where no Justice Seat, Swanimote, or Court of Attachment had been holden for sixty years next before the first year of King Charles' reign. And here we have the last of the Chief Justice as an effective minister; for Dugdale, writing in 1666, and giving an account of the Law Courts and legal institutions of the country, makes no mention of any Court of the Justices of the Forest as then in existence.

By Charles II.[3] the property qualification for pursuit of game was still further extended, and William and

---

[1] Gardiner, *Personal Government*, vol. ii. pp. 73, 172, 182.
[2] 16 Car. I., c. 16.   [3] 22, 23 Car. II., c. 25.

Mary[1] introduced the pillory, with imprisonment, for offenders against their Game Laws. Justices of the Peace were empowered to try all such offences; and by the time of Queen Anne, the Chief Justice of the Forest and his Courts had ceased to exist, or even to be had in remembrance, except for the purpose of supplying sinecure offices, with respectable stipends, in the gift of the Crown.[2] In 1817, an Act of Parliament,[3] reciting that the duties of the Chief Justices of the Forests north and south of the Trent, had in a great measure ceased through the disafforesting of many of the great forests and the inclosure of others, and that, nevertheless, these officers were in receipt of considerable emoluments, abolished the offices of Chief Justice of the Forest after the determination of the then existing interests, and transferred their jurisdiction to the Chief Commissioner of H.M. Woods and Forests without any additional stipend.

---

[1] 3, 4 W. & M., c. 10.

[2] In 1811 the Chief Justice of the Forest was in receipt of a salary of £3,466 13s. 4d. per annum.—P. Lewis, *Historical Enquiries*, etc., p. 20.

[3] 57 Geo. III., c. 61.

CHAPTER V.

(A.D. 1485-1660.)

I.

Henry VII.—The Star Chamber—The Rack—The Privy Council
—The Exchequer Chamber—Collar of S S.—Its supposed
Origin—Bestowed on the Offices of Chief Justice and Chief
Baron—Suits in Forma Pauperis—Cardinal Wolsey as Chan-
cellor—The Chancellor's Mace and Bag—Court of Wards
and Liveries—Court of Requests—High Commission Court—
Westminster Hall under Edward VI.—The Courts in the
time of Queen Mary—Sir Nicholas Throckmorton and the
Jury—Revival of Business under Queen Elizabeth—Bacon,
the first Queen's Counsel—Barons promoted to Equality with
Judges of King's Bench and Common Pleas—Cursitor Barons.

HENRY VII. after the battle of Bosworth Field found
himself in the position of a sovereign with a kingdom
much divided in affection between the conflicting claims
of the Yorkist and the Lancastrian families, but on the
whole, sincerely desirous of tranquillity, and willing to
accept the union of the two roses, in Henry of Lancaster
and Elizabeth of York, as a sufficient guarantee of a
durable peace. One natural result of the intestine conflicts which had distracted the country for many years, was
that, during such period, certain families became for the
moment great and powerful, surrounding themselves with
partizans and retainers whom they kept in their pay and

could summon at their need. The general spirit of lawlessness which was the product of the times led persons,
though possessed of some means and position, to attach
themselves for support and protection to one or other of
the great houses; so that there was hardly a man under
the rank of a noble who did not wear the livery or token
of some titled and powerful clan. The great nobles thus
assumed the character almost of independent rulers, and
when two or three combined against the Crown, it was
with much difficulty that they were reduced into subjection. Attempts had been made in previous years to
mitigate the danger, by reducing the number of retainers
permitted to each nobleman, and by forbidding the gift
of liveries. These usually took the form of parti-coloured
garments with which the histories and the costumes of
the middle ages have made us sufficiently familiar. A
continuance of such a condition of society was obviously
inconsistent with the preservation of public peace and
private security, and accordingly the King, after the immediate flush of his victory, obtained from Parliament an
Act dealing with these evils. His success in this respect
was owing in a great measure to his own power, to the
temporary exhaustion of the rival factions, and to the
general desire of all parties for the passing of any such
laws as would ensure to the country for the present, at all
events, a freedom from intestine commotions. In the
absence of those favourable conditions it is not probable
that such extended powers would have been conferred
upon him.

The theory of the King's personal presence and partici-

pation in the administration of justice is recognised in
every scheme of monarchical government. And thus,
although the Curia Regis, or Court of the King's Justice
Hall, came to an end in the reign of Henry III., and its
duties were thereafter discharged by various courts and
judges, yet the spirit and the practice of the regal
participation in the ordering of justice still subsisted.
The King no longer sat as supreme Justiciar in either of
the Common Law Courts or even in the Court of Chancery, yet his Royal prerogative of personally doing justice
was still exercised in the *Curia Regis in Camera*, or
Court of the King in private Council ; a court, afterwards
unfavourably known as the STAR CHAMBER, or *Camera
Stellata*, from the fact that the roof of the chamber in
which the King's Council sat at Westminster was orna-
mented with golden stars. This Court, the origin of
which is somewhat obscure, was formerly composed of the
King, when he chose to sit, which he probably did frequently in the early days, the Lords of the King's Privy
Council, the Chancellor, the Treasurer, and the Chief
Justices. Its earliest records now extant date from the time
of Edward III. ; it was then called *Camera Stellata*,[1] was
held by prescriptive right, and as Camden says, *vetustate
antiquissima, dignitate honoratissima*, in age most antient, in dignity most honourable. During the early period
it sat but seldom, three reasons for which are given
by Coke.[2] First, that cases of sufficient magnitude to
warrant its intervention rarely occurred ; secondly, that

---

[1] *Close Roll*, 29 Edw. III.   [2] *Inst.*, vol. iv. p. 61.

it dealt with no cases that other courts could sufficiently punish; and thirdly, that it was not expedient unduly to withdraw the Privy Councillors and the Chief Justices from their daily avocations.

Of the cases civil and criminal recorded, some by Coke and some by Crompton,[1] those before the accession of Henry VII. answer to the description given to them in the *Institutes*, and appear to have been matters which the Courts of Chancery and of Common Law could not very satisfactorily have dealt with. It exercised, like all other courts, the power of fine and imprisonment, but did not touch either life or limb. To a Court thus established, exercising its functions with the moderation and reserve which distinguished its proceedings till the end of the civil wars, no great objection could be taken. But upon this jurisdiction, which still survives in the prerogative of mercy inseparable from the Crown, a court was constituted, or rather, I should say, was reconstituted by Henry VII., of which the results were disastrous, not only to the country, but also to the Crown.

It is not, I think, to be imputed to the King, that in re-creating this Court of Star Chamber, or in converting an antient common law into a statutory tribunal, he necessarily contemplated any interference with the action of the Common Law Courts, or any attack upon the liberties of his subjects. I am disposed to think that he resorted to the Court of Star Chamber as being the only existing

---

[1] Fol. 29, *De Court de Starre Chamber and matters avant le Counsell le Roy.*

court sufficiently honourable, and at the same time sufficiently powerful, to deal with the great and masterful interests which would thus become subject to its orders. Its institution is dealt with in terms of characteristic difference by the two great lawyers of the Elizabethan era. Sir Edward Coke[1] speaks of it as a high and honourable court "which ought to be kept within the proper limits." Lord Bacon[2] describes it as "one of the sagest and noblest institutions of the kingdom," and says that the Act[3] which confirmed its authority was principally aimed at the suppression of force and the two chief supports of force, combination of multitudes and maintenance or headship of great persons.

The Court, thus constituted for the first time by Statute, provided that the Chancellor, to whom was afterwards added the Master of the Rolls (who attended frequently in the reigns of Elizabeth and James I.), the Treasurer, the Keeper of the Privy Seal, or any two of them, with a Bishop, and a Lord of the Privy Council, and the two Chief Justices, or two Common Law Judges in their absence, should hear complaints of unlawful maintenance, giving of liveries, retainers, riots and unlawful assemblies, and complaints against sheriffs, with power to call the accused parties before them and to examine them, and, if found guilty, to punish them according to due form of law. The act was, however, according to Sir Edward Coke, only declaratory of the procedure of the antient court, in

---

[1] *Inst.*, vol. iv. p. 60. [2] *Spedding*, vol. vi. p. 85.
[3] 3 Hen. VII., c. 1.

which the information, now ordered to be laid before the
Chancellor, was formerly directed to be laid before the
king himself. In one respect, however, he points out that
it was introductory of a new law, inasmuch as it empowered the court to examine the defendant upon oath, on
interrogatories or otherwise, according to discretion, and
thus opened up a procedure entirely unknown before that
period.[1] Its jurisdiction, though not extending to sentences of death or loss of limb, did, however, in addition
to fine and imprisonment, extend to the infliction of pillory, whipping, and in cases of great enormity, such as
slander of Queen Elizabeth,[2] cutting off the ears.

The Chancellor, now grown great in his office, was the
president of the court, which was held at Westminster,
as nearly as can be ascertained on the site now occupied
by the Speaker's house, in a large room on the river side
of the buildings. Its days of sitting were every Wednes-
day and Friday in term, unless either was the first or
last day of term; but it sat after term to finish cases
already begun. It appears to have commenced business
at eleven o'clock, as we hear from Cavendish,[3] that
Wolsey, when Chancellor, sat in the Court of Chancery
till eleven, when the court rose, and that he then left to
preside in the Star Chamber.

The jurisdiction of examining defendants, thus newly
conferred upon the court, though probably not inserted
by Parliament with any view of increasing the powers
then vested in the Crown, was held not only to authorize

---

[1] *Inst.*, vol. iv. p. 62.   [2] 23 Eliz., cap. 3.
[3] *Life of Wolsey*; Foss' *Judges*, vol. v. p. 261.

the examination of such persons by *vivâ voce* questions or by written interrogatories, but also to enforce answers where the parties were reluctant, or to obtain further and better answers when those already given were not satisfactory to King and Council. For this purpose it was held that recourse might be had to the system of examinations practised abroad, and thus the rack was administered in England with at least a semblance of legality. I am not able to say who was the first unhappy person to suffer under this system of violence and oppression; but the last, as far as is known, was Peacham, to whom the rack was administered in 1614, under the orders of the Star Chamber, in the presence of Lord Bacon, when Attorney-General [1]

Nor was it by this practice alone that the Court of Star Chamber became hateful to the people, for it had an element of procedure which should be foreign to all courts, and which stamped it as a pronounced respecter of persons. For although it assumed the right to put defendants to the rack, it held itself incompetent to administer torture to any person of the rank of nobility.[2] The high-handed transactions of this court, with its excessive fines and immoderate imprisonments, are, however, matters of general history, and it was abolished by the Long Parliament in 1642.[3]

The original jurisdiction of the PRIVY COUNCIL to

---

[1] *State Trials*, vol. ii. p. 872. Peacock's case (1619–20) was later; but it is doubtful if he was ever submitted to the rack. Spedding's *Bacon*, vol. xiv. p. 78.

[2] *State Trials*, vol. ii. p. 773.   [3] Stat. 15, Car. I., c. 10.

summon parties before them and take their depositions before either sending them for trial before the Common Law Judges, or remitting them for further examination before a justice of the peace, was not dealt with by the Long Parliament. It was resorted to on numerous occasions by the Commonwealth, and exists even at the present day, when it is beyond doubt that the Secretary of State may arrest a supposed criminal, and bring him before the Privy Council for examination, without any intervention of a justice of the peace. This course was actually pursued in the case of Oxford, who attempted the life of Her Majesty in 1840.[1]

The early difficulties of King Henry's reign were not confined to the treatment of his subjects; but as the king had himself been outlawed by Richard III., and as many of his staunchest supporters were in the same condition, though they were then sitting in his first parliament, he was much troubled as to the possible legal position of himself and his friends, and the constitutional method of avoiding future misfortunes. He accordingly referred the whole matter to the Common Law judges, who, under the presidency of Sir William Hussey, Chief Justice of the King's Bench, met in the EXCHEQUER CHAMBER,[2] and delivered their judgment, that while in the case of a king, the succession to the throne purges all antecedent disabilities; yet that, in the case of a subject, an Act of Parliament is required to reverse an attainder. This

---

[1] Reg. *v.* Oxford, 9 Car. and P. 525.
[2] Bacon's *Life of Henry VII.* Spedding, vol. vi. p. 37.

opinion has always been recognised as sound in law, and decisive of the points then raised for their determination.

This Court had then become known and recognised as the Council-chamber of the judges, where they met together when they were consulted by the King, when in the case of an equality of votes in their particular court the judges of both benches came together and gave their opinions, or when they set aside the judgments of inferior courts,[1] including those of the Court of Exchequer, in which event, however, the Treasurer and the Chancellor sat with the other judges.[2] From this time forward, therefore, the Exchequer Chamber, which was strengthened by the addition of the barons of the Exchequer, when the latter under Queen Elizabeth became Common Law judges, continued till the year 1875 to be the Court of Appeal from the Common Law Courts, and for the hearing of writs of error.

At or about this time the chiefs of the King's Bench, the Common Pleas, and the Exchequer were decorated by the Sovereign with the Collar of SS., which has ever since remained the insignia of their high office. There is a well-recognised legal tradition to this effect, and like many other legal traditions, it will bear the test of examination. The origin and the history of this collar have given rise to much learned discussion.[3] The letter

---

[1] *Bacon*, Spedding, vol. vi. p. 37.   [2] Coke, *Inst.*, vol. iv. p. 62.

[3] See *Notes and Queries*, Series 1, vol. ii.; Series 4, vols. ii., ix., x.; Series 6, vols. ii., iii. Planché, *Dictionary of Costume*, p. 126. *Gentleman's Magazine*, vol. xvii. p. 478; vol. xviii. p. 853, 595. *Retrospective Review*, vol. i. p. 302 ; vol. ii. pp. 156, 504. Foss' *Judges*, vol. vii. p. 17. Dugdale, *Orig. Jud.*, fol. 102.

S on the chain is accounted for in various ways. It is suggested to represent *Souvenir*, as used by John of Gaunt; or *Soverayne*, as used by Henry IV.; or *Seneschallus*, the Steward of the Household; or *Sanctus, Sanctus, Sanctus*, of the Salisbury Liturgy. Some antiquaries, wishing to find a connection between the emblem on the collar and the course of justice, suggest that it should be attributed to S. Simplicius, a Roman advocate of great piety, who for his religious opinions was drowned in the Tiber. Whatever may be the accuracy of the former suggestions, and they are all supported by cogent reasons, the theory of the beatified barrister is beyond my acceptance. The collar itself was not one of personal dignity, like that of the Order of the Garter or of the Bath, given by the sovereign and worn by the knight till his death, but was a badge or insignia of livery attached to certain offices entitling the holders to wear the collar so long only as they retained the several offices to which the dignity was appurtenant. This custom, which required the Chief Justice if promoted to the office of Chancellor, to which the collar was not appurtenant, to resign its use, finds a familiar instance in the portraits of Sir Edward Littleton, which show him with the collar of SS when painted as Chief Justice, and without it in his portraits as Chancellor.

The badge or livery of SS appears to have originated with John of Gaunt, "time-honoured Lancaster," whose coat of arms in the window opposite his tomb in old St. Paul's was encircled by this collar.[1] It did not,

---

[1] A copy of this window, taken by C. Nicholas, Lancaster Herald,

1. *Tracing from a window in Old St. Paul's, opposite the tomb of John of Gaunt, showing the collar of SS.*

2. *A Sketch from the Monument of Gower, the poet, in S. Saviour's, Southwark, showing the collar of SS.*

3. *Engraving of Richard III., with the Yorkist collar of suns and roses.*

See page 176.

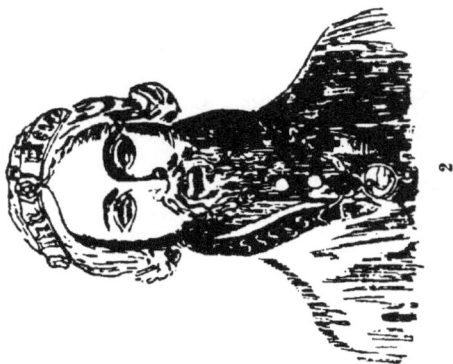
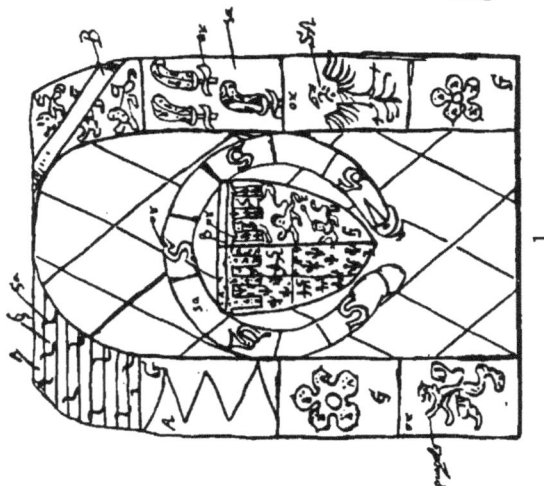

Face page 177

however, at that time, present the gorgeous appearance we now recognise, for it was then made of leather with golden S's sewn upon it. It was worn on some occasions by Richard II. out of respect to his uncle, and was adopted by Henry IV.[1] (grandson of John of Gaunt) as one of his badges. It thus became the token, badge or livery of the Lancastrians, as distinguished from a collar of roses and suns[2] adopted by the Yorkists. Henry V. continued to use the collar of SS, and it is said that he gave to each gentleman who fought in armour at the battle of Agincourt, the right to wear it. Henry VI. undoubtedly used it, and his portrait, which represents him bearing the collar of SS, is in the National Portrait Gallery. Henry VII., after his accession, resumed the collar with the addition of the portcullis being the badge of the Beaufort family. A Tudor rose or other ornament was also worn as a pendant in the place of the hart or the swan used by Richard II. and Henry IV.[3] It was also made entirely of silver or golden links. The only instance, however, in which it is suggested that a judge wore this collar before the reign of Henry VII., is that of Sir Richard Newton, who died in 1449, and was Chief Justice of the Common Bench under

---

before the fire of London, is preserved among the Lansdown MSS. at the British Museum.

[1] He ordered a gold collar with S's and jewels at a cost of £385 6s. 8d. money of that day. *Issue Roll*, 8 Henry IV., Devon's *Issues of the Exchequer*, 305.

[2] See Planché's *Dictionary of Costume*, p. 124.

[3] One of the earliest specimens of the collar is to be found on the effigy of the poet Gower in St. Saviour's, Southwark. He died in 1408.

Henry VI. A monument, supposed to be that of the
Chief Justice and his wife, is in the parish church of
Yatton, Somerset. The monument, according to a drawing in the British Museum, shows a figure with a coif
and with bare feet, somewhat resembling an ecclesiastic,
but wearing a short sword and what appears to be a
bottle suspended at the right side. The robe is long, of
a pattern which may be either legal or ecclesiastical,
with a tippet and what may be a collar of SS or of any
other device. His wife lies beside him. The drawing
has an endorsement that the figure is thought to be that
of one of the Newton family, formerly a warrior and
afterwards a religious.

In Collinson's *History of Somerset*,[1] the tombs are
described, but no mention is made of any collar. The
design would seem to be of the fifteenth century, but even
this is not without doubt. Lady Newton, the Judge's
widow, died in 1475, in the reign of Edward IV., when
the collar of SS was not in vogue, and the inscription
on the marble is effaced. If, therefore, as is possible,
the monument was erected at a later period by some
member of the family, the ornament may well have been
then added. Whatever may be the explanation, the
appearance of this collar on the effigy of a judge in the
fifteenth century is quite unique. The next judge in
order of date whose effigy shows the collar is Sir Thomas
More, whose portrait, painted by Holbein in 1527,[2] shows

---

[1] Bath, 1741, vol. iii. ; " Yatton."
[2] In the possession of Louis Huth. See *Tudor Catalogue*, No.

him in black velvet with the collar of SS and the port-cullis, and with the Tudor rose as a pendant. Sir Thomas More, however, was not Lord Chancellor at the time this portrait was painted. His appointment as Chancellor was not made till October, 1529, after the fall of Wolsey. But, in 1527, he was a Privy Councillor, Chancellor of the Exchequer, and sub-Treasurer of the Royal House-hold, in either of which offices he would have been entitled to wear the collar of SS. Except therefore for the doubtful case of Sir Richard Newton no effigy of any judge on glass, in marble, in brass, or in picture, can be found which bears the collar before the time of Henry VII. The effigies of Sir John Cockayne, Chief Baron, under Henry IV.;[1] of Sir William Gascoigne,[2] the cele-brated Chief Justice under Henry IV. and Henry V.; of Sir William Hawkford[3] and Sir John Fortescue, Chief Justices under Henry VI.; and of Sir John Billing,[4] Chief Justice under Edward IV., in Wappenham Church, Northampton, still exist. They were all distinguished judges and none of their effigies show any trace of the collar of SS. Edward IV. and Richard III., being Yorkists, made no use of the collar of SS, and none of the Chiefs under Henry VII. have left either portraits or sepulchral monuments to throw any light on the question.

---

94. *Dictionary of National Biography*; Hans Holbein, vol. xxvii. p. 108.

[1] Dudgale, *Orig. Jud.*, fol. 100.   [2] Planché, p. 427.

[3] Foss' *Judges*, vol. iv. p. 325.

[4] Baker's *Northampton*, p. 730.   Bridge's *Northampton*, *Wap-penham*.

The first judge, accordingly, who *without doubt* appears
with this decoration, is Sir Richard Lyster, Chief Baron
in 1529, and Chief Justice of the King's Bench in 1545.
He died in 1554, and was buried at St. Michael's Church,
Southampton, where his monument shows him wearing
the collar of SS with his judicial robes.[1]   From this
period the chiefs of the three courts invariably appear
upon their tombs or in their portraits decorated with
the collar of SS.   This, it may fairly be said, carries the
date no further back than the reign of Henry VIII.
But that monarch was no great admirer of the Common
Law judges.   He preferred, at least after the death of
Wolsey, to do his business through the Privy Council,
the Court of Star Chamber, and the High Court of Parliament.   Henry VII., on the other hand, conducted matters
in the Star Chamber as if it were a Court of Common
Law, and kept well within legal bounds.   He owed
much to his lawyers, advised with them frequently, and
attended in person at the serjeant's feasts.[2]   He made
many valuable reforms in the law, in the direction of
public liberty and convenience, and many minor improvements in the procedure.   Among others he gave to poor
litigants the privilege of suing *in forma pauperis*,
thus relieving them of the payment of any fees, and
entitling them to have attorneys and counsel provided
for them free of cost.   Thinking it better, as he is
reported to have said, that poor men should thus be
enabled to bring vexatious actions than that their poverty

---

[1] Foss' *Judges*, vol. v. p. 307.
[2] Bacon: Spedding, vol. vi. p. 158.

Contemporary Portrait of Sir Edward Coke, by Simon van de Pass, an engraver, who was born at Utrecht in 1591, came to England about 1613, and died at Copenhagen about 1614. The portrait shows the golden collar of SS, with the portcullis and the Tudor rose. The ring suspended from the neck by a string is a personal ornament in no way connected with the collar.

ILLUSTRISS · D.no EDOVARDUS COKUS EQV · AVR · QVONDA TOT.P ANGL. IUDEX ET IUST.

Vultum (clare) tuum sculptor cum inciderit, arti
    Diffidit solers sculptor et ipse suæ:
Artem materies quoniam superaret, et una
    Contulerant vultus Dijs, Deaq́s suos:
Si tam cælestis videatur corporis vmbra,
    Quantum cius menti reris inesse decus.

Si. Passæus
sculp: Lon..

Comp.es Holland
excudit.

A. H. con

Face page 181.

should disable them to sue for their just rights.[1] An addition to the honour and dignity of the chiefs of the three courts would thus more probably have come from King Henry VII. than from either of his immediate ancestors or successors. The collar of SS was still worn by the chiefs of the three courts until their amalgamation in the Supreme Court of Judicature in 1875. Each chief, according to custom, provided his own collar, except in the Common Pleas, where the collar followed the office. Lord Coleridge, as the last Chief Justice of the Common Pleas, thus succeeded to the collar worn by Sir Edward Coke; and in order that the memory of that great judge and the insignia of his high office may still be venerated, he has by his will entailed it as an heirloom upon such of his heirs as shall succeed to the title of Lord Coleridge. The present Lord Chief Justice of England, upon those occasions when it is customary to wear the collar of SS, appears in the antient scarlet of his office, bearing the golden chain of his eminent predecessor, Sir Alexander Cockburn, who entailed the Collar of the Queen's Bench upon all holders of the office of Lord Chief Justice.

The reign of Henry VIII. is filled with materials of history, but for juridical as well as historical convenience it may be regarded as composed of two epochs, divided by the fall of Wolsey. Up to that event, which occurred in 1529, the king had interfered but little if at all with the course of justice, interesting himself mainly with foreign affairs, and carrying on the policy of his

---

[1] Bacon : Spedding, vol. vi. p. 160. Stat. 3 Henry VII., c. 8.

father. To Wolsey we owe the promotion of the Master of the Rolls to be a permanent Chancery judge, who took precedence, according to Sir Matthew Hale, between the two Chief Justices.[1] He added splendour and dignity to the office of Chancellor. He appeared in court with ample retinue, preceded by officers bearing maces, and he caused the Great Seal, which up to his time had modestly reposed in a little white leather bag, to be borne before him in a bag of crimson velvet, embroidered with the arms and badges of England.[2] This, with some additions of gold embroidery devised by James I., is the bag in which the great seal is now customarily borne before the Lord Chancellor of England.

Wolsey, who was one of the last of the clerical Chancellors,[3] and who carried himself, not only in home and foreign affairs, but also in Chancery, with the high hand which for a time jumped with the inclinations of his royal master, sat assiduously at the hearing of suits, and in the forty-four articles against him, four only refer to his conduct as Chancellor. In article 20 it is charged that on divers occasions he had examined into matters that had already been decided at Common Law, and had made

---

[1] Hargrave's *Tracts*, p. 300.

[2] An interesting account of his splendour as Chancellor is given in Cavendish's *Life of Wolsey*, written in or about 1557. See also some remarks on the bags provided for the Great Seal by different monarchs.—Foss, vol. v. p. 88.

[3] His ecclesiastical successors were Goodrich, Bishop of Ely under Edward VI.; Gardiner, Bishop of Winchester, and Heath, Archbishop of York under Mary; and Williams, Dean of Westminster under James I. This was the last clerical Chancellor.

some successful parties restore to the other side the fruits of their judgments. By article 21 it is charged that he granted injunctions without having the parties properly before him : by article 26 that he not only issued injunc- tions to stay proceedings at law, but sent for the Common Law judges, and commanded them with threats to defer any judgment in such suits ; and by article 31 that he removed by writ of certiorari from the assize at York into his own court certain indictments against his officers for taking 5 per cent. as their fees on probates of wills. But no suggestions of bribery, malversation, or partiality in his court were made against him. No details of his alleged misconduct in his office, such as are given of other charges against him, are to be found in his im- peachment ; and considering the strenuous exertions of the Court party to secure his ruin, I think it may fairly be said that his thirteen years' tenure of the Chancellor- ship was not stained by any moral blemish.

His ambition, however, was as unbounded as his power, and there is little doubt that in looking down as he did upon the Judges and the doctrines of the Common Law, he brought the judgments of those courts before him, inquired into the propriety of their decisions, and granted injunctions to stay their execution in cases where he was of opinion that they were excessive or unjust. This course appears also to have been followed by his succes- sor, Sir Thomas More, although the agreeable manners and mild corrections of the latter seem to have reconciled the judges to his interference with their tribunals.[1]

---

[1] *Dictionary of National Biography*, Thos. More.

Complaints, constant and well-founded, of the numerous exactions and peculations of the officers who dealt with the incomes and lands of the royal wards, especially in the cases of Empson and Dudley under Henry VII., led to the establishment of a Statutory Court[1] after the fall of Wolsey, called the COURT OF THE KING'S WARDS. It is more commonly known as the Court of Wards and Liveries, by reason of the increased jurisdiction afterwards conferred upon it. It was intended originally for the relief of the subject; was a Court of Record, and took over much of the business in this respect that was formerly transacted by the barons of the Exchequer. The chief officer of the court was the Lord Treasurer, who had the assistance of the three chiefs, if he so desired, with that of the King's Serjeant and the Attorney of the court, together with Surveyors and other officers.

A painting by an unknown artist of the time of Queen Elizabeth[2] shows Lord Burleigh sitting in the Court of Wards with the mace beside him, surrounded by the Surveyors and Attorneys of the court, while the Queen's Serjeant, in scarlet robe, is in attendance, and two serjeants in parti-coloured gowns are arguing. The court failed, however, to give any satisfaction, as the whole system of wardship and feudal tenures had become hateful to the people, and after an attempt by James I. to get rid of it by arrangement,[3] it was suppressed in 1646,

---

[1] 32 Henry VIII., c. 46.

[2] In possession of the Duke of Richmond. It is engraved in *Vetusta Monumenta* by the Society of Antiquaries.

[3] Coke, *Inst.*, vol. iv. p. 202.

and ultimately abolished by Statute at the Restoration.[1] It was situated in Old Palace Yard, between the back of Westminster Hall and the antient building known as Edward the Confessor's Hall. A passage led to it from the Court of Chancery, so that the Chancellor, if so disposed, might either from his private room in Westminster Hall or from the Court of Chancery, when sitting in the Hall, pass directly to the Court of Wards.

A COURT OF REQUESTS which can best be described as an emasculated Court of Chancery, holding perhaps the same relation to that Court that the small debts Courts held to the Common Pleas, was also established in this reign. It was intended to be a relief to the Chancellor, and as such it entertained certain appeals from the Court of Admiralty. But it followed the fate of other courts of the Tudors, and was abolished in 1641.[2] It was held near the Court of Wards in Old Palace Yard, and a staircase led directly from it to the Painted Chamber in the House of Lords.

The COURT OF HIGH COMMISSION, originated by Henry VIII. to hear appeals and to try heresy and other ecclesiastical matters, disused under Philip and Mary and erected by Elizabeth, was one of those unconstitutional tribunals which, with the Star Chamber and the Court of Requests, was swept away by the Long Parliament in 1641.

The policy of non-interference with the judges and their courts continued under Edward VI., Mary, and Elizabeth. Several Protestants holding office under

---

[1] 12 Car. II.   [2] Stat. 16 & 17, Car. i. c. 10.

Mary, and several Catholics, including Sir Edward Saun-
ders, the Lord Chief Justice, retaining their places under
Elizabeth. With the accession of Edward VI., however,
trade began to decrease, and litigation consequently
diminished, so that the courts were less frequented, and
Westminster Hall became as much a market for merchan-
dize as a temple for justice. Houses, formerly used by the
Exchequer officers and others, were let out to innkeepers,
who had taverns adjoining called *Paradise*, *Purgatory*,
and *Hell*. Stalls and shops were put up against the
sides of the Hall, and flags, taken in various campaigns
where our troops had been engaged, hung from the roof.
This occupation of the Hall, however, continued long after
the return of business. Under the Commonwealth there
were leading out of the Hall two refreshment houses
known as *Heaven* and *Hell*, referred to in Hudibras[1] and
Pepys'[2] description of Westminster Hall and his flirta-
tions with the shop-girls during the reign of Charles II.
are well known to all interested in the social England of
that period.

Bad, however, as was business under Edward VI., it
was worse during the reign of Queen Mary, so much so
indeed that in the year 1557, there was only one serjeant
(Bendlowes) and one counsellor (Foster) in attendance in
the Common Pleas and Queen's Bench respectively. It
is also stated by Stow, and it may to some extent account
for this desertion of the courts, that at the time of
Wyatt's rebellion there was so much fear of a general

---

[1] Part iii. canto ii. v. 224.   [2] Pepys, vol. i. p. 16.

Queen Elizabeth's Bed-chamber, facing the Abbey, and communicating with the Great Court and other rooms of the Officers of the Exchequer.

See page 187.

Queen Elizabeth's
Bed-Chamber

Face page 187.

rising in London, that the serjeants and counsel attending the courts " pleaded in harness." And certainly the spectacle of two learned gentlemen, clad in plate armour, with their swords and helmets beside them, arguing a demurrer, was not one to encourage litigation. Mary's reign was also distinguished by a flagrant interference with the courts in the case of Sir Nicholas Throckmorton. This gentleman being tried for high treason, was acquitted by the unanimous verdict of the jury. For this act of justice and independence they were brought before the Star Chamber, questioned, reprimanded, and fined in various sums ranging from £60 to £2,000 each,[1] and imprisoned till payment.

No sooner, however, was Elizabeth on the throne than the business of the courts at once revived. " The spaniels came into the field,"[2] as it was said, " when there was plenty of game," and the roll of serjeants and of counsel rapidly increased. Westminster Hall and the Courts of Law became places of common resort, the Queen, habitually occupying the Palace of Westminster, had a set of apartments adjoining the Hall with a spacious and decorated bedroom facing the Abbey. She used the great Court of Exchequer, from time to time, as a ball-room, and the gallery as a chamber for music. The chestnut pillars of the court were restored by her in 1570, when the chief officers of state, Sir Nicholas Bacon, the Lord Keeper; Dudley, Earl of Leicester, Master of the Horse; William Cecil, Principal Secretary of the Queen; William

---

[1] *State Trials*, vol. i. p. 864. [2] Foss, vol. v. p. 339.

Paulet, Marquis of Winchester, Treasurer of England; Walter Mildmay, Kt., Chancellor of the Exchequer; and James Dyer, Kt., Chief Justice of the Bench, had their names carved on the bases of the columns supporting the gallery.

At the same time the Bar began again to flourish. The Inns of Court frequented as in the days of Fortescue by sons of country gentlemen, noblemen and squires, who regarded a certain training in those hospitia as part of a liberal education, spent large sums in feasts and entertainments, for which their members were assessed according to their standing in the Inn. They patronised the players and had plays frequently acted in the hall of their Inn. They kept Christmas with great cheer and hospitality. They entertained the sovereign and attended at Court, taking part in masques, tournaments and barriers. The number of serjeants was gradually increased by appointment of the Crown, but the customary feasts and the gold rings which etiquette required the serjeants to give to the judges and courtiers on these occasions became so heavy a tax on their income that lawyers of position, who did not aspire to be judges, frequently begged to be relieved from the acceptance of this honourable degree. And Bacon, who himself was never a serjeant-at-law, persuaded the Queen to create a new rank, that of QUEEN'S COUNSEL, and to nominate him the first of that honourable brotherhood, a rank which was afterwards confirmed to him by James I.[1]

---

[1] Spedding, vol. x. p. 78.

The various devices described by Sir Matthew Hale [1] by which the King's Bench and the Common Pleas (as the Court was then commonly called) endeavoured to attract business to their own court and to drive it from their neighbour by lowering costs and expediting causes, had resulted in a considerable multiplication of suits in both courts, while the abstraction from the Court of Exchequer of the numerous cases relating to the king's wards, widows and idiots, now disposed of by the Treasurer in the Court of Wards and Liveries, left the Exchequer comparatively unoccupied for a great part of the year. The barons also, who had for many generations been, with the exception of the Chief baron, selected from clerks in the Exchequer office, or other persons without a sound legal training, now began to enter at the Inns of Court, to engage in the study of the law, and to qualify themselves for judicial posts. Some of the barons had in this way become readers and benchers of their Inn,[2] although I do not find that any had yet been

---

[1] " A Discourse concerning the Courts, etc."; Hargrave's *Tracts*, p. 359.

[2] The earliest instance I have found of a baron of the Exchequer holding office at the Inns of Court is that of Richard Illingworth, a baron of the Exchequer, who was elected Governor of Lincoln's Inn, 22 Henry VI. (A.D. 1444). Dugdale, *Orig. Jud.*, fol. 257. In 11 Edward IV. (A.D. 1472), Nicholas Statham, a baron of the Exchequer, was elected Reader of that Society. The first baron holding office in the Inner Temple was —— Blagge, Governor, 3 Henry VIII. (A.D. 1512). The first baron at Gray's Inn was John Petyte, Reader, 9 Henry VIII. (A.D. 1518). The first at the Middle Temple was Nicholas Lake, Reader, 26 Henry VIII. (A.D. 1535).

called to the degree of the coif, or become serjeants-at-law.   In view of this improved legal status of the barons and of the increase of business in the two other courts, the practice was adopted of appointing the barons to the same duties as the justices, requiring them to be serjeants before their appointment, and sending them on Circuit to act with the others in trying prisoners and causes as well as the not very frequent matters which arose touching the revenue.   In 1579 Robert Shute[1] was appointed second baron of the Exchequer with the same rank and duties as the puisne judges of the other courts, and from that date forwards each succeeding baron of the Exchequer was a trained lawyer and received his patent in similar form.

This elevation of the barons, however, to the same rank as the justices necessitated the appointment of an additional officer with special duties as regarded the revenue.   He was called a cursitor baron, was to be present at the counting in the Exchequer, and to see that the King's prerogative in fees and fines was duly guarded.   There was also committed to him the ceremonial duty of notifying the sovereign's assent to the election of the lord mayor and sheriffs, and of addressing the lord mayor when he came into the Exchequer on each 9th of November to invite the Chief baron and the rest of the Common Law judges to dinner at Guildhall. He was not necessarily, therefore, a trained lawyer. His post was not judicial, his pay was much less than

---

[1] Dugdale, *Chronica Series*, fol. 94.   Foss, vol. v. p. 410.

that of the other barons, and his position was in all respects inferior to that of the other judges of the three
courts.   Little is recorded of the duties or the proceedings of these cursitor barons from the time of
Elizabeth to that of Victoria.   The reformers of this
reign have abolished many sinecure offices, and the cursitor barons having no longer any duties to perform,
were not reappointed after the year 1856.[1]   Their only
surviving historical record is to be found in a published collection of speeches by Baron Tomlins, a cursitor
under Charles I. and the Commonwealth.   They are long,
and would now be considered in bad taste ; but they
probably were adapted to the period in which he lived,
and to the company whom he addressed.[2]

II.

Treatment of the Judges by the Stuart Kings—Sir Edward Coke
—Felton's Case—Constitution of the Courts on the King's
Death—No Judges on his Trial—Appointment of Judges—
The Admiralty—Arrears in Chancery—Lord Chancellors
and Lord Keepers—Projected Reform—Interference with
Judges—Baron Thorpe and Justice Newdigate—Counsel
sent to the Tower—Courts and Costumes of Judges—Wigs
and Bands—Judges in Parliment—The Upper Bench—Special
Commissions.

THE same method of dealing with offences against the
Crown through the medium of the Privy Council, the
Star Chamber and Parliament that had been adopted

---

[1] Stat. 19, 20, Vic. c. 86.

[2] A specimen of one of the speeches is given in Foss, vol. vi.
p. 27.   The original is in the British Museum.

under the Tudor sovereigns was pursued during the reigns of King James and King Charles, and no modification was made in the procedure or in the constitution of the Courts of Common Law. King James, shortly after his accession, sat in the King's Bench, but he was not so far encouraged by the judges as to induce him to try causes or to deliver judgments. The Chancellors, holding their office during pleasure, continued as under the Tudors, to be subservient to the Crown, and in great measure responsible for the calamities that followed, a responsibility from which it is impossible to exclude the great name of Bacon. The personal interference, however, of the Sovereign with the duties of the judges, the taking of what was described as their auricular confessions, the giving of royal orders to postpone the hearing and decision of suits, the reprimands dealt out to them from time to time, and the payments extracted from them on their appointments, reduced the position of the Bench to almost its lowest degradation, and would perhaps have affixed a permanent stigma upon it had it not been for the courageous and patriotic resolution of not a few of the judicial staff.

First and greatest among these was Sir Edward Coke, Lord Chief Justice successively of the Common Pleas and of the King's Bench, whose early intolerance of language and demeanour, in some of the State prosecutions under Queen Elizabeth and King James, has tended to obscure the great services which, apart altogether from his legal attainments, he afterwards rendered to his country, and for which he has hardly received his full tribute of jus-

tice. Sir Randolph Crew, Chief Justice of the King's
Bench, Chief Baron Walter and Chief Justice Heath of
the Common Pleas, whose places were at a later date
sacrificed to their independence, should also be mentioned
with respect. Mr. Gardiner [1] pays a high tribute to
the personal character, the honesty and the purity of the
judges under King Charles, but thinks that they were
bound too much by the strict letter of the law, without
considering what the result might be of giving present
effect to laws that had long, by common consent, fallen
into disuse. And he suggests that the King took advantage of this habit of theirs in formulating the questions
he submitted for their determination. In support of this
view he takes the case of the forests, where for three
centuries people had lived, had reclaimed and cultivated
land, had erected mills, and had built villages and towns
with the knowledge and tacit assent of successive
sovereigns, and yet the judges held, in answer to the
King's request, that as there was no license and no disafforesting by the King, the whole of these lands, villages
and towns were still subject to the Forest, and not to
the Common Law, and that the farms, lands and houses
reclaimed from the forests, and occupied by generations
of owners, were forfeit to the Crown as purprestures
or assarts. It may be that Mr. Gardiner is right in his
theory, and, if so, we may find some compensation in this,
that if the genius of the age brought forth judges of abstruse and technical minds, it also enriched the time with

---

[1] *Personal Government*, vol. ii. pp. 71–77.

great antiquaries and archæologists. For to that age we owe Bacon, Coke, Selden the greatest of legal antiquaries, Camden the historian, Prynne, Dugdale, Spelman, Weever and his inimitable collection of funeral monuments and antiquities, Sir Robert Cotton whose library was the foundation of the British Museum, Jeake the historian of the Cinque Ports, Hobbes author of the *Leviathan*, Harvey the physician, and Sydenham the father of medicine.

In one matter King Charles followed in the steps of his ancestor, King Henry VII., for he called the judges together in 1628 to inquire whether Felton, who had murdered the Duke of Buckingham, and had confessed his guilt, could be put upon the rack to compel him to disclose the names of his supposed associates. They were assembled in the Exchequer Chamber under Chief Justice Richardson, of whom it was said that he paid £17,000 for his place,[1] and notwithstanding the King's expressed desire that Felton should be racked, they made the declaration against the use of torture to which I have already referred. Felton had also in terms expressed penitence for his act, and his willingness that the hand with which he dealt the blow should be struck off while he was yet living. A further question was accordingly submitted, whether it could not be held, as Felton had given an implied consent to the striking off of his hand, that such addition might lawfully be made to the sentence to be passed upon him, and the judges were sig-

---

[1] Foss' *Judges*, vol. vi. p. 208. Walter Yonge's *Diary*, p. 97.

nificantly informed that if they were of opinion in the affirmative, the King would not exert his prerogative to prevent it. They replied, however, that the sentence for Felton's offence being defined by law, they had no power to add anything to it.[1]

The quarrels of the King with the Long Parliament, his flight from London, and the subsequent outbreak of hostilities, threw the Courts of Law into comparativo disorganization. Sir Edward Littleton, the Chancellor, joined the King at Oxford, taking with him the Great Seal, which precluded for a time the issuing of writs. Sir Robert Heath, re-appointed after his removal in 1634, sat at Oxford as Lord Chief Justice, and followed his master's fortunes to his death. The Parliament, on the other hand, removed the Ship Money judges, and filled their places after a time with serjeants more in sympathy with the Puritan cause. In the meantime the courts sat regularly in Westminster Hall,—sometimes constituted by a single judge, sometimes by two,—and struggled man-fully with the increasing list of causes. The possibility of holding circuits depended upon the locality of the contending armies; but they were not wholly abandoned, and in the west and south, where there was little fight-ing, assizes were held with remarkable regularity. Early in 1648 there was a full call of serjeants by order of Parliament, and from these serjeants, chiefs were ap-pointed to the various courts, Serjeant Rolle to the King's Bench, Sir Oliver St. John to the Common Pleas, and Serjeant Wilde to the Exchequer.

---

[1] *State Trials*, vol. iii. p. 371.

At the death of King Charles (30th January, 1648-9), all the Courts were fully manned. A chief and three puisnes sat in each, exclusive of the King's Chief Justice and Chancellor, who, as in the time of Henry VI., were discharging nominal functions beyond the realm. But no judge sat on this famous trial. A proposed commission for the trial of the King contained the names of certain judges, but the proposal was rejected by the Lords, and the Court, over which Serjeant Bradshaw presided, was composed exclusively of members of the House of Commons.

It had long been held, as an established custom of the Common Law, that the demise of the Crown determined all judicial appointments,[1] and the first act of a new sovereign had always been to appoint, usually to re-appoint, the judicial staff. Acting on this principle, it became necessary for the Commonwealth at once to fill up the vacant offices. It was proposed to re-nominate all the judges then sitting; but before any steps could be taken in this direction, a declaration was required from Parliament that the fundamental laws of the country should be continued, and that the judges should administer justice accordingly.[2] Upon this being passed, in terms settled at a meeting of the judges, six of the twelve, including the three chiefs, accepted re-appointment, and six puisnes were afterwards added. Of the retiring judges, Baron Atkins accepted a judgeship in

---

[1] The judges, being consulted by Queen Elizabeth, declared this to be the case.—Dyer, *Rep.*, fol. 165.

[2] Whitelock, vol. ii. p. 528. Scobell's *Acts, etc.*, 9 Feb., 1648-9.

1650, and in 1653, Sir Matthew Hale, who, whether a Puritan or a Royalist at heart, had been, while at the bar, the foremost defender of cavaliers, and the trusted adviser of King Charles in the times of his greatest adversity, was appointed to the Common Bench.

The judges thus appointed went forthwith upon circuit, and endeavoured by conciliatory charges and careful methods to induce a respect for the law, and a confidence in its administration by the executive. Their duties at this time, as judges of assize, were multifarious, and were not, as in the present day, confined to the trial of prisoners and of causes. They had inherited from their predecessors, from the earliest times, the duty of administering upon appeal all the important affairs of the county. They sat as magistrates, took informations, committed prisoners for trial, and admitted them to bail. The repairs of roads, bridges, gaols and churches were submitted for their adjudication. They heard appeals from magistrates and from overseers of parishes on questions of relief, in cases of poverty or of sickness. Some of them went under the escort of troops when the country was unquiet, and two of them, Baron Gates and Baron Rigby, died at Croydon of the plague, which attacked them in court. Most of the others also risked a similar fate, while ordering the necessary precautions to be taken in various counties and towns, where this scourge was beginning to make itself felt.

Returning to London, they sat with regularity in their several courts and discharged their duties both there and on their circuits with intrepidity and integrity, not scrupling to resign rather than comply with what they regarded as contrary to law—and they have as judges left behind them a name which for probity and learning is not surpassed by any bench of judges, at any period of our national history. The name and the judgments of Chief Justice Rolle still hold their place in our libraries, and the encomiums passed upon him by the collected judges of Charles II., to be found in the preface to his reports, show him to have been a discreet, a learned and an impartial judge. No fewer than nine of the Commonwealth judges also held office under Charles II., and were among the best of those that sat in his reign. Sir Matthew Hale, Lord Chief Baron of the Exchequer and Lord Chief Justice of the King's Bench, Sir Edward Atkins, Sir John Archer, Sir Hugh Windham and Sir Thomas Tyrrell, were among the most conspicuous examples.

The successful warfare of the Commonwealth, more especially upon the high seas, threw duties upon the Court of the Admiralty which, for many years, it had not been called upon to discharge. For this purpose therefore the appointments to the Admiralty were of great importance, both in regard of cases of prize and of various contracts arising out of the extended maritime commerce protected by our flag. Among the civilians occupying seats on the Admiralty Bench were Dr. Exton and Dr. Godolphin. They were both men of considerable erudition, to whom the country is indebted for many learned expositions of the maritime law. The *Maritime Dicæologie* of the former and the *Orphan's Legacy* of the latter of these learned authors are among their numerous works.

In the appellate jurisdiction of the Privy Council the Protector on more than one occasion sat as President, and according to the records of that body heard appeals from Jersey and other parts.[1] He also acted as arbitrator in a suit between the daughter and the legatees of Sir Theodore Mayerne, the celebrated physican who attended upon Charles I., and afterwards upon Cromwell, and died leaving a large fortune which was the subject of litigation. This, according to Whitelock,[2] he decided in November, 1657, "very justly." Except in these two instances he personally took no part in the trial of causes, leaving all such matters to his Attorney General, Edward Prideaux, who maintained the dignity and the prestige of the former attorneys by wearing his hat during the trials, being the only person who remained covered in court except the judges.

The great difficulty of the Commonwealth, however, appears to have been in the reform of the Court of Chancery. Owing to the troubles of the previous reign, and it may be to some extent to the inefficiency of the Chancellors and their staff, the court was blocked with arrears. It was said that 20,000 causes stood for judgment in the Court of Chancery, many of them ten, twenty or thirty years old, and that in some not less than 500 orders had been passed.[3] Vigorous attempts were accord-

---

[1] *Mercurius Politicus*, No. 385.   [2] *Memorials*, vol. iv. p. 312.
[3] *Parliamentary History*, vol. iii. p. 1412.

ingly made to cope with these arrears. There had arisen on occasions, certainly during the Tudors, some question as to the relative position of the Chancellor and the Keeper of the Great Seal. To dispel any doubt on this head, an Act[1] had been passed in 1563, declaring that the Keeper of the Great Seal always had by the Common Law the same place and authority as if he were Lord Chancellor of England. And Selden, when his friend Bacon was about to be appointed, wrote a short but learned treatise[2] to show that the Keeper of the Great Seal was always, in effect, in the same position as the Chancellor. There was however a substantial difference between a Lord Keeper and a Lord Chancellor, which was not affected by the statute. For although the Lord Keeper and the Lord Chancellor were equally Speakers of the House of Lords, yet the former, if not a peer, which indeed was not usual, had no power to sit as a peer, or to participate in the debates, and he might accordingly have to put the question of his own impeachment without being able to say a word in his defence, while the Lord Chancellor as a peer, which he usually was, could always, according to the practice of the Lords, leave the Woolsack and take part in the debates and votes of the House. At a somewhat later date, Sir Robert Henley complained that, being Lord Keeper and Speaker of the House of Lords, though not a peer, he had to put the question that his judgments in the Court of Chancery be reversed on

---

[1] Stat. 5 Eliz. c. 18.

[2] *A brief Discourse touching the office of Lord Chancellor of England, etc.*

appeal, without being permitted, before doing so, to explain the grounds of his opinions or the reasons for his judgments.[1]

Under the Commonwealth, as under King Charles I. and the Long Parliament, the Great Seal was put into Commission, for there had been no Lord Chancellor since the fall of Lord Bacon in 1621. The Keepers of the Great Seal of the Commonwealth, by sitting as early as 7 a.m., and as late as 7 p.m. (an unheard of innovation for those times), grappled with, and to some extent reduced, the mass of arrears. Their attempt was not, however, altogether successful, and Parliament tried to effect by legislation what the industry and goodwill of the Chancery judges had failed to accomplish. A well-meaning but impracticable Ordinance [2] for dealing with cases in Chancery was passed in August, 1654; but beyond bringing about the retirement of Bulstrode Whitelock, who refused to attempt its application, and the threatened but unaccomplished resignation of the Master of the Rolls,[3] no recognisable improvement was made in that regard.

The Protector, however, was unable to keep his hands altogether off the judges, and although the scruples of Sir Matthew Hale and of Justice Atkins, as to the superseding of trial by jury in the various Commissions for trying the royalists, were so far respected as to put no

---

[1] Campbell's *Lives of the Chancellors*, vol. v. p. 186.

[2] Scobell's *Acts*, fol. 324; and see Whitelock's *Memorials*, vol iv. pp. 191–207.

[3] Whitelock, vol. iv. p. 206.

impediment in the way of their continuance in office, yet the removal of Baron Thorpe and of Justice Newdigate stands on a different footing. The actual reason of their resignation is not very clear. Whitelock[1] says, " they were put out of their places for not observing the Protector's pleasure in all his commands," but he gives no particulars. The fact, so far as I have been able to ascertain it, was, that these two judges, acting according to their duty as committing magistrates as well as judges of Assize, did not see in the conduct of certain royalists in the North such overt acts as were necessary to establish a *prima facie* case of high treason. Their views were reported to the Council in London, and shortly after their return to Westminster, the resignations of these two judges were tendered and accepted, and they returned as serjeants to their practice at the Bar. It was the only case however of the removal or resignation of judges under the Commonwealth for what may be described as political reasons. An instance in which the Bar suffered for freedom of speech is more clearly defined, and more generally agreed upon. One, Cony, a Turkey merchant, having refused to pay the import duty on certain Spanish wines, had been committed to the custody of the Serjeant-at-Arms by order of the Council of State. He thereupon applied to the Upper Bench for a writ of *habeas corpus*, calling upon the Serjeant-at-Arms to show why he was held in custody, and why he should not be discharged. His application was supported by Serjeant Maynard, Serjeant Twisden, and Mr. Wadham Windham. Serjeant

---

[1] *Memorials*, vol. iv. p. 101.

Twisden, in the absence of Serjeant Maynard, argued that the Protector had no power to levy any duties or customs, and that according to law none were then payable either by Cony or by any other person, thus directly impeaching the validity of the orders of the then executive, and claiming on behalf of the community the right to refuse payment of all taxes and excise.[1] The subject matter of this speech was brought before the Council of State, who, drawing no distinction between the counsel, and assuming that they all concurred in the line adopted by Serjeant Twisden, sent the three learned gentlemen to the Tower, from which they were only released on humble petition and apology. This course, though usually considered as high-handed and autocratic as any action of the Stuarts, was not without its justification in view of the state of the country, and the danger likely to arise from the promulgation of doctrines subversive of the first elements of settled government. The discussion, however, of this question touches on the domain of politics, and as such is beyond the scope of this work.

In the matter of courts, of officers, and of costume, the judges of the Commonwealth differed but little from their predecessors, except that the King's Bench was called the UPPER BENCH, a name by which it also seems to have been occasionally known in previous reigns. The keepers of the Great Seal wore a robe described by Whitelock, the historian of the epoch, as "a handsome velvet gown," closely resembling that worn by Lord

---

[1] *State Papers Domestic*, 18th May, 1665.

Bacon in the portrait in Lord Verulam's collection. The
Common Law judges wore their scarlet, as we know from
certain petitions presented to the Protector praying that
the judges who went Circuit in their scarlet, and were at
times escorted by a troop of horse, should no longer be
permitted to " affright the country with their blood-red
robes and their state and pomp." [1] And Chief Justice
Glyn, as we know from his portrait, wore with his scarlet
gown the collar of SS. Serjeants wore their coifs and
striped gowns ; but the Bar, under the rank of serjeant,
wore their own hair trimmed in such device as was prescribed by fashion and not forbidden by the regulations
of the Inn to which they belonged. The head-dress of
the judges, the serjeants, and the Bar had from the very
earliest periods been fixed and determined. The judges
wore the coif and the velvet cap over their own hair,
with their beards and moustaches as they thought fit.
Serjeants wore the coif, while counsel wore " a serious
dress " of the costume of the period. Ruffs were in
fashion during Elizabeth and James I., when judges
and counsel wore them. These were supplanted by a
broad lace collar, which was in fashion under Charles I.,
and by white linen bands under the Commonwealth. In
the reign of Charles II. the monarch and people of position assumed the periwig, a fashion imported from
France, where it was patronized by Louis XIV., and
gradually left off wearing beards and moustaches. Some
of the judges, but not all, accordingly wore their judicial

---

[1] *State Papers addressed to Oliver Cromwell*, fol. 99.

robes with the periwig in place of the coif; and this diversity of head-dress among the judges continued during the reign of James II., when Sir Thomas Street, one of the judges who was in office in 1688, still wore his own hair with the coif and the black velvet cap.[1] The Bar, being younger than the judges, took more generally to the prevailing fashion, and wore first the long and then the short wig. In course of time, mainly under William III., all classes of the community, including bishops and clergy, wore the long or the short wig, judges and counsel being included in the number; and the serjeants, to indicate their status, wore a black patch on a white silk ground, fastened on to their wigs as a substitute for the black cap and the white coif. The lawyers, however, who followed the public taste in assuming periwigs, failed to follow it in leaving them off. The bishops, who continued to wear their wigs long after the public had ceased to do so, gave up the practice some fifty years ago; but judges and counsel have continued till to-day the bands of the Commonwealth along with the head-dress of the Restoration, which is no more any portion of antient or traditionary legal costume than were the ruffs of Queen Elizabeth or the lace collars of Charles I. And thus it happens that, by a very perversity of conservatism, that head-dress, which in the seventeenth

---

[1] Foss, vol. vii. p. 17. In the highest Courts of Appeal, viz. the House of Lords and the Privy Council, the judges now sit without wigs or robes of office. The Lord Chancellor presiding in the former, wears his robes as Speaker of the House of Lords and not as judge.

century was worn alike by kings and by courtiers, by clergymen and by soldiers, by Jeffreys on the bench, and by Titus Oates in the dock, has become in the nineteenth century the distinct characteristic of the advocate and the judge. King James I., interfering with the Inns of Court, as with most other of his subjects' affairs, had ordered that barristers were not to come to the hall of their Inn with their cloaks, boots, swords, spurs or daggers, showing that their ordinary habits were those of the gentlemen of the period, and further that none were to be admitted into the Society who were not gentlemen by descent. These directions were repeated by Charles I., and seem to have been very generally followed, and it was not, I conceive, till the middle of King Charles' reign, if not later, that counsel under the rank of serjeants, when employed in court, took to wearing silk or stuff gowns, and thus became " gentlemen of the long robe.''

Upon the promulgation of the new Constitution and the establishment of a Commonwealth " without a king or a house of lords," the position of the judges towards Parliament was materially changed, and they became eligible for election as members of the legislature. According to antient practice, the judges were regarded as auxiliaries and assistants of the peers. At the commencement of each Parliament, writs were issued under the Great Seal, commanding the attendance of the judges of the King's Bench and the Common Pleas, and such of the barons of the Exchequer as were of the coif, together with the Master of the Rolls, to attend the House of

Lords when the peers should require their presence or their advice. When called in to assist the peers, they sat either on the woolsack with the Chancellor, or on other seats provided for them within the House.[1] They were also required for other purposes, sometimes to consider and advise on bills relating to real estate, and sometimes to carry messages to the Commons : for as the formal etiquette of Parliament required a message from the Commons to be brought to the Lords by five members of the Lower House, so the Lords in communicating with the Commons sent their messages by the hands of two of the judges.[2] These duties of the judges were held, reasonably enough, to be inconsistent with their being members of the House of Commons, and down to the period of the Commonwealth, the Common Law judges had never occupied that position. When, however, there was no longer a House of Lords, and the duties and liabilities of the judges in relation to the peers had ceased to exist, the reason for their exclusion from the other House no longer operated to their prejudice, and accordingly, during the interregnum, several of the Common Law judges were also members of Parliament. Among them Lord Chief Justice Glyn, of the Upper Bench, was also M.P. for Chester; Oliver St. John, Lord Chief Justice of the Common Bench, was M.P. for Totnes; Sir Matthew Hale, a justice of the Common Bench, was M.P. for the county of Gloucester, and Baron Hill, of the Exchequer, was M.P. for Bridport.

---

[1] May's *Parliamentary Practice*, p. 236.　　[2] *Ibid.*, p. 448.

On the erection of a House of Lords by Cromwell, the old practice revived, old precedents were followed, the judges were reinstated as assistants to the peers, and the respectful message from the Lords to the Commons, in January, 1658, asking the latter to concur in fixing a day for public fasting and humiliation, was brought from the Painted Chamber by Justice Windham and Baron Hill, two of the Common Law judges.[1] A further message was sent by the Lords in the month of February by the hands of Justices Windham and Newdigate.[2]

In London the judges still sat at Westminster, but the Courts of Chancery and of the Upper Bench were removed from the end to the side of the Hall, so that the four courts were on one side, the shops on the other, and the end unoccupied.[3] Among the visitors to the Hall during the early days of the Commonwealth it is related, though not perhaps upon very good authority, that Charles II., in the disguise of a woman, after the battle of Worcester, saw the judges sitting in their courts, and the flags that Oliver had taken from the Scots.[4]

They were all, Lord Keepers and judges alike, appointed for life during good behaviour; they were for-

---

[1] *Mercurius Politicus*, No. 399.

[2] *Ibid.*, No. 401. The custom of sending messages by the judges has only recently been discontinued. The message in reference to the Prince of Wales' Annuity, in 1863, was brought from the Lords by two judges, as was also that in reference to Princess Louise's Annuity in 1871. Messages are now brought by the respective clerks of the two Houses.—May's *Parliamentary Practice*, p. 450.

[3] Whitelock, vol. iii. p. 383.   [4] *Ibid.*, vol. iii. p. 361.

bidden to take any fee, perquisite, or reward, and in consideration of this they were given salaries of £1,000 [1] per annum, charged on the customs revenue, and those of them who went circuit were allowed to charge their expenses, in addition to their salary.

Although impartial opinion gives credit to the judges of this period for their conduct in the judicial office, yet a prospect of return to the old constitutional methods was undoubtedly received with acclamation by the people. Many causes, most of them unconnected with judicial procedure, contributed to this result. Among them, however, must probably be reckoned the trial of cavaliers by tribunals, constituted for the purpose by Special Commission, where they were tried as if before the House of Peers—before a large number of commissioners, presided over by a judge. The erection of this class of tribunal, necessary perhaps at that period for obtaining tranquillity in the State, is not without apparent justification; but although the commissioners hardly convicted without sufficient evidence, yet their proceedings were unpopular, and much sympathy was shown for the accused, inasmuch as it was well known that some of the judges had refused to sit on these commissions or to try treasons without the intervention of a jury.

The restoration of royalty was accordingly welcomed with rapture. The bells that rang in the new system were thought to ring out the servility and the corruption

---

[1] Equal to about £5,000 a year of the present value of money.

P

of the old, and to herald the advent of a race of judges irremovable and incorruptible, discharging their functions without regard to the wishes of the Crown. That such was the ultimate result of the re-action against the methods of the Tudors and of the Stuarts is undoubted; but it was not accomplished without the judicial bench passing through a phase of servility and corruption at the end of the century, to which there had hitherto been no parallel, and which, happily for England, cannot recur.

CHAPTER VI.

FROM THE RESTORATION TO THE ERECTION OF THE
SUPREME COURT OF JUDICATURE. .
(A.D. 1660-1873.)

Effect of the Commonwealth on Law and Procedure—The Restoration—Policy of Retrogression—Appointment of Judges—Removal of Judges—The Rebuilding of London— Sir Matthew Hale—King James II.—Judges after the Revolution—Their Tenure of Office—Their Integrity — Complaints of the Judicial System—Mercantile Code established by the Judges—Partial Abolition of the Ecclesiastical Courts—The Court of Probate—The Court of Divorce—Proposals for a Supreme Court—Erection of a Supreme Court of Judicature in 1873—The High Court of Justice and the Court of Appeal—Further Consolidation of the Courts— Suggested Fusion of Law and Equity—Further Division of the High Court—The Chancellor and the Lord Chief Justice —The Royal Courts of Justice—Former alterations in the Courts—The Removal from Westminster to the Strand.

THE rule of the Protector was of too short a duration to enable him to secure those ameliorations in the law and in the practice of the courts, the accomplishment of which was the ambition of himself and of the party who gave him their support. Most of the reforms which he introduced were just and well considered; they have of late years been received with general approval, and now form part of our legal procedure. Had Cromwell lived another fifteen or twenty years they would probably have become recognised and established as the law of the land,

and the country would not have been compelled to suffer
under the old cumbrous system for another two hundred
years. As it was, these various beneficent alterations,
the reform of the Court of Chancery, the relief of unhappy debtors from life-long imprisonment by means of a
system of discharge in Bankruptcy, the bringing of wills
and administrations from the Ecclesiastical tribunals to
the courts at Westminster, the introduction of the English language into pleadings and Courts of Justice, the
abolition of the complicated system of fines and re-
coveries, and the mitigation of punishments in criminal
cases, though embarked upon by the Protector, had been
so short a time either in operation or under discussion,
that the people of England had no sufficient opportunity
of considering their value; nor had they anywhere
become accustomed to changes, which, at his death, had
not yet passed from the stage of innovations into that of
accepted doctrines of the law.

The effect of the legal improvements under the Commonwealth did however show itself, on the first blush of
the Restoration, in the many beneficent statutes then
enacted. But after the disbanding of the army and the
trial and execution of the regicides, the country gave
itself up so thoroughly to the acceptance of the new
King, that there seemed to be no reason, in prudence or in
policy, to revert even for good to the experience of the
last twenty years. There was a general spirit of make-
believe so as to get rid of the spectre of the Commonwealth, and to conduct public affairs as if there had been
no interval between the death of the first Charles and the

accession of the second. The first year of Charles II. was called in all statutes and public documents the twelfth year, the mace was altered from the Commonwealth to the Stuart type, the courts were restored to the end of Westminster Hall, and the English tongue which had been introduced by the Long Parliament was reconverted into the unknown tongue of the Anglo-Norman French. But in the meantime many dangerous innovations had gone never to return. The Court of Star Chamber, the Court of Wards, and the Court of High Commission had been abolished, and the Chief Justice of the Forest, though a feeble effort was made after the Restoration to reconstitute his office,[1] was no more heard of, except as a pensioner on the civil list. Good and learned men were appointed as judges; they held their office during good behaviour, and in the early part of the reign there was no interference with their duties or their opinions. During the latter period, however, their patents were again drawn *durante bene placito* during the King's good pleasure, and no less than nine, exclusive of the Chancellors, were removed for causes more or less political, the varying phases of the Popish Plot providing in many instances the reasons for their dismissal.

The reign of Charles II. provides the first instance in which the judges of the Common Law Courts consented to take upon themselves public functions other than those incident to the duties strictly pertaining to their office. The circumstances were exceptional, and whatever

---

[1] Stephen's *History of the Criminal Law*, vol. i. p. 138.

opinion may be held as to the employment of judges
of late years on commission and inquiries, the judges
of the Restoration undoubtedly conferred an obligation
upon London and the country which should ever be
held in remembrance. The great fire of 1666, which
stamped out the plague, nearly stamped out London
with it. The extent of the devastation wrought by the
fire is described by Pepys, by Evelyn, and by Stowe.
One of the acts for the rebuilding of London declares
that "the City of London . . . was for the most part
burnt down and destroyed . . . and now lies buried
in its own ruins." And another recites that the greatest
part of the houses in the City of London, "and some in
the suburbs thereof, have been burnt . . . by the late
dreadful and dismal fire," and the position of freeholders,
occupiers, lessees, and others liable to pay rents, and without means to rebuild, or in many cases to identify the
boundaries of their property, was pitiable in the ex-
treme. To remedy this distress, so far as was practicable, an Act[1] was passed in 1667 by which a special
court of judicature was established, consisting of the
judges of the King's Bench, the Common Pleas, and the
"Barons of the Coif of the Exchequer," for the time
being, or any three of them sitting together, with powers
of a most extensive character, to settle without charge
all disputes between landlords, tenants, proprietors,
occupiers, adjoining owners and others, so that their
various boundaries might be ascertained, and the re-

[1] 19 Car. II., c. 2.

building of the City be proceeded with at once. Their jurisdiction was summary and without appeal, except where an order was made by less than seven judges, when, upon the assent of the Lord Chief Justice and the Lord Chief Baron, the matter might be reconsidered by all the judges together. They could terminate leases, could order new leases to be granted, with or without condition as to payment, or otherwise; could make orders, notwithstanding the coverture, minority, or incapacity of the parties for or against whom such orders were made; and they proceeded, as directed by the Act, without the formalities or technicalities of courts of law or equity, *sine forma et figura judicii.* By a subsequent Act[1] of the same session, rules and orders were laid down for the rebuilding of the City. It contained the well-known provision for building in brick or stone, and embodied a modified form of betterment,[2] by which those whose houses were improved in value, by new or enlarged streets or thoroughfares, were to contribute, in proportion to their advanced values, towards a fund to be employed for the general rebuilding and improvement of the City, and for the compensation of those whose lands or houses had been compulsorily taken for that purpose.

Acting under the authority of these and certain amending statutes,[3] the judges, most prominent among whom

---

[1] 19 Car. II., c. 3.   [2] Cl. 26.

[3] Stat. 19 Car. II., c. 2, limited the powers of the judges to 31 Dec., 1668; Stat. 22 Car. II., c. 11, extended them to 29 Sept., 1671; Stat. 22 & 23, Car. II., c. 14, further extended them to

were Sir Orlando Bridgman, Lord Chief Justice of the
Common Pleas, and Sir Matthew Hale, Lord Chief Baron
of the Exchequer, sat day by day at a court which they
erected in Cliffords Inn, and there they superintended
the rebuilding of the City. The work went on without
impediment or delay; the judgments of Sir Matthew
Hale and his colleagues were unreservedly accepted, and
within six years of the outbreak of the fire their duties
had determined, and London was rising again from its
ashes.

The Lord Mayor, Aldermen, and Commonalty of
London, recognising the obligations they were under
to the several judges who took part in the deliberations
and orders at Cliffords Inn, commissioned Nathaniel
Wright, a distinguished artist of the period, to paint
their portraits, and these are still on the walls of the
Council Chamber at Guildhall, with an inscription
recording the facts. Burnet, referring to the action
of the judges about the rebuilding of London, speaks
in the following terms of Sir Matthew Hale:[1]—

" Nor did his administration of justice lie only in that
court: he was one of the principal judges that sat in
Cliffords Inn, about settling the difference between land-
lord and tenant, after the dreadful fire of London—he
being the first that offered his service to the City, for

---

29 Sept., 1672, when they expired. In consequence of a disastrous
fire at and about the Navy Office in January, 1673, the judicature and power of the judges were revived, and continued in
operation till 25 July, 1675, 25 Car. II., c. 10.

[1] *Life of Sir Matthew Hale.*

accommodating all the differences that might have arisen
about the rebuilding of it—in which he behaved himself to the satisfaction of all persons concerned, so that
the sudden and quiet building of the city, which is justly
to be reckoned one of the wonders of the age, is in no
small measure due to the great care which he and Sir
Orlando Bridgeman (then Lord Chief Justice of the
Common Pleas, afterwards Lord Keeper of the Great
Seal of England) used, and to the judgment they showed
in that affair; since, without the rules then laid down,
there might have otherwise followed such an endless
train of vexatious suits, as might have been little less
chargeable than the fire itself had been.   But without
detracting from the labours of the other judges, it must
be acknowledged that he was the most instrumental in
that great work; for he first, by way of scheme, con-
trived the rules, upon which he and the rest proceeded
afterwards, in which his readiness at arithmetic and
his skill in architecture were of great use to him."

Under King James II. the storm which had destroyed
his father and imperilled the monarchy burst forth again.
The violence and irregularity of Scroggs, Jeffreys and
others of the Common Law judges of this reign, in matters touching the Crown and the prerogative, went far to
engender the second Revolution, which, shorter and less
bloody than that against Charles I., accomplished, by its
unanimity and moderation, the results for which the country had previously striven through years of bloodshed
and disorder.

From the accession of William and Mary to the year

1873 no change took place in the composition of the courts,
in the tenure of the judges, or in the character of their
duties and obligations. They held their office as under
the Commonwealth, and under the old custom of England *quamdiu se bene gesserint*, during good behaviour,
and their removal even under this clause could only be
effected by the Crown, on the joint address of both Houses
of Parliament.[1] Their salaries were fixed and ascertained. Lord Chief Justice Holt, one of our best chiefs
of the Common Law, succeeded Sir Robert Wright, one of
our worst, and from that time forward judges have followed each other in quiet if not in monotonous succession;
and no single instance has occurred, during the two
hundred years that have elapsed since the Revolution, in
which an English judge has been removed from his office,
or in which an address has been voted by either House
of Parliament with a view to his displacement.

The quiet hum-drum administration of the law by
judges, whose position removed them from the arena of
party strife and political warfare, and whose sole object
had been to deal out impartial justice alike between king
and subject and between man and man, accentuated, as
time went on, certain anomalies of our procedure and
certain irregularities of our system. That the development of these defects in our procedure has been gradual
and slow is due to the careful action of the judges, who,

---

[1] 12 & 13 William III. c. 2. The only judge who has ever been
removed by the Crown on such resolutions was Sir Jonah Bar-
rington, Judge of the Court of Admiralty in Ireland, who was
dismissed in 1830.

so far as the system would permit, have relieved these anomalies and equalised these apparent inequalities. The Common Law, which after all is very much what the judges make or declare it, being founded on the dictates of natural justice, has been adapted, so far as is practicable, to the changes of the time and the requirements of the age, and a notable addition was made to that branch of our law by the elaborate code of mercantile usages, established by Lord Mansfield and his colleagues, aided by special juries of the City of London.

In 1857, a new departure was made in the administration of justice. The outcry against the cost, the delay, and the prolixity of proceedings in the Ecclesiastical Courts, had attracted the attention of the public; a Royal Commission had reported on the abuses of their system, and bills were introduced into Parliament to abolish their jurisdiction, except in so far as it might be of a purely ecclesiastical character. They were accordingly divested of all power to entertain suits relating to probate of wills, and grants of administrations, to declare the validity of marriages, and to pronounce divorces *à mensa et thoro*, and such jurisdiction was conferred upon a new Court of Common Law which was to sit in Westminister Hall, and to be held in two divisions called respectively the COURT OF PROBATE and the COURT FOR DIVORCE AND MATRIMONIAL CAUSES. The great public advantage which accrued from the first of these new tribunals was, that it enabled the same court to adjudicate finally upon all questions relating to the succession to real as well as to personal

estate. These the Ecclesiastical Courts were not competent to entertain, for although they could by their
procedure bind the next of kin, and all persons claiming
to be interested in the personal estate, they had no power
to decide questions relating to the land or to bind the
heir, which could only be done by process at Common
Law. The result of this divided jurisdiction was, that
there might be a decision one way in the Ecclesiastical
Courts as to the personalty and another way at Common
Law as to the real estate, the validity of the same
document being in either case the subject of litigation ; a state of things which was neither creditable to
our legal procedure nor satisfactory to testators and
legatees. To effect the necessary change of jurisdiction
it was enacted that the right of succession to the goods
of a deceased person should no longer vest primarily in
the Bishop in whose diocese they might be found, but
that it should vest in the Queen,[1] who now has the
legal custody of all goods and chattels of a deceased
person from the hour of his death to the issuing of a
grant of administration to his next of kin, or of a probate
of his will to his executor. The position of the Church
as the heir of a deceased man's personal estate thus came
to an end. It had been for many centuries a beneficial
heirship, but as the power of the Church had diminished,
its interest in dead men's goods became of less and less
value, until the claims of the Church ceased to have any
operation, except for the perception of fees on grants of

---

[1] 20 & 21 Vic. c. 77.

probate or on letters of administration. The privilege
of issuing these grants, however, it still retained, and its
Courts and judges still tried the right of succession to
personal estate until the year 1857, when the powers it
had exercised for so many years passed away to the
Crown. The procedure was then adapted to modern
ideas, witnesses were examined *viva voce* in open court,
a concise form of pleading was introduced, and parties
could, upon application, have any disputed matters of fact
tried by a jury.

Questions as to the personal relations of husband and
wife had always been referred to the Ecclesiastical
tribunals, but the abuses of their procedure had affected
the trial of these causes to so great an extent that the
doors of justice were, in this respect, closed to all but
those of independent means. The power of granting
divorces enabling the divorced parties to marry again
had up to this period been retained in the hands of the
Legislature, where proceedings were taken by way of a
private Bill followed by a private Act. Here again,
however, the cost of carrying a Bill through both Houses
made the procuring of a statutory divorce, though
attainable by the rich, out of reach of the poor. And
accordingly in the same Session that Parliament dealt
with the succession to goods by instituting the Court
of Probate, it provided a speedy and comparatively in-
expensive mode of dealing with matrimonial troubles.
It constituted a Court for Divorce and Matrimonial
Causes in England, transferring to it all the jurisdiction formerly exercised in matters matrimonial by the

spiritual courts, and conferring upon it, in addition, power to grant divorces *à vinculo matrimonii* in certain cases specified in the Statute.[1]

There remained to the civilians, as the only remnant of their secular jurisdiction, the right to try maritime causes in the Court of Admiralty. Such privilege, however, could not long survive the recent innovations, and in 1873 the High Court of Admiralty ceased to be an independent tribunal, and its jurisdiction and authority were transfered to the judges of the Supreme Court, of which it then became, and has since remained, a component part.

This reform of the antient ecclesiastical procedure, the successful bringing of the new courts into line with the old, and the rapid extension of business in Westminster Hall, gave rise to a strong feeling among the lawyers and the public, that the decentralization of our courts, with the consequent limitation of the powers of each, had grown to an extent which was detrimental to the suitor, and amounted, in many cases, to a denial of justice. The systems of Law and Equity it was said, with some truth, had become so divergent that a man who might on the same question rightly succeed at law, might also rightly fail in equity. The fifteen judges of the Common Law Courts were unable efficiently to help each other, and numerous concurrent jurisdictions were a snare to the litigant. The cost of procedure under our varying systems was out of all proportion to the result attained,

---

[1] 20 & 21 Vic. c. 85.

and the law encouraged appeals which were numerous and unsatisfactory. These evils, as it was thought, might be remedied by combining our divided courts and jurisdictions under one Supreme Court of Judicature. " We must bring together," said Lord Selborne,[1] in presenting his Bill to the House of Lords in February, 1873, " our many divided courts and divided jurisdictions by erecting or rather re-erecting—for after all there was in the beginning of our constitutional system one Supreme Court of Judicature—a Supreme Court, which operating under convenient arrangements, and with a sufficient number of judges, shall exercise one single undivided jurisdiction, and shall unite within itself all the jurisdictions of all the separate superior Courts of Law and Equity now in existence." His Lordship accordingly took as his model the Curia Regis of the Norman Kings as it existed before the division of the courts. Acting on this principle, the High Court of Chancery, the Court of Queen's Bench, the Court of Common Pleas at Westminster, the Court of Exchequer, the Court of Admiralty, together with the Courts of Probate and Divorce (erected in 1858), and the Court of Bankruptcy, were by the Statute[2] that was enacted in 1873, united and consolidated into one Supreme Court of Judicature.[3] This

---

[1] *Hansard*, vol. 214 p. 337.

[2] The first Judicature Act was passed in 1873 to come into operation in 1874. This not being practicable, its operation was postponed till 1875. In that year the second Judicature Act was passed, and in Michaelmas term of 1875, the judges took their seats as members of the Supreme Court.

[3] The Supreme Court of Judicature is, however, only a col-

was divided into two sections, the HIGH COURT OF
JUSTICE, being a Court of First Instance, with power to
hear appeals from Inferior Courts, and the COURT OF
APPEAL, having an exclusive appellate jurisdiction over
the High Court, and over certain other courts which it
was not then proposed to abolish. To the High Court
were committed all the powers of the Court of Chancery,
both in Equity and Common Law, of the Queen's Bench,
of the Common Pleas at Westminster, of the Court of
Exchequer as a Court of Revenue as well as a Court of
Common Law, of Courts of Assize erected from time to
time by Commissions from the Crown, and of the Court
of Admiralty. The original position of the Chancellor,
as a Common Law as well as an Equity Judge, and the
status of the Common Pleas, as constituted to sit in *aliquo
loco certo*, to wit Westminster, were thus formally and
legally recognised. All the powers and authorities then
consolidated and committed to the Supreme Court of
Judicature were held and exercised by the Supreme
Court of the Norman Kings before the increasing multiplication of causes, towards the end of the reign of King
Henry III., rendered a division of the courts and a re-
arrangement of the business necessary in the public

lective name for the judges composing the High Court and the
Court of Appeal. The only occasion when a Supreme Court is
constituted is when the judges meet together in council once a
year to frame a report to the Secretary of State, and to suggest
any improvements they may think right to bring before him.
It thus exercises one of the functions of the Exchequer Chamber
which was formerly the council room of the judges.

interest. All questions relating to the goods of a deceased person, as distinct from his lands, were beyond the jurisdiction of the Curia Regis, and were settled by the Bishops in their Diocesan Courts. All questions of marriage, of separation, and of alimony, or provision for a wife, were tried in the Ecclesiastical Courts, and Courts of Bankruptcy were not then invented.

Subsequent legislation, with the same object, has abolished the Court of the Master of the Rolls and the Courts of Common Pleas and Exchequer, leaving all the Common Law and Equity business to be transacted by the High Court, of which the Chief Justice of the Queen's Bench, under the style of Lord Chief Justice of England (a title which Bacon jealously scrupled to allow to Coke), is the permanent president.[1] The High Court sits in two divisions, of which the Chancellor is the head of the Chancery, and the Lord Chief Justice, sitting in the Queen's Bench Division with an *ex officio* right to sit also in the Court of Appeal, is the head of the Common Law. The Master of the Rolls, having no longer a court of his own, but still holding his position as second permanent judge, next after the Lord Chief Justice of England, and before the chiefs of the Common Pleas and Exchequer, so long as they remained, sits as the head of one of the divisions of the Court of Appeal, and is no longer of necessity a Chancery lawyer.

That much advantage has accrued to the public

---

[1] "President" is a title with a Norman flavour, which now, for the first time, finds a place in the Courts of Chancery or of Common Law.

Q

through this re-arrangement of business cannot, I think, be denied. The pleading and the practice of the courts have been assimilated and simplified, and the power given to each court to deal completely in a single action with all differences between the parties, has reduced the cost and the delays of litigation. In one respect, however, upon which great stress was laid not only by laymen, but by the lawyers who were concerned in the change, it seems to have been productive of but little result. It was believed by some, and hoped by others, that by the unification of the courts, by the assimilation of procedure, and by making the judges interchangeable, there might be accomplished, what is commonly known as, the fusion of Law and Equity. And much reliance was placed upon the argument that, as in all countries but those deriving their legal constitution directly from ourselves, no distinction exists between law and equity, and one set of courts disposes of all questions that arise in human affairs, so, in our country also, a similar arrangement of courts would accomplish the like results. A great distinction, however, is to be observed between the judicial system of England and its children, and that of other nations in Europe and their descendants. It is to be found in this, that our law is greatly of a customary character, that there is no statutory sanction in regard to much of it, and that there is with us no such code or *corpus juris* as exists in other countries, to which reference may be made for the decision of all disputed questions, and outside of which are no legal rights or obligations. Until, therefore, we find ourselves in the same position as other nations in respect of this codification of our law and procedure, this fusion will be as impracticable as the fusion of oil and water. By shaking the vessel which holds the liquids there may be produced what appears to be a fusion of the two, but a few moments of repose will show the two elements as clear and as separate as before. And it is no disparagement of our lawyers to say, that what Cromwell, supported by his judges and his lawyers, all hot and in full cry to deal with the Chancery and its equitable doctrines, was unable to effect, they also, even in times of quiet and good will, have failed to accomplish. The actual nomenclature of the courts recognised by the Judicature Acts as the Chancery and the Queen's Bench Divisions, seemed to point to the impracticability, for the present, at all events, of any true amalgamation, and the experience of twenty years has shown that this anticipation has been well founded. To carry out this scheme of fusion, however, the description of the Chancery judges was altered. They ceased to be Vice-Chancellors, and became justices of the High Court, and as such were, in the first instance, sent on circuit to try Common Law cases and prisoners, taking their turns with the judges of the Queen's Bench. But the practice was soon abandoned. The Chancery judges remained in London trying their causes, they reverted to the black silk gown of the Vice-Chancellor, the Chancery Bar became once more composed of lawyers who made equity and conveyancing their special study, Chancery appeals were specially allocated to one of the divisions of the Court of Appeal, and whether from their convenience of access, or from other causes, the Equity judges have attracted to their courts the greater portion of the work of the country. The dividing line between the two jurisdictions, simplified and improved in their course of procedure, has thus become once more clear and accentuated, and there is every indication that the present working of those courts is satisfactory to the public and to all branches of the legal profession.

Nor has it been altogether possible in other respects to carry out in its entirety the original scheme of the promoters of the measure. The division of the Supreme Court, which was found necessary in the time of Edward I., has been found equally necessary now, though it has not been carried out in the same form as at that period. The business of the Probate and Divorce Courts, though removed from the control and procedure of the Ecclesiastical Courts, has been put into a separate Division, together with the Court of Admiralty, which has been equally removed from the control of the civilians. The Court of Bankruptcy has a court with officers and offices of its own. A separate Court sits for the trial of Railway and Canal cases, and within the present year an attempt has been made to erect a tribunal of commerce by the constitution of a court for the special hearing and determining of mercantile cases, to be presided over by one of our most eminent commercial lawyers.

One of the results of this alteration of our procedure, has been to make some change in the relative positions of the Lord Chancellor and the Lord Chief Justice. That such a scheme as that of the Supreme Court should require for its satisfactory development a lawyer and an administrator, directly responsible to Parliament, would seem to have been inevitable. And in the absence of any Minister of Justice, who in other countries, without being a judge, is by virtue of his office responsible for the successful working of the machinery of the courts, the Lord Chancellor, as the person most nearly approaching to such an official, would also seem to be the person indicated for the purpose. It is commonly said, and with truth, that to combine the legislative, the judicial, and the executive duties in one and the same person, would be to create an autocracy fatal to our liberties and to our constitution. And it is argued that the great success of the English constitution is derived from the fact that these three functions are always distinct and independent. Thus the legislature which makes the laws, leaves it to the Courts and the Executive to declare and to enforce them; the Courts construe and give effect to the laws as they emerge from Parliament, without either questioning or enforcing them, and the Executive, without questioning the law or its construction by the judges, carry out the orders they receive from Parliament or from the Courts. The proposition must, however, be received with this qualification, that such distinct authorities must act in accord, though independently, in carrying out their respective duties or their conflicts, and the consequent deadlock of justice will bring into existence a state of anarchy, the actual antipodes of absolutism, and probably the worse condition of the two. Of the possible coincidence of the three powers in a single person, the Chancellor is a standing and perhaps a solitary example. As a peer, as Speaker of the House of Lords, and as a member of the cabinet which originates legislation, he represents the first of these functions; as President of the Court of Appeal, with a Common Law and a statutory right of sitting as a judge of First Instance, if he so desires, he represents the second; and as the creator of judges, and justices of the peace, with administrative duties in regard to the Supreme Court and various others, he represents the third. M. de Franqueville, a distinguished member of the Academy of France, to whom our judicial system, in its various aspects, presents a study of unceasing interest, speaks of the English Chancellor as a living image of the Trinity, embodying in his own person the three independent elements of government.[1] And it is, I think, to this combination of duties and responsibilities in the Chancellor that we must look for the future development and successful working of the Supreme Court of Judicature. The Chancellor, under the Judicature Acts, is President of the Court of Appeal, of the High Court, and of the Chancery Division of the High Court; but he is seldom seen in the Court of Appeal, and never, as far as I am aware, in the High Court. Many years have passed since he sat as a judge of First Instance, or even as a judge of appeal in the Court of Chancery, and the Acts specially provide (from an excess of

---

[1] *Système Judiciaire*, vol. i. p. 42. "Il est une image vivante de la Trinité; il est à la fois le centre, et le lien des trois grands pouvoirs de l'état."

caution) that he is not a permanent judge of any of the courts in which he sits, and that his appointment is not, as that of the other judges, "during good behaviour." Whenever he sits in any court he is entitled to preside, a precedence to which the customary rights of his office fully entitle him; but I think that the days of the Chancellor sitting in Equity, or even in Appeal, are rapidly coming to a close, and that, except when a press of business may demand his presence in the Court of Appeal, the Chancellor will be found in future to confine his duties to the House of Lords, and to the solution of the many administrative questions relating to the judicature of the country, that must constantly demand his attention.

The Lord Chief Justice, on the other hand, is advanced in his position and responsibilities from that of Lord Chief Justice of the Queen's Bench to that of the actual Lord Chief Justice of England, yielding place only to the Chancellor, if he should wish, on any occasion, to form part of his court. He is a member of the Court of Appeal, where he is President when sitting in the absence of the Lord Chancellor, and he is the permanent President of the Queen's Bench Division. He holds office during good behaviour, and can only be removed by the Crown after a joint address of both Houses of Parliament. He is thus essentially the permanent chief of the judges. Becket, as Chancellor, was the second man in the kingdom, the Chief Justiciar being the first; but the Justiciar was then the legislator and minister, as well as the chief judge, and now that the positions are reversed, the Chancellor, as legislator, Cabinet Minister, and administrator, takes prece-

dence of the Chief Justice. The former more nearly resembles the Minister of Justice of modern Europe, the
latter the Chief Justiciar of the Normans and the Plantagenets.

Whether the effect of the Judicature Acts is to alter
the customary position of the Chancellor, to derogate
from his high and exceptional position, to make him one
of the judges, to bring him within the quaint but well-
recognised description of a Chief Justice, *primus inter
pares*, the first among equals, and thus to make him the
representative of their body, is more difficult to determine. It has been the subject of friendly discussion
between distinguished holders of the respective offices ;
but without taking sides in a matter which King Charles
would have said "appertaineth not to the common
people," it would appear, to the independent observer,
that the tenure, the power of appointments, and the
administrative duties of the Chancellor, though necessarily
pertinent to his high office, are inconsistent with his
position as a chief judge, co-equal and co-ordinate with
the others, and that if the intention of the statute was to
confer that position upon him, it was contrary to English
usage, if not unconstitutional.

The anticipated re-arrangement of business and aggre-
gation of the courts necessitated, according to public
opinion, the bringing together under the same roof of all
the courts composing the Supreme Court of Judicature.
Attempts had previously been made to deal with these
courts. The half open enclosures at the end of the hall,
within which the Courts of Chancery and King's Bench

Sir John Soane's Plan of the Courts in and about Westminster Hall, in 1795, before their demolition, showing the position of the Court of Exchequer, the Court of Common Pleas, the inclosures for the Courts of Chancery and King's Bench at the end of the Hall, and the Court of Requests. Original in the Grace Collection in the British Museum.

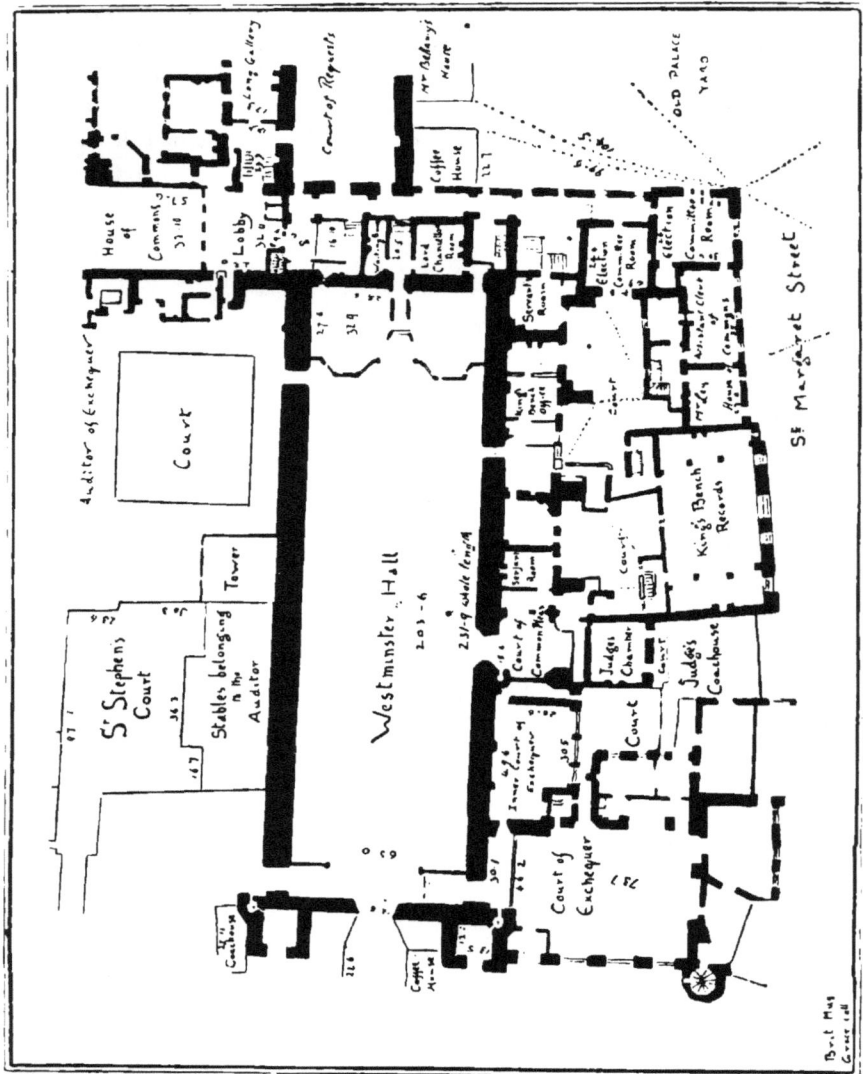

Face page 233.

Copy of the Plan of Westminster Hall by Mr Soane in 1793

formerly sat, had, after the removal of the shops, been
hidden by a graceful Tudor screen, which, reaching nearly
to the chestnut roof, separated them from the turmoil
and bustle of the hall. The increase of business and the
want of further accommodation had, at a later date, led to
the courts being taken from inside the hall and located
in a building erected by Sir John Soane, in 1822, on the
western side overlooking the Abbey. To make way for
this building, various old houses, the great rooms and
the Court of the Exchequer, Queen Elizabeth's apartments, and other historical memorials, were pulled down
and removed. The courts, then erected, survived the fire
of 1834 ; but they were felt to be unsuitable both from
their size, their situation, and their numbers for the new
experiment to be tried in our judicial procedure. After
a delay of some fifteen years, spent in discussion and
in building operations, the new temple of justice was
eventually completed in the year 1882. On the 4th
December of that year, Her Majesty opened the Royal
Courts of Justice, and the judges and barristers of the
day bade adieu for ever to their courts and their
chambers in Westminster Hall. Sir John Soane's courts
were then entirely removed. The old walls of the hall
showing the masonry of Rufus, Becket, Richard II.,
Henry VII., and Elizabeth, with many masons' marks
identified with the period, were for a time exposed to
view, and then again closed up and preserved for the
contemplation of future generations.

Many familiar scenes have thus passed away. The
Exchequer Chamber, which was for centuries the Court

of Consultation, and afterwards a Court of Error for the judges, has been replaced by the Court of Appeal, a more stately and in many respects a more competent tribunal. The modern method of raising the revenue of the sovereign has abolished the special functions of the Court of the Exchequer. The law terms of inconvenient shortness have given way to law sittings of ever-increasing length. The quarterly peregrinations of the Bench and the Bar between the city of Westminster and the city of London no longer recur. The serjeants, who took part in the administration of justice from the first recognition of advocacy in our system are seen no more, and brotherly compliments passing among the judges, and between them and the Bar, are now meaningless expressions, as there are no longer any " brothers of the coif." The judges at Nisi Prius, discarding the black silk robe which they formerly wore, have assumed the violet gown, which dates back to the time of Edward I., and which, Dugdale says, they used to wear when they sat at Nisi Prius in London or West-minster.[1] The red casting hood, however, which was part of their costume, has been abandoned for a red sash worn somewhat unmeaningly over the shoulder. The arm-chair of the Chancery judge has supplanted the padded and cushioned *bench*, which gave the name and the style to the King's and the Common Benches in Westminster Hall. The quaint regulations, by which at certain periods the junior Bar had precedence in the Queen's Bench, have come to an end, the postman and the tubman have dis-

---

[1] *Orig. Jud.*, fol. 102.

appeared from the Exchequer, Masters in Chancery have been abolished, and the Prothonotary has gone from the Common Pleas. These and many other amendments in legal procedure have doubtless enured to the public good. But while we may recognise this removal of the courts from Westminster as a necessary and consequential addition to Lord Selborne's scheme, yet we may be pardoned the regret that it was not possible to carry out the new system in the antient hall of justice. Looking back over a period of nearly eight hundred years, during which law and justice had their throne in Westminster Hall, and mindful of the great scenes that those walls have witnessed, the meeting of the early English Parliaments, the Norman and the Plantagenet kings in their pomp and splendour, occupying the judgment-seat beside the great fathers of our law, the trial and deposition of King Richard, the trial and condemnation of King Charles, and the impeachment of Warren Hastings, and in view of the long line of honourable and learned lawyers who have sat in the courts that occupied or environed the antient hall, we, who are old enough to have practised in Westminster Hall, but have not outlived the respect for immemorial traditions, or learned to despise the teaching of antiquity, may at least have this satisfaction, that we have trodden the floor of the Aula Regia, and have striven to transplant its traditions and associations into the new field of forensic labour.

ADDENDA

A few words as to the works referred to in the preceding pages may not be out of place. "In quoting of books," says Selden in his *Table Talk*, "quote such authors as are usually read; others you may read for your own satisfaction, but not name them. Quoting of authors is mostly for matter-of-fact, and then I cite them as I would a witness: sometimes for a free expression, and then I give the author his due, and give myself praise for reading him." Acting on this good worldly advice, I have referred to those authors that are accessible to the student, and have done little more than indicate the lines upon which he may pursue a course of thorough and complete investigation into the subject-matter of this sketch. The absence of codification in our law involves an absence of precise information as to the modifications in our procedure and our Courts of Justice. Changes which are gradual and uneventful make little impression on the time, and are seldom recorded in contemporaneous annals or histories of the period. They are thus very difficult of ascertainment, and the evidence frequently has to be gathered from a mass of loose and undigested material.

Taking, therefore, Selden's advice on the quotation of authors, I cite, in reference to the Anglo-Saxon period, the following works :—

The Ancient Laws and Institutes of England, comprising *Laws enacted under the Anglo-Saxon Kings, from Æthelbirht to Cnut ; the Laws called Edward the Confessor's ; the Laws of William the Conqueror, and those ascribed to Henry I.* Edited by B. Thorpe, published London, 1840. A book absolutely indispensable to any student of the Anglo-Saxon period.

The Anglo-Saxon Chronicle, edited by Thorpe. London, 1861.

Kemble's Codex Diplomaticus ævi Saxonici. London, 1839. (6 vols., 8vo.) Being a collection of Charters and other documents of the Anglo-Saxon period.

Sir Henry Ellis' Introduction to Domesday Book. London, 1833.

Anglo-Saxon Charters, published some in text, some in reproduction by the Record Commissioners.

Stubbs' Select Charters, from the earliest date to Edward I. Oxford, 1888. Many of these are, however, taken from *The Ancient Laws and Institutes.*

The above may be said to be the evidences or witnesses of the period. Of the writers, I quote *Sir Francis Palgrave's History of the Anglo-Saxons.* London, 1837.

Lappenberg's History of the Anglo-Saxon Kings. London, 1845. (2 vols.). *Lappenberg's History of the Anglo-Norman Kings.* London, 1857.

Reeves' History of the English Law, from the time of the Romans to the death of Elizabeth. London, 1869.

(3 vols.) With notes by Finlason. A book of much re-search, but over-loaded with the notes of the learned editor, who holds strong views as to the place which the Roman Civil Law held in our antient jurisprudence.

Stubbs' Constitutional History of England. Oxford, 1883. (3 vols.) *Freeman's Norman Conquest.* Vol. i. Oxford, 1867.

Sir James Stephens' History of the Criminal Law. London, 1883. (3 vols.)

Pollock and Maitland's History of the English Law before the time of Edward I. Cambridge, 1895. (2 vols.).

Essays in Anglo-Saxon Law. Boston, U.S. 1876. These essays, by distinguished American writers, are a most remarkable contribution to the history of this period.

Taking the next period, from the Norman Conquest to the accession of Edward I., we have at the early part but little information beyond the chroniclers and the judicial rolls, which began about the time of Henry II. Added to these is the work of *Glanvil on the English Laws*, a copy of which, translated and edited by Beames, was published in London, 1812.

Placita Anglo-Normanica : Law cases from William I. to Richard I., by M. M. Bigelow, London, 1879, and *History of Procedure in England from the Norman Conquest*, by the same author. London, 1880. The several publications of the *Selden Society* also bear upon this period.

Dialogus de Scaccario, first published by Madox in 1708, and to be found in Stubbs' *Charters*, pp. 168–248.

A work by Richard, Bishop of London, High Treasurer in the reign of Henry II., and written in the Red Book of the Exchequer. Over this period perhaps the most valuable works are *Madox's History and Antiquities of the Exchequer of the Kings of England, from the Norman Conquest to the end of the reign of Edward II.* London, 1708. (2 vols. 4to.) This gentleman, a most laborious and exact writer and antiquary, was a barrister of the Middle Temple, and made this subject a life-long study, gaining his information from original sources, and referring, in profuse and minute detail, to the original writs, rolls and charters from which his knowledge was obtained.

The History of the Life of King Henry II., and of the age in which he lived, with a History of the Revolution of England from the death of Edward the Confessor to the birth of Henry II., by George, Lord Lyttleton, London, 1767 (3 vols. 4to), is a book of almost as much research and authority as that of Mr. Madox.

Freeman's Norman Conquest (6 vols.) with the *Reign of William Rufus.* 1882. (2 vols.).

Pollock and Maitland's History; Hubert Hall's Antiquities of the Exchequer, London, 1891. *Court Life under the Plantagenets,* London, 1890, contains many interesting extracts in the Appendix.

The public records also begin during this period, but a life-time would not suffice for a proper study of the wealth of historical and judicial lore to be found in those pages. The introductions to the various series, however, will repay the perusal of any student.

For the next period, to the eve of the Wars of the Roses, materials are abundant. *Bracton*, published by the Record Commissioners, edited by Sir Travers Twiss, Q.C., 1883 (3 vols.). The *Mirror of Justices, written originally in the old French, long before the Conquest, and many things added by Andrew Horne,* translated into English, and published in London, 1768.

Fleta, seu Commentarius Juris Anglicani "sic nuncupatus, sub Eduardo rege primo seu circa, annos abhinc cccxl. ab anonymo conscriptus, atque è codice veteri autore ipso aliquantulum recentiori nunc primum typis editus," by John Selden, London, 1647.

Sir John Fortescue on the Laws of England, written in the reign of Henry VI. first published in London in 1537 : a book which gives the earliest detailed account of the mode and time of the sittings of the judges in their various courts.

John de Britton, edited by Kelham in 1762.

The Paston Letters, London, 1872 (3 vols.), extending from 1422 to 1509, edited by James Gairdner, contain numerous references to the litigation in the Paston family, and throw light upon the social life of this period.

From the accession of Henry VII. materials are still more abundant. We have *Bacon's Life of Henry VII., Cavendish's Life of Wolsey,* and the greatest of all works on the history, the jurisdiction and the procedure of our courts, the *Institutes of Sir Edward Coke.* The fourth part, concerning the Jurisdiction of Courts, is that to which reference is chiefly made. It was first published in 1644, and was written by the Lord Chief Justice, after his retirement from public affairs, at Stoke Pogis.

R

Origines Juridiciales, or *Historical Memorials of the English Laws, Courts of Justice, Form of Tryal, etc.,* London, 1666, by Sir William Dugdale, who held various offices, and was before his death Garter King-at-Arms, is a book of great authority on all matters connected with the Courts, the Judges, and other officers of Justice. It contains what he calls *Chronica Series* or a complete list of judges, so far as can be ascertained, from the Conquest to the reign of Charles II. In the reign of Elizabeth, *R. Crompton, of the Middle Temple,* wrote his work on *The Authority and Jurisdiction of the Queen's Courts.* It was published in 1594, and went through many editions.

Among other books of this period, *The Charters of the Cinque Ports, by Samuel Jeake,* Puritan town clerk of Rye, is a valuable addition to our historical knowledge, as giving in minute detail, after the manner of Madox in his *History of the Exchequer,* an account of the antient customs, jurisdiction and procedure of these old Admiralty Courts, from the time of the Confessor to that of King Charles II. The book, which has been accepted as an authority in the Courts and in Parliament, was for long consulted in MS., having been written in 1678; but in 1728 it was published at the expense of Chief Baron Gilbert, with the sanction of his brother judges.

During this period also, John Selden, Sir Henry Spelman, Prynne, Sir Matthew Hale, Whitelocke, in his *Memorials of Public Affairs,* published in 1682, and numerous other lawyers and antiquaries contributed to the legal literature of the age. And the full reports of cases tried in the Courts add to our knowledge of their constitution and procedure.

The general literature connected with this subject, in addition to that already referred to, may be fairly said to be comprised in the following :—*The State Trials* (34 vols.) which, extending from 1163 to 1820, give a chronological history of the most important trials in our various Courts. The earliest accounts given in these volumes are hardly reports of the trials themselves, but are reprints of more or less contemporaneous accounts, in pamphlets and broadsheets, of what was generally believed to have been the course of the trial there discussed. In the progress of time, however, more accurate notes of the trials were taken, and from about the time of James I. the reports are probably fairly accurate. *The Lives of the Norths*, London, 1826 (3 vols.), including that of Lord Keeper Guildford ; *The Antiquities of the Inns of Court*, by William Herbert, London, 1804; the various English histories of the older type, together with *Macaulay's History*, *Hallam's Constitutional History* and his *History of the Middle Ages*, and *Green's History of the English People*, London, 1883 (4 vols.).

Froude's History from the fall of Wolsey to the death of Elizabeth, London (12 vols.), and *James Rawson Gardner's History from the Accession of James to the Protectorate*, London, 1863–1894 (14 vols.). Both Mr. Froude and Mr. Gardner have dug into the bowels of the time for illustrations of their work, and enter, as all such writers must, into the action of the Courts and the Judges, under whom wrongs were permitted and rights were secured. *Lord Campbell's Lives of the Chancellors*, London, 1846 (7 vols.) and his *Lives of the Chief Justices*, London, 1849 (3 vols.).

In these very amusing and instructive volumes Lord Campbell, who held successively the offices of Lord Chief Justice and Lord Chancellor, discusses most of the doubtful questions that have been raised as to the growth and authority of the Courts, and although his works have been subjected to criticisms, and errors have been shown in matters of minor consideration, yet they have survived the carpings of the day, and are accepted as substantially accurate in their historical details. But pre-eminent above all others in this particular department of literature, is to be found the late Mr. Edward Foss, who made the *Lives of the Judges since the Norman Conquest* the study of his life, and after a preparation of many years, and an exhaustive search through old records and county histories, produced his *Lives of the Judges*, in 9 volumes. The first volume was published in 1848, the last in 1864. It is a work of great erudition and of ceaseless labour. His sketches of the various reigns, his interpolations of antiquarian lore and of quaint anecdotes, render his book, though unattractive in title, yet thoroughly readable, not alone by students of the law and its professors, but by all who take an interest in the progress of our judicial life.

I also strongly recommend *Le Système Judiciaire de la Grande Bretagne*, by Le Comte de Franqueville, a member of the Institute. (2 vols.) Paris, 1893.

I have included in this sketch a chapter on the Courts of the Forest. It is a subject of which the legal literature is not extensive. John Manwood, a member of Lincoln's Inn, published in 1578 *A Treatise on the Forest*

Laws, which is the standard work on that department of the law. It was, even at that time, very obscure, the Crown not being too anxious to assert rights which might give rise to contests, and the officers of the Forests, resting their position and their claims upon custom rather than upon statute. Manwood describes the Forest Law as being in his time gone "clean out of knowledge," as not being contained in any existing treatise, but lying scattered here and there in the year-books, or in antient records stowed away and not accessible to the public. His treatise however was admirably conceived and nearly complete, and rapidly went through several editions. Crompton, in his work on the jurisdiction and authority of the Courts, devotes 120 pages of black letter to the consideration of the forests, and sets out various writs which were issued to enforce the process of these Courts. These Elizabethan writers were followed by Sir Edward Coke, who, in his *4th Institute*, goes at length into the history and the jurisdiction of the Chief Justice and the subordinate officers of the Forests, and a little book on the *Game Laws and Statutes*, London, 1707, brings the subject down to the time of Queen Anne. *A Collection of Pleas of the Forest* is, I understand, in course of preparation, and will, I have little doubt, throw very considerable light upon the law and the procedure of these Courts.

Historical Enquiries concerning Forests, etc., by P. Lewis, London, 1811, and *Pearson's Historical Maps*, London, 1869, review the subject of the Forests from the standpoint of the nineteenth century, while the disputed

Forest Law of Canute, together with those of the Confessor and Henry I. are to be found in the *Ancient Laws and Institutes*. *The Carta de Foresta* of Henry III., which is the Great Charter of the Forest population, is printed by Stubbs among his select Charters, along with other documents bearing upon this subject.

INDEX

Butler & Tanner, The Selwood Printing Works, Frome, and London.

www.ingramcontent.com/pod-product-compliance
Lightning Source LLC
Chambersburg PA
CBHW031406270326
41929CB00010BA/1341